PHP for Absolute Beginners

Jason Lengstorf

Apress®

PHP for Absolute Beginners

ISBN-13 (pbk): 978-1-4302-2473-0

ISBN-13 (electronic): 978-1-4302-2474-7

Printed and bound in the United States of America 9 8 7 6 5 4 3 2 1

Lead Editor: Michelle Lowman
Technical Reviewer: Gordon Forsythe
Editorial Board: Clay Andres, Steve Anglin, Mark Beckner, Ewan Buckingham, Tony Campbell, Gary Cornell, Jonathan Gennick, Michelle Lowman, Matthew Moodie, Jeffrey Pepper, Frank Pohlmann, Ben Renow-Clarke, Dominic Shakeshaft, Matt Wade, Tom Welsh
Project Manager: Debra Kelly
Copy Editor: Patrick Meader
Compositor: Lynn L'Heureux
Indexer: John Collin

Distributed to the book trade worldwide by Springer-Verlag New York, Inc., 233 Spring Street, 6th Floor, New York, NY 10013. Phone 1-800-SPRINGER, fax 201-348-4505, e-mail `orders-ny@springer-sbm.com`, or visit `http://www.springeronline.com`.

For information on translations, please e-mail `info@apress.com`, or visit `http://www.apress.com`.

Apress and friends of ED books may be purchased in bulk for academic, corporate, or promotional use. eBook versions and licenses are also available for most titles. For more information, reference our Special Bulk Sales–eBook Licensing web page at `http://www.apress.com/info/bulksales`.

The source code for this book is available to readers at `http://www.apress.com`. You will need to answer questions pertaining to this book in order to successfully download the code.

For my dad, who showed me that nothing stands between a bear and its honey.

Contents at a Glance

■About the Author xiv

■About the Technical Reviewer.. xv

■Acknowledgments.. xvi

■Introduction... xvii

■Chapter 1: Setting Up the PHP Development Environment...3

■Chapter 2: Understanding PHP: Language Basics 29

■Chapter 3: Passing Information with PHP 69

■Chapter 4: Working with Databases 97

■Chapter 5: Building the Entry Manager 125

■Chapter 6: Adding Support for Multiple Pages... 157

■Chapter 7: Updating and Deleting Entries 187

■Chapter 8: Adding the Ability to Upload Images 207

■Chapter 9: Syndicating the Blog... 263

■Chapter 10: Adding a Commenting System to Your Blog 283

■Chapter 11: Adding Password Protection to Administrative Links 311

■Chapter 12: Finishing Touches... 341

■Index 369

Contents

■About the Author xiv

■About the Technical Reviewer xv

■Acknowledgments xvi

■Introduction xvii

■Chapter 1: Setting Up the PHP Development Environment 3

Why You Need Apache, MySQL, and PHP 3

   Drilling Down on PHP 3

      Stable/Production vs. Development Releases 4

      How PHP Works 4

      Server-Side vs. Client-Side Scripting 4

      What Apache Does 5

   Store Info with MySQL 5

Installing PHP, Apache, and MySQL (the Hard Way) 6

   Installation Made Easy 6

   Installing XAMPP 6

      Step 1: Download XAMPP 7

      Step 2: Open the Installer and Follow the Instructions 7

      Step 3: Test XAMPP to Ensure Proper Installation 11

Choosing a Development Kit 15

   Benefiting from SDKs and IDEs 15

   Choosing the Right SDK 18

      The Eclipse Foundation and PDT 18

Installing and Using the Eclipse PDT 18

   Step 1: Downloading the PDT 19

   Step 2: Unpacking the PDT Archive 19

   Step 3: Choosing Your Project Workspace 20

   Step 4: Creating Your First Project 23

Step 5: Creating a File 26
Step 6: Writing Your First Script 27
Summary 28
Chapter 2: Understanding PHP: Language Basics **29**
Embedding PHP Scripts 29
Alternative Delimiters 30
Short Tags 31
HTML <script> Tags and ASP-Style Delimiters 31
Variables and Datatypes 32
What Is a Variable? 32
Storing Values in a Variable 32
Understanding Strings 33
Understanding Integers 37
Understanding Floating Point Numbers 37
Understanding Boolean Values 37
Understanding Arrays 38
Sending Data to the Browser as Output 41
The Different Output Commands 41
The print() Statement 41
The echo() Statement 42
The printf() Statement 43
The sprintf() Statement 45
Commenting Your Code 46
Inline vs. Block Comments 46
Other Comment Styles 47
Operators 47
Arithmetic Operators 48
Arithmetic Assignment Operators 48
Comparison Operators 50
Error Control Operators 51
Incrementing/Decrementing Operators 52
Logical Operators 52
String Operators 54
Control Structures 54

if, else, and else if 55

while and do-while 56

for 58

foreach..59

break..60

switch 61

continue...62

return 63

include, include_once, require, and require_once...63

goto...65

User-Defined 66

Returning Values from Functions 67

Summary..68

Chapter 3: Passing Information with PHP...**69**

Superglobal Arrays..69

Variable Scope...70

$GLOBALS..73

$_SERVER...74

$_GET...77

URL Encoding..78

Accessing URL Variables 78

$_POST...82

$_REQUEST..84

$_FILES..85

$_SESSION 89

Using session_destroy()..92

$_COOKIE..93

Summary..95

Chapter 4: Working with Databases..**97**

The Basics of MySQL Data Storage...97

Manipulating Data in MySQL Tables..98

Creating and Deleting Databases 99

Deleting Databases Using DROP..99

Creating Databases Using CREATE 100

The CREATE TABLE Statement...100
    Data Types in MySQL..102
    Understanding PRIMARY KEY..102
    Understanding AUTO_INCREMENT...102
    Indexes in MySQL...103
The INSERT Statement...103
The SELECT Statement...105
The UPDATE Statement...107
The JOIN Statement..108
The DELETE Statement..109
Opening a Connection 109
PHP's MySQL Extension...109
The MySQLi Extension 111
    Using Prepared Statements...111
    Using MySQLi..112
    Using Prepared Statements with MySQLi 113
PHP Data Objects (PDO)..116
    Rewriting Your Example in PDO 116
Table Structure and a Crash Course in Planning...118
Planning Database Tables 118
The Shortcut Selector (*) 122
Summary..122
Recommended Reading..122

■Chapter 5: Building the Entry Manager 125
Planning the Entry Database Table 125
Creating the Entry Input Form 128
Create a Script to Process the Form Input 132
Performing the Initial Verification..133
Connect to the Database 134
    Keeping Database Credentials Separate 134
    Connecting to the Database in update.inc.php...135
Save the Entry to the Database 135
Retrieve the Entry's Unique ID and Display the Entry to the User..............................136
Displaying the Saved Entries..138

Planning Our Scripts 139

    Separation of Logic in Programming 139

    Mapping Your Functions to Output Saved Entries 140

    Writing the Database Functions 141

    Writing the Business Function 148

    Writing the Presentation Code 149

Fix the Redirect 155

Summary 156

■**Chapter 6: Adding Support for Multiple Pages** **157**

Add a page Column to the entries Table 157

Modify Your Functions to Accept Page Parameters 158

    Accepting Page Information in the URL 158

    Using the Page Information to Filter Entries 159

Modifying admin.php to Save Page Associations 165

Saving Page Associations 168

Using .htaccess to Create Friendly URLs 170

    What .htaccess Does 170

    Using Regular Expressions 171

    Creating Your .htaccess File 171

        Step 1: Turn on URL Rewriting 171

        Step 2: Declare the Base-Level Folder for Rewriting 172

        Step 3: Set Up a Rule to Stop Rewriting for Certain File Types 172

        Step 4: Set Up a Rule for Admin Page Access 173

        Step 5: Set Up a Rule for Page-Only URLs 174

        Step 6: Set Up a Rule for Page-and-Entry URLs 174

        Trying It Out 175

    Creating Friendly URLs Automatically 175

        Step 1: Add a url Column to the entries Table 176

        Step 2: Modify functions.inc.php to Handle URLs 176

        Step 3: Modify index.php to Handle URLs 178

        Step 4: Write a Function to Create Friendly URLs Automatically 180

        Step 5. Modify update.inc.php to Save URLs in the Database 182

Adding a Menu 184

Creating Different Viewing Styles for the Pages 185

Summary 186

■**Chapter 7: Updating and Deleting Entries** **187**

Creating Administrative Links 187

Displaying Administrative Links 188

Passing URL Values to admin.php with .htaccess....................................190

    Modifying the Original Admin Rule 190

    The New Admin Rule 191

Populating Your Form with the Entry to Be Edited 191

Updating Entries in the Database...194

Handling Entry Deletion...197

Confirming Your Choice to Delete an Entry 200

    Handling Your Submitted Confirmation Form 201

Removing Deleted Entries from the Database 203

Summary...205

■**Chapter 8: Adding the Ability to Upload Images** **207**

Adding a File Input to the Admin Form...207

Accessing the Uploaded File 208

    A Quick Refresher on the $_FILES Superglobal Array 208

    Object-Oriented Programming..211

        Drill Down on Objects 211

        Why Objects Are Useful 212

Writing the Image Handling Class 218

    Saving the Image...219

        Checking for Errors Using Exceptions.....................................221

        Saving the File 223

    Modifying update.inc.php to Save Images.......................................225

        Using try...catch with Exceptions 226

    Creating a New Folder 228

    Renaming the Image..236

        Determining the File Extension...237

Storing and Retrieving Images from the Database 240

    Modifying the entries Table 241

    Modifying update.inc.php to Save Images.......................................241

    Modifying retrieveEntries() to Retrieve Images 244

    Modifying index.php to Display Images..246

Adding a Function to Format Images for Output 246

Resizing Images 248

Determining the New Image Dimensions 249

Adding a Property for Maximum Dimensions 249

Creating the Method to Determine New Width and Height 250

Determining Which Image Functions to Use 252

Resampling the Image at the Proper Size 254

Adding Your New Method to processUploadedImage() 258

Summary 260

Chapter 9: Syndicating the Blog 263

What Is RSS? 263

What Is XML? 264

Creating an RSS Feed 264

Describing Your Feed...265

Creating Feed Items..266

Using Existing Functions to Minimize Effort 266

What Is a GUID? 271

What Is a Publishing Date? 272

Publishing Your Feed 278

Adding the Feed to the Blog 278

Using the <link> Tag to Signify an RSS Feed...278

Adding an RSS Link 279

Summary 281

Chapter 10: Adding a Commenting System to Your Blog 283

Creating a comments Table in the Database 283

Building a Comments Class..285

Building the Comment Entry Form 286

Modifying index.php to Display the Comment Form..287

Storing New Comments in the Database 289

Modifying update.inc.php to Handle New Comments...291

Retrieving All Comments for a Given Entry 293

Displaying Comments for a Given Entry 296

Modifying index.php to Display Entry Comments 302

Deleting Comments 304

    Creating a Confirmation Form 305

    Removing the Comment from the Database...306

    Modifying update.inc.php to Handle Comment Deletion 307

Summary 310

■ **Chapter 11: Adding Password Protection to Administrative Links** **311**

Adding an admin Table to the Database 311

Adding Administrators in the Database...312

    Building an HTML Form 312

    Saving New Administrators in the Database 315

        Dealing with Passwords 316

        Saving the Admin...316

Hiding Controls from Unauthorized Users 318

    Modifying index.php 318

    Modifying comments.inc.php 323

    Modifying admin.php 325

Creating a Login Form..328

Displaying Controls to Authorized Users 330

Logging Users Out 337

    Adding a Log Out Link...337

    Modifying update.inc.php to Log Out Users...339

Summary 340

■ **Chapter 12: Finishing Touches** **341**

Email Validation...341

    Adding a Method to Validate Email 342

    Validating Email Addresses 343

    Saving Comments in Sessions 344

        Displaying the Stored Comment Information..345

    Adding Error Messages..348

        Identifying Errors in saveComment() 348

        Modifying update.inc.php 349

        Matching Error Codes in showCommentForm()...350

Basic Spam Prevention 353

    Creating a Basic Logic Question..354

Generating Random Numbers...354

Obfuscating the Values...354

Adding the Math Question to the Form...355

Adding the Challenge Question to the Form 356

Verifying the Correct Answer...358

Adding the Verification into saveComment()..359

"Post to Twitter" Link..362

Creating a Shortened Link with http://bit.ly..363

Generating an Automatic Status Update for Twitter 365

Displaying the Link on Entries 366

Summary..368

■**Index** **369**

About the Author

Jason Lengstorf is a software designer and developer based in Missoula, MT. He runs a web design/development effort called Ennui Design that specializes in custom web applications ranging from simple informational web sites to full-on content-management systems.

When not glued to his keyboard, he's likely to be found standing in line for coffee, brewing his own beer, lifting heavy things, or pretending to know something about wine.

About the Technical Reviewer

 **Gordon Forsythe** has been developing web applications using PHP since 2000. He has worked on many open source applications and has developed programs for various fields, including education, health care, real estate, and telecommunications. He currently resides in Phoenix, AZ, with his wife, three cats, two dogs, and five fish.

Acknowledgments

I owe the most thanks to my parents, Wendy and Wally Lengstorf, and to my brother and sister, Kyle and Carly. If you guys hadn't been so forgiving during my many years of troublemaking, I'd probably still be living out of a bag in a van somewhere. I'm especially thankful to my dad, who taught me that software isn't about degrees or certifications, but determination.

To Nate Green, my oldest friend and biggest inspiration — this had better move me up to Friday or Saturday! Thanks for showing me that there's no such thing as too young, too bold, or too ambitious.

To my friends Kyle Hibler, Mike Scialabba, and Taylor Selig: keep at it. Someday you'll write books, too, and then you'll be as cool as Nate and I. Thanks for putting up with my geekiness and letting me be on Team Cobra.

I also can't forget to thank Chris Coyier. My clumsy article on his web site was my springboard into this project, and I am sincerely grateful that he took a chance on some punk kid from Montana.

Michelle Lowman, thanks for reading that article and giving me a shot. And for putting up with my incessant questions. And dealing with my utter lack of experience. I really appreciate it, and it's probably the only thing that got me through this project alive.

Gordon Forsythe, thanks for keeping my code clean. Without you, my code might have ended up held together by duct tape. And Patrick Meader, thank you for all your time spent poring over my bad English. This book would have been a grammatical disaster without your help.

Debra Kelly, you came into this project halfway through and managed to somehow put us ahead of schedule. I don't know how you did it, but thanks!

And finally, to all my geeky friends: Rob MacKay, Mike Conaty, Robert Banh, Brenley Dueck, Drew Douglass, Andy Sowards, Tomo Kawai, Chad Engle, and the whole #DCTH crew — thanks for asking questions, providing answers, and reminding me why I do what I do.

Introduction

On February 18, 2009, I received this email:

Hello Jason,
I'm looking for someone to write PHP for Absolute Beginners, *and I was wondering if you would be interested. I like your Simple CMS tutorials; they look like just the thing for this type of book. Please let me know if you are interested.*

Thanks!
Michelle Lowman

I, of course, assumed it was some kind of joke. I replied with something like, "Yeah, okay, sure. I'll write a book." And then a contract showed up in the mail.

Now, not even six months later, the book is almost ready to go to press, and I'm happy to say that I'm proud of the result.

This book is the book I wish I'd had when I first started programming. It assumes no knowledge of PHP, but it doesn't spend hundreds of pages on programming theory or the history of the language. Sure, it covers that, but what I really wanted to do was jump right in and teach you how to build something that you could *use*. I chose a blogging application because it feels like everybody has a blog these days, and why shouldn't *you* know how to build one?

In this book, I've tried to write exactly the way I'd teach you one-on-one: you should feel comfortable with what's being discussed, but not bored. The material should move quickly, but remain easy-to-follow. I also want you to feel like you're learning, not memorizing. And most importantly, when you've finished this project, I want you to turn around and build another one — this time without any help.

PHP is a great language, and it provides developers with the ability to build pretty much anything they can imagine when paired with a database and some good ol' HTML. However, it can also seem intimidating. It's not visual like front-end design, there's all this theory involved, and it's just, you know, *harder*.

But that doesn't have to be the case, and it's my sincere hope that this book will allow you to get your hands dirty with PHP without ever feeling intimidated, lost, or hopeless. It wasn't long ago that I was struggling through complex, boring how-tos on PHP, so I know how it is to feel completely overwhelmed by the massive amounts of information about the language. It's my sincere hope that I've written a book that will allow you to learn everything you need to know in a far less stressful manner.

So take a deep breath and turn the page. Let's do this!

PART 1

■ ■ ■

Getting Started

Before you can get your hands dirty, you'll need to get a development environment set up and familiarize yourself with the basics of PHP. These first few chapters assume no knowledge of PHP and will walk you through the steps required to build a local development environment on your computer.

CHAPTER 1

■ ■ ■

Setting Up the PHP Development Environment

Getting a working development environment put together can be intimidating, especially for the absolute beginner.

To follow along with the project in this book, you'll need to have access to a working installation of Apache, PHP, and MySQL, preferably on your local machine. It's always desirable to test locally, both for speed and security. Doing this both shelters your work-in-progress from the open Internet and decreases the amount of time spent uploading files to an FTP server and waiting for pages to reload.

Why You Need Apache, MySQL, and PHP

PHP is a powerful scripting language that can be run by itself in the command line of any computer with PHP installed. However, PHP alone isn't enough in order to build dynamic web sites.

To use PHP on a web site, you need a server that can process PHP scripts. Apache is a free web server that, once installed on a computer, allows developers to test PHP scripts locally; this makes it an invaluable piece of your local development environment.

Additionally, dynamic websites are dependent on stored information that can be modified quickly and easily; this is the main difference between a dynamic site and a static HTML site. However, PHP doesn't provide a simple, efficient way to store data. This is where a relational database management system like MySQL comes into play. This book's examples rely on MySQL; I chose this database because PHP provides native support for it and the database is free, open-source project.

■**Note** An open-source project is available for free to end users and ships with the code required to create that software. Users are free to inspect, modify, and improve the code, albeit with certain conditions attached. The Open Source Initiative lists 10 key provisions that define open-source software; you can view this list at www.opensource.org/docs/osd.

Drilling Down on PHP

PHP is a general-purpose scripting language that was originally conceived by Rasmus Lerdorf in 1995. Lerdorf created it to satisfy the need for an easy way to process data when creating pages for the World Wide Web.

■**Note** PHP was born out of Rasmus Lerdorf's desire to create a script that would keep track of how many visits his online resume received. Due to the wild popularity of the script he created, Lerdorf continued developing the language. Over time other developers joined him in creating the software; today, PHP is one of the most popular scripting languages in use on the Internet.

PHP originally stood for "Personal Home Page" and was released as a free, open source project. Over time, the language was reworked to meet the needs of its users. In 1997, PHP was renamed to the current "PHP: Hypertext Preprocessor."

At the time I write this, PHP 5.2.9 is the latest stable release available, but versions 5.3 and 6 are both scheduled for release in the near future. PHP 4 is still in use on a number of servers, but support has been discontinued. Many hosting companies let developer use either PHP 4 or PHP 5 on their sites.

Stable/Production vs. Development Releases

Many software products will have a *development release* available, alongside the current, stable release. This is a way for the development community to test an upcoming version of a product; this helps the product's creators work bugs out of the system.

After a proposed release has been tested to a satisfactory level, its creators mark it as the current production release. Users reasonably expect the production software they use to be free of major defects or bugs; calling a version a stable/production release is a way for the product's creators to let potential users know that, in the opinion of the product's creators, all major issues have been worked out, and that it is safe to use this software for mission-critical applications.

How PHP Works

PHP is generally used as a server-side scripting language; it is especially well-suited for creating dynamic web pages. The scripting language features integrated support for interfacing with databases such as MySQL, which makes it a prime candidate for building all manner of web applications, from simple personal web sites to complex enterprise-level applications.

Unlike HTML, which is parsed by a browser when a page loads, PHP is *preprocessed* by the machine that serves the document (this machine is referred to as a server). All PHP code contained with the document is processed by the server *before* the document is sent to the visitor's browser.

PHP is a scripted language, which is another great advantage for PHP programmers. Many programming languages require that you compile files into machine code before they can be run, which is a time-consuming process. Bypassing the need to compile means you're able to edit and test code much more quickly.

Because PHP is a server-side language, running PHP scripts on your local machine requires installing a server on your local machine, as well. The examples in this book rely on the Apache web server to deliver your web pages.

Server-Side vs. Client-Side Scripting

The Internet features two main kinds of scripting: *server-side* and *client-side.* Client-side scripting is comprised mainly of JavaScript, which is responsible for many of the web features that you can actually *see* happening, such as pop-up windows, some animations, and other site features like drop-down menus. The reason this is called "client-side" scripting because the code is executed on the user's machine, after the page has been loaded.

Using client-side scripts enables you to make changes to a page without requiring a page refresh; it also facilitates initial form validation and simplifies making improvements to the user interface.

However, using client-side scripts requires that the users have JavaScript turned on or that their browsers support the script you have written. This means you should not use client-side scripts for user authentication or the handling of anything sensitive, due to the user's ability to modify and/or disable your client-side scripts.

Server-side scripting is performed on the site's hosting server before the page is delivered to the user. This means that any changes that must be made by the script require a page refresh.

Using server-side scripting is great for user authentication, saving changes to database information, retrieving entries for display, and many other tasks.

The downside of server-side scripts lies mainly in the required page refresh. Because the script is processed before it is delivered to the browser, the user doesn't have access to the inner workings of the code. This makes server-side scripts the best choice for handling any sensitive information.

■**Caution** Server-side scripting is better suited to handling sensitive information than client-side scripts, but you still must take care to protect sensitive data. We'll spend more time on basic security later in the book.

Serving web pages with Apache HTTP Server is the most popular web server on the web; it hosts nearly half of all web sites that exist today. Apache is an open-source project that runs on virtually all available operating systems.[1] Apache server is a community-driven project, with many developers contributing to its progress. Apache's open-source roots also means that the software is available free of charge, which probably contributes heavily to Apache's overwhelming popularity relative to its competitors, including Microsoft's IIS and Google's GWS, among others.

On the Apache web site (www.apache.org), Apache HTTP Server is described as "an effort to develop and maintain an open-source HTTP server for modern operating systems including UNIX and Windows NT. The goal of this project is to provide a secure, efficient, and extensible server that provides HTTP services in sync with the current HTTP standards."

What Apache Does

Like all web servers, Apache accepts an HTTP request and serves an HTTP response. The World Wide Web is founded on web servers, and every website you visit demonstrates the functionality of web servers.

I've already mentioned that, while HTML can be processed by a web browser, programming languages such as PHP need to be handled by a web server. Due to its overwhelming popularity, Apache is used for testing purposes throughout this book.

Store Info with MySQL

MySQL is a relational database management system (DBMS). Essentially, this means that MySQL allows users to store information in a table-based structure, using rows and columns to organize different pieces of data. This structure is similar to that of Microsoft's Access database.

The examples in this book rely on MySQL to store the information you'll use in your PHP scripts, from blog entries to administrator information; it is that approach that allows your site to be *dynamic*.

---

1 Wikipedia, "Apache HTTP Server," http://en.wikipedia.org/wiki/Apache_(HTTP_server)

■**Note** *Blog* is short for *weblog*, which is an online journal for an individual or business.

Installing PHP, Apache, and MySQL (the Hard Way)

One of the biggest hurdles for new programmers is *starting*. Before you can write your first line of PHP, you must first download Apache and PHP, and usually MySQL, and then fight through installation instructions that are full of technical jargon you might not understand yet. This experience can leave many developers feeling unsure of themselves, doubting whether they've installed the required software correctly.

In my own case, this hurdle kept me from learning programming for *months*, even though I desperately wanted to move beyond plain ol' HTML. I unsuccessfully attempted to install PHP on my local machine not once, but *three* different times before I was able to run my first PHP command successfully.

Installation Made Easy

Fortunately, the development community has responded to the frustration of beginning developers with several options that take all the pain out of setting up your development environment, whether you create applications for Windows, Mac, or Linux machines. These options include all-in-one solutions for setting up Apache, MySQL, and PHP installations.

The most common all-in-one solution is a program called "XAMPP" (`www.apachefriends.org/en/xampp.html`), which rolls Apache, MySQL, PHP, and a few other useful tools together into one easy installer.

XAMPP is free and available for Windows, Mac, and Linux, so this book assumes you will use it as your development environment.

■**Note** Most Linux distributions ship with one flavor or another of the LAMP stack (Linux-specific software that functions similarly to XAMPP) bundled in by default. Certain versions of Mac OS X also have PHP and Apache installed by default.

Installing XAMPP

Enough background: You're now ready to install XAMPP on your development machine. This process should take about five minutes and is completely painless.

■**Note** A good habit to get into is to create separate *development* and *production* environments. A development environment is for testing projects for bugs and is generally sheltered from the world at large. A production environment is reserved for fully functional, publicly available projects.

Step 1: Download XAMPP

Your first task is to obtain a copy of the XAMPP software. Head over to the XAMPP site (`www.apachefriends.org/en/xampp.html`) and download the latest version (0.7.4 for Mac, 1.7.1 for Windows, and 1.7 for Linux at the time I write this).

Step 2: Open the Installer and Follow the Instructions

After downloading XAMPP, find the newly downloaded installer and run it. You should be greeted with a screen similar to the one shown in Figure 1-1.

■**Note** All screenshots used in this book were taken on a computer running Mac OS X 10.4.11. Your installation might differ slightly if you use a different operating system. XAMPP for Windows offers additional options, such as the ability to install Apache, MySQL, and Filezilla (an FTP server) as services. This is unnecessary and will consume computer resources even when they are not being used, so it's probably best to leave these services off. Additionally, Windows users should keep the c:\xampp install directory for the sake of following this book's examples more easily.

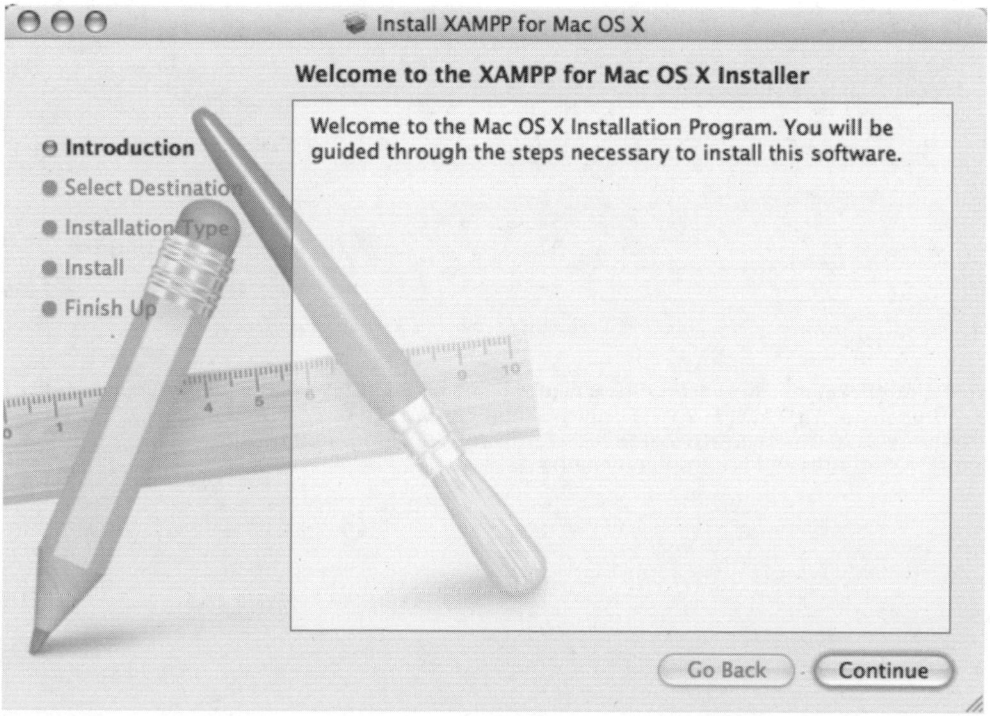

Figure 1-1. The introductory screen for the XAMPP installer on Mac OS X

Click the Continue button to move to the next screen (see Figure 1-2), where you can choose the destination drive you want to install XAMPP on.

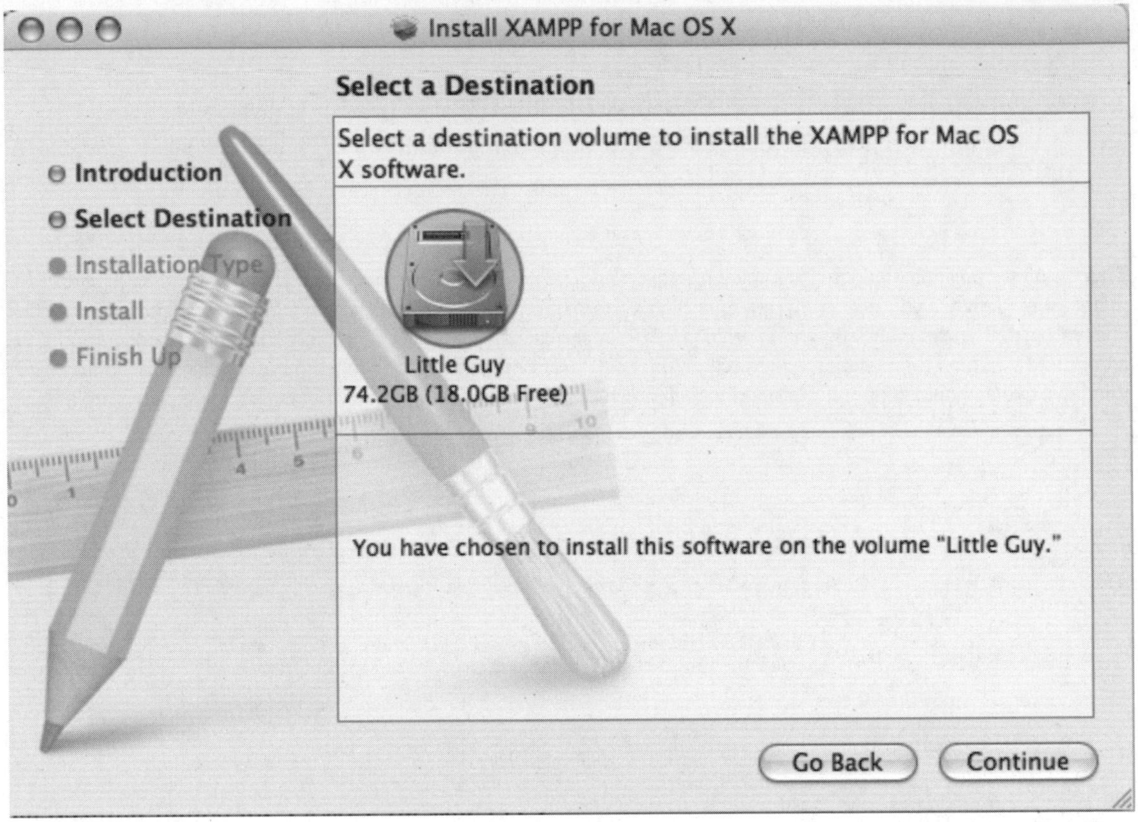

Figure 1-2. Select a destination drive on which to install XAMPP

The installation wizard's next screen (see Figure 1-3) asks what type of installation you prefer. This is your first time installing XAMPP, so the only available option is a basic installation of XAMPP.

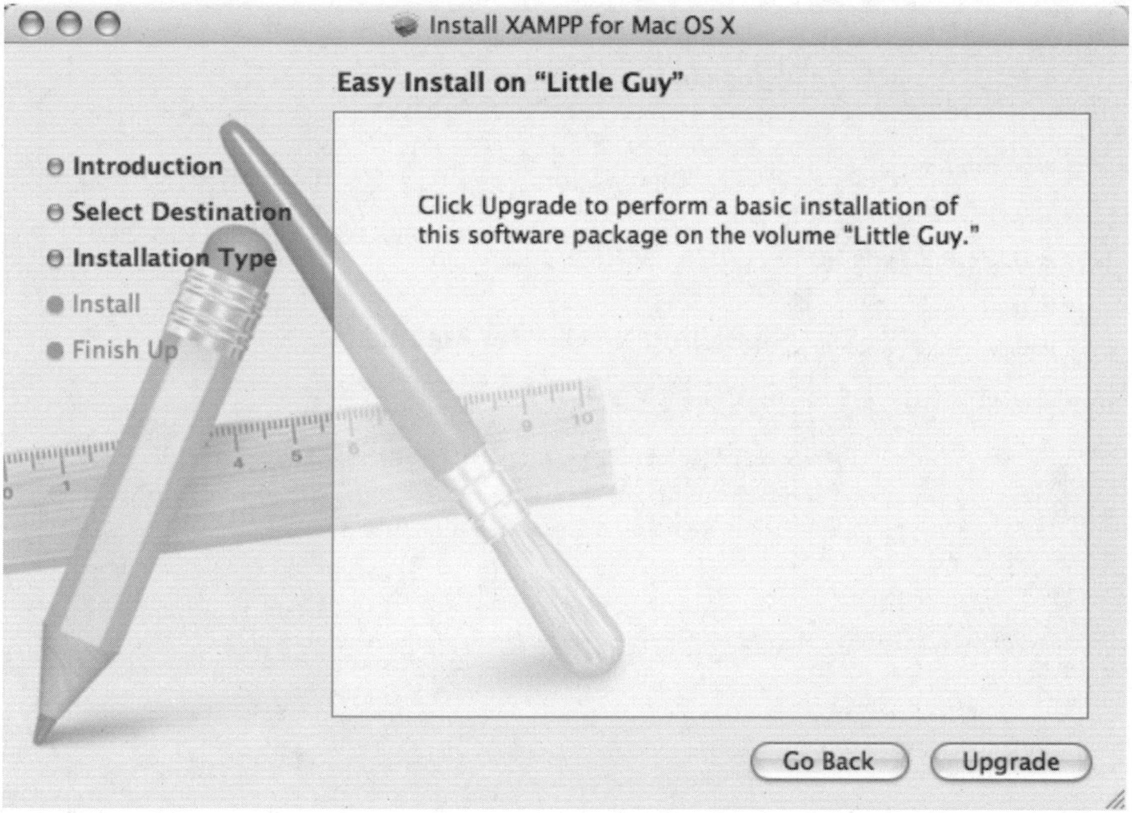

Figure 1-3. *XAMPP gives you only one option the first time you install it*

Clicking "Upgrade" brings up a screen that shows the progress of XAMPP as it installs on the selected drive (see Figure 1-4).

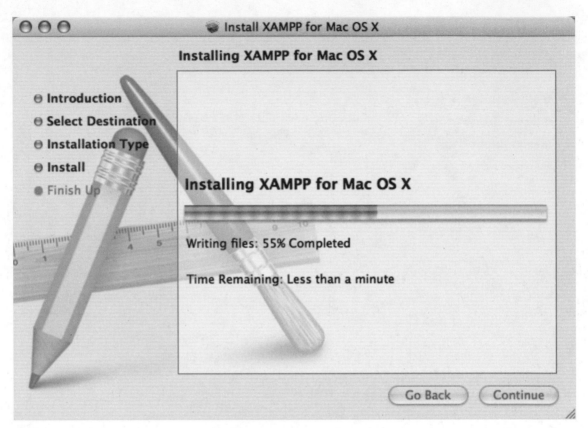

Figure 1-4. Watch the installer's progress for XAMPP for Mac OS X

Installation requires a minute or two to complete, whereupon the installer displays the final screen (see Figure 1-5), which confirms that the installation was successful.

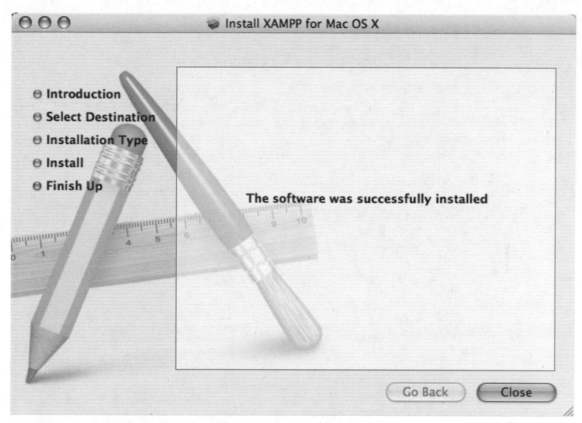

Figure 1-5. Successful installation of XAMPP brings up this screen

Step 3: Test XAMPP to Ensure Proper Installation

So far you've used the XAMPP wizard to install Apache, PHP, and MySQL. The next step is to activate the trio of applications.

Open the XAMPP Control Panel

You can activate the just-installed applications by navigating to the newly installed xampp folder and opening the XAMPP Control Panel (see Figure 1-6).

■**Note** When opening the XAMPP Control Panel you may be prompted for your password. This has no effect on the services themselves and should not affect the projects covered in this book.

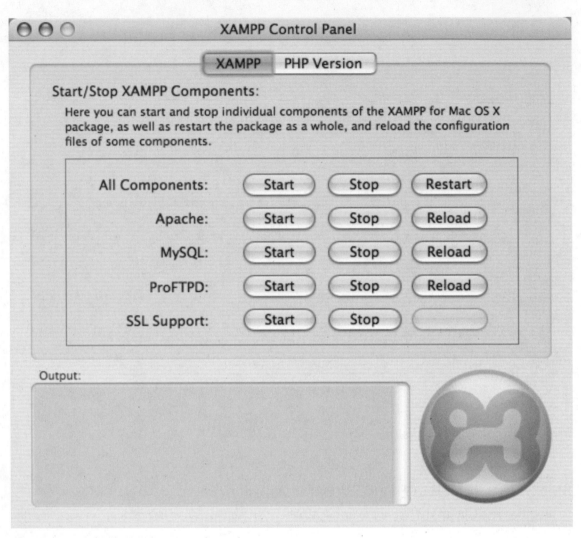

Figure 1-6. *Inside the XAMPP control panel*

Activating Apache, PHP, and MySQL on your development machine is as simple as clicking the "Start" button next to both Apache and MySQL on the XAMPP Control Panel. You might be prompted to confirm that the server is allowed to run on your computer, and you might be required to enter your system password. After you do this, the "Output" panel should start displaying a series of messages (see Figure 1-7); the final message displayed should say, "XAMPP for (*operating system here*) started."

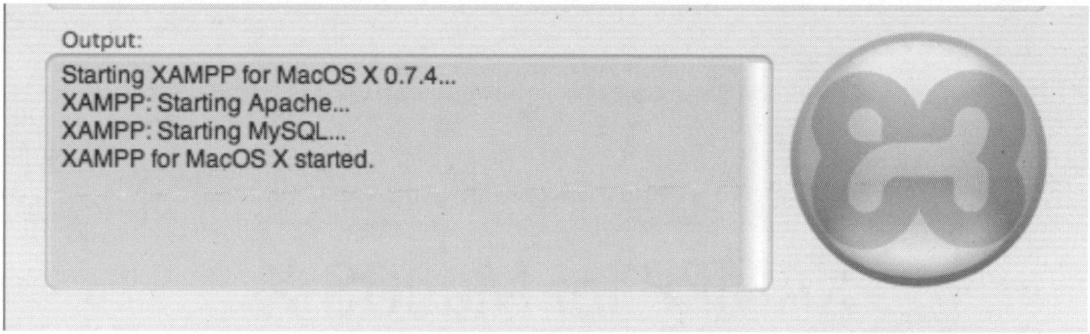

Output:

Starting XAMPP for MacOS X 0.7.4...
XAMPP: Starting Apache...
XAMPP: Starting MySQL...
XAMPP for MacOS X started.

Figure 1-7. *Starting XAMPP services*

■**Note** There is also an FTP (file transfer protocol) option available in XAMPP. FTP provides a method for moving files between networks. The examples in this book don't require this option, so there is no need to activate it in the XAMPP control panel.

Verify That Apache and PHP Are Running

It's a simple matter to check whether all the services are running properly on your development machine. Simply open a browser and go to this address: `http://localhost`. If everything has gone correctly, you'll be redirected to `http://localhost/xampp/index.php` (see Figure 1-8).

If this screen loads, you've installed Apache and PHP on your development machine successfully!

If you do *not* see this screen, the XAMPP online community is extremely helpful and most installation issues have been addressed in the Apache Friends forum at `http://www.apachefriends.org/f/viewforum.php?f=34`.

The address, `http://localhost`, is an alias for the current computer you're working on. When using XAMPP, navigating to `http://localhost` in a browser tells the server to open the root web directory; this is the `htdocs` folder contained in the XAMPP install directory.

Another way to use your server to access the root web directory on your local machine is to navigate to the *IP address*—a numerical identifier assigned to any device connected to a computer network—that serves as the "home" address for all HTTP servers: `http://127.0.0.1`.

Figure 1-8. Visit the XAMPP homepage at http://localhost

Verify That MySQL Is Running

You can verify that MySQL is also running by going to the Tools menu and choosing "phpMyAdmin." This should bring up the screen shown in Figure 1-9.

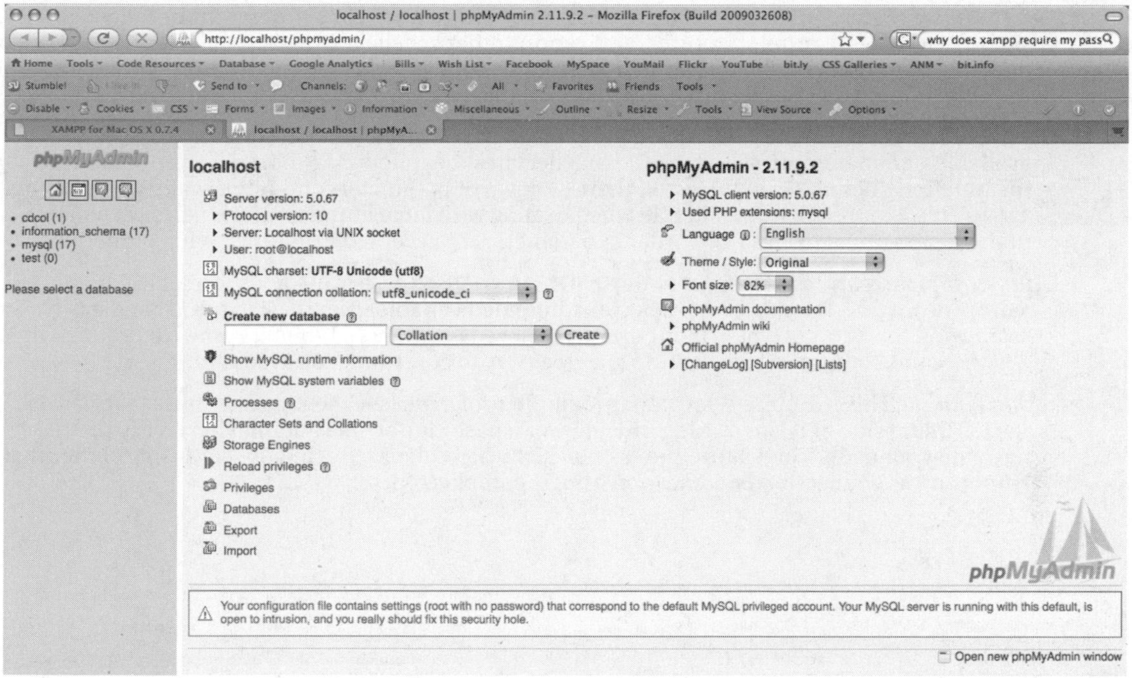

Figure 1-9. MySQL is running if phpMyAdmin loads without error

Now that have MySQL running on your development machine, you're ready to start running PHP scripts. Note that if you're a Windows user, you might need to navigate to C:\xampp\php\php.ini and locate the following lines to verify that magic_quotes_gpc is set to Off:

```
; Magic quotes for incoming GET/POST/Cookie data
magic_quotes_gpc = Off
```

Choosing a Development Kit

Your development machine is now running all the necessary programs for programming with PHP. The next step is to decide how you're going to write your scripts. PHP scripts are text-based, so you have myriad options, ranging from the simple Notepad.exe and text-edit programs to highly specialized software development kits (SDKs) and integrated development environments (IDEs).

Benefiting from SDKs and IDEs

There's nothing wrong with coding in a plain text editor, but using an SDK and/or IDE for development can bring you many benefits, including:

- *Syntax highlighting:* This is the ability to recognize certain words in a programming language, such as variables, control structures, and various other special text. This special text is highlighted or otherwise differentiated to make scanning your code much easier. For example, the color coding on the left makes this code less daunting to look at (see Figure 1-10).

- *Built-in function references:* When you enter the name of a function, this feature displays available parameters, as well as the file that declares the function, a short description of what the function does, and a more in-depth breakdown of parameters and return values (see Figure 1-11). This feature proves invaluable when dealing with large libraries, and it can save you trips to the PHP manual to check the order of parameters or acceptable arguments for a function.

- *Auto-complete features:* Common to most SDKs and IDEs, this feature adds available variables to a drop-down list, allowing you to select the intended variable from the list quickly and easily, saving you the effort of typing it out every time (see Figure 1-12). When it comes to productivity, every second counts, and this feature is a great way to contribute to saved time.

- *Code Folding:* This feature lets you collapse snippets of code (see the plus and minus toggles on the left-hand side of Figure 1-13), reducing workspace clutter-free and making it easy to navigate your code. This feature proves especially helpful for reducing the confusing clutter that springs up as your scripts become increasingly complicated.

```
static function buildMenu($menu_array, $url_array, $is_sub=FALSE)
{
    $attr = ($is_sub) ? ' id="menu"' : ' class="submenu"';
    $menu = "<ul$attr>";
    foreach($menu_array as $id => $properties) {
        echo 'ID: ', $id, '<br />';
        foreach($properties as $key => $val) {
            if(is_array($val)) {
                $sub = buildMenu($val, $url_array, TRUE);
            } else {
                $sub = NULL;
                $$key = $val;
            }
        }
        $sel = ($id==$url_array[0]) ? ' class="selected"' : NULL;
        $menu .= "<li><a href=\"$url\"$sel>$display</a></li>$sub";

    }
    $menu .= '</ul>';

    return $menu;
}
```

```
static function buildMenu($menu_array, $url_array, $is_sub=FALSE)
    {
        $attr = ($is_sub) ? ' id="menu"' : ' class="submenu"';
        $menu = "<ul$attr>";
        foreach($menu_array as $id => $properties) {
            echo 'ID: ', $id, '<br />';
            foreach($properties as $key => $val) {
                if(is_array($val)) {
                    $sub = buildMenu($val, $url_array, TRUE);
                } else {
                    $sub = NULL;
                    $$key = $val;
                }
            }
            $sel = ($id==$url_array[0]) ? ' class="selected"' : NULL;
            $menu .= "<li><a href=\"$url\"$sel>$display</a></li>$sub";

        }
        $menu .= '</ul>';

        return $menu;
    }
```

Figure 1-10. *The left-hand side shows code with syntax highlighting; the right-hand side shows the same code with no syntax highlighting*

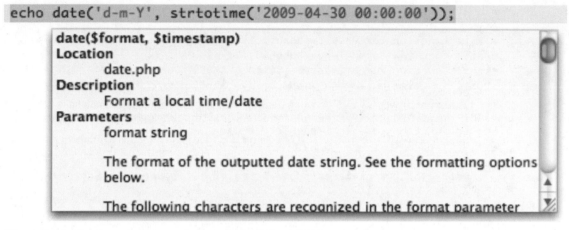

Figure 1-11. Viewing a function reference in the Eclipse PDT

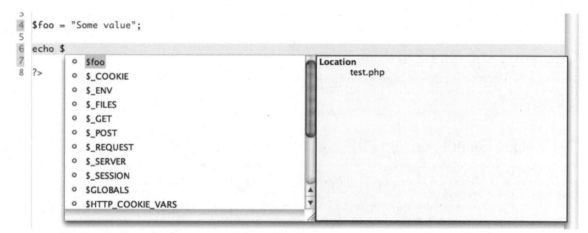

Figure 1-12. Taking advantage of autocomplete in the Eclipse PDT

```
  3⊖class Utilities
  4 {
  5⊕    static function textPreview($body, $limit=45)▢
 39⊕    static function formatImageThumb($e, $class=NULL)▢
 53⊕    static function formatImage($e, $link=FALSE)▢
 85⊕    static function buildMenu($menu_array, $url_array, $is_sub=FALSE)▢
108⊕    static function curry($func, $arity) {▢
123⊕    static function replaceTags($transformations, $matches)▢
128⊖    static function copyrightYear($created)
129    {
130        $current = date('Y', time());
131        return ($current>$created) ? $created.'-'.$current : $current;
132    }
133 }
134
135 ?>
```

Figure 1-13. *Code folding in the Eclipse PDT*

Choosing the Right SDK

You have many choices when it comes to choosing development tools, and it should be noted that there's no wrong answer when selecting yours. If the tool feels right, and makes sense to you, that's really all that matters.

The Eclipse Foundation and PDT

The exercises in this book rely on the popular open source Eclipse SDK and more specifically on the PHP-specific PDT IDE. PDT stands for PHP Development Tools, and this IDE provides a free IDE option for beginning developers.

The team responsible for overseeing Eclipse notes, "Eclipse is an open source community, whose projects are focused on building an open development platform comprised of extensible frameworks, tools and runtimes for building, deploying and managing software across the lifecycle."

Essentially, this means that Eclipse is a group of people working together to create the best available tools for developers—at no cost to the developer.

Installing and Using the Eclipse PDT

Installing and setting up the Eclipse PDT requires six steps.

Step 1: Downloading the PDT

Get started by navigating to the PDT download page (http://www.eclipse.org/pdt/downloads/) and scrolling down to the All-In-One downloads section. Select your operating system, then choose a mirror for downloading (generally, the default mirror will be highlighted and will work just fine).

Step 2: Unpacking the PDT Archive

After the file finishes downloading, unzip the file. A folder called "eclipse" should appear in the same directory as the downloaded archive.

Drag this folder into your Programs or Applications folder (or wherever you want to keep it) and open it up. There will be a purple icon that says "Eclipse"; double-clicking the icon launches the IDE and brings up the loading screen (see Figure 1-14).

Figure 1-14. *Loading the Eclipse PDT screen*

Step 3: Choosing Your Project Workspace

After a moment, a dialog box will pop up (see Figure 1-15) that asks you to select your workspace. You'll be working with XAMPP, so set the path to the XAMPP htdocs folder (see Figure 1-16). You can find this in the xampp folder you installed previously.

Figure 1-15. *Selecting your workspace in the Eclipse PDT*

Figure 1-16. *Selecting the htdocs folder from the XAMPP installation*

Selecting this folder and checking the "Use this as the default and do not ask me again" box enables you to tell Eclipse to create new projects in the htdocs folder automatically, which simplifies testing your code.

After clicking "Choose," close the welcome screen that shows up by clicking the "X" in the tab at the top, next to "Welcome" (see Figure 1-17), which takes you to the editor.

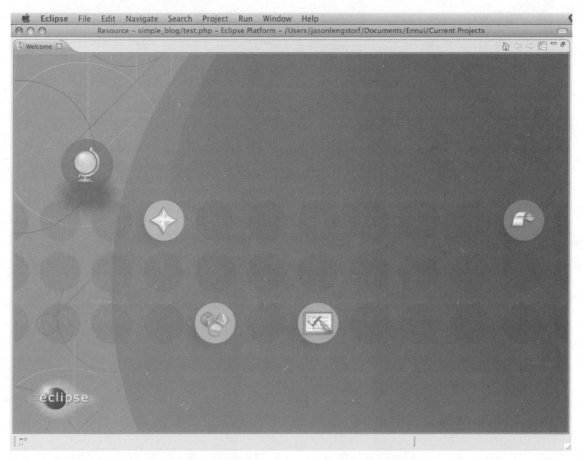

Figure 1-17. *Clicking the "X" next to "Welcome" closes the welcome screen*

Step 4: Creating Your First Project

You're almost to the point where you can code a simple blog. The next step is to create a project. Do this by clicking the New Project icon, which is at the top left of the Eclipse toolbar (see Figure 1-18).

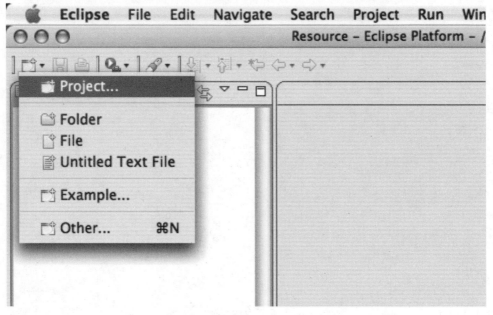

Figure 1-18. Creating a new project in Eclipse

Select "New Project..." from the drop-down menu that pops up. This brings up a new dialog (see Figure 1-19); select "PHP Project" from the list of project types and click "Next."

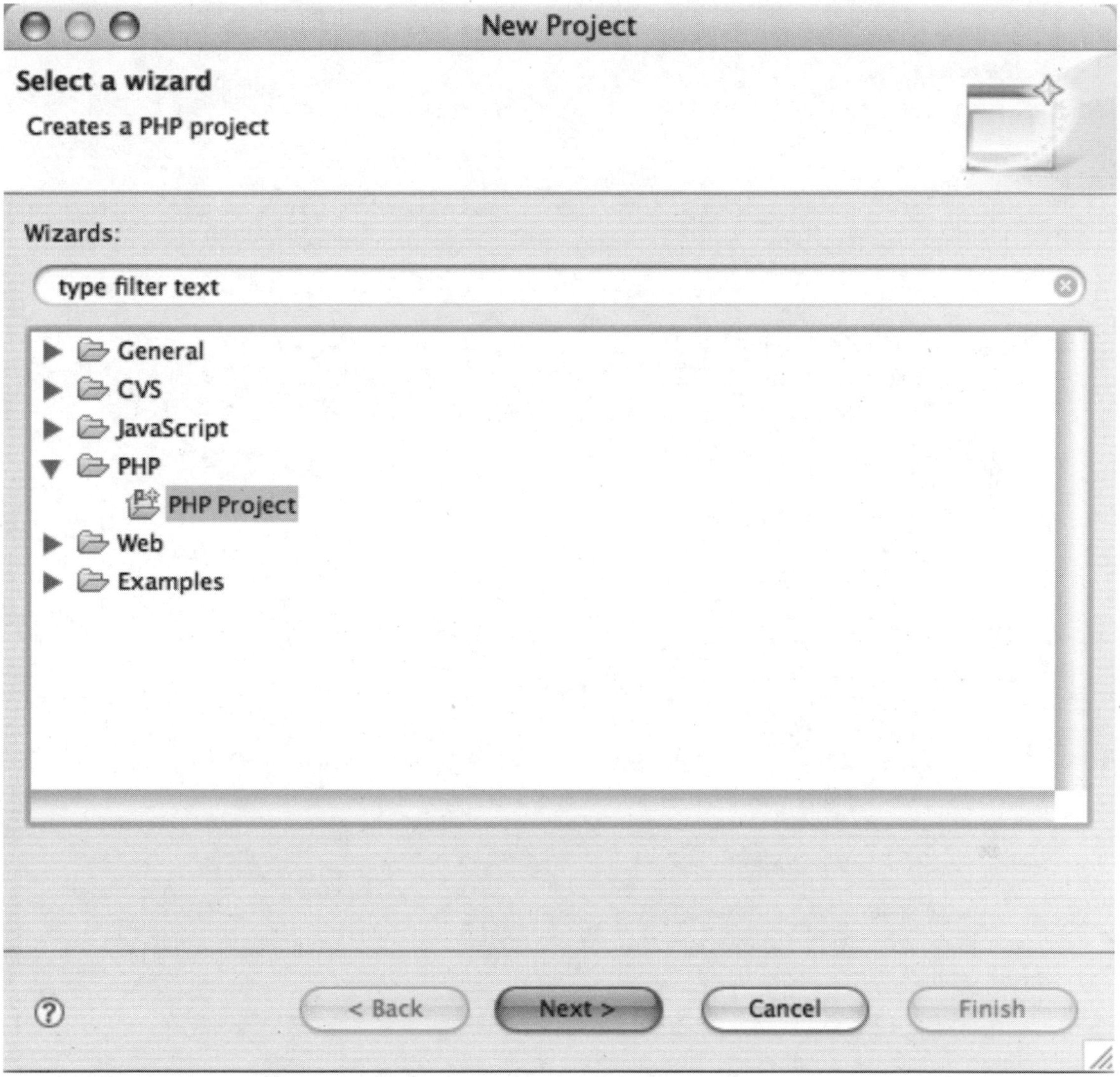

Figure 1-19. *Creating a PHP project*

The next dialog presented asks you to name your project and provides some customization options for the project (see Figure 1-20). Name the project "simple_blog" and leave all the settings at their default values.

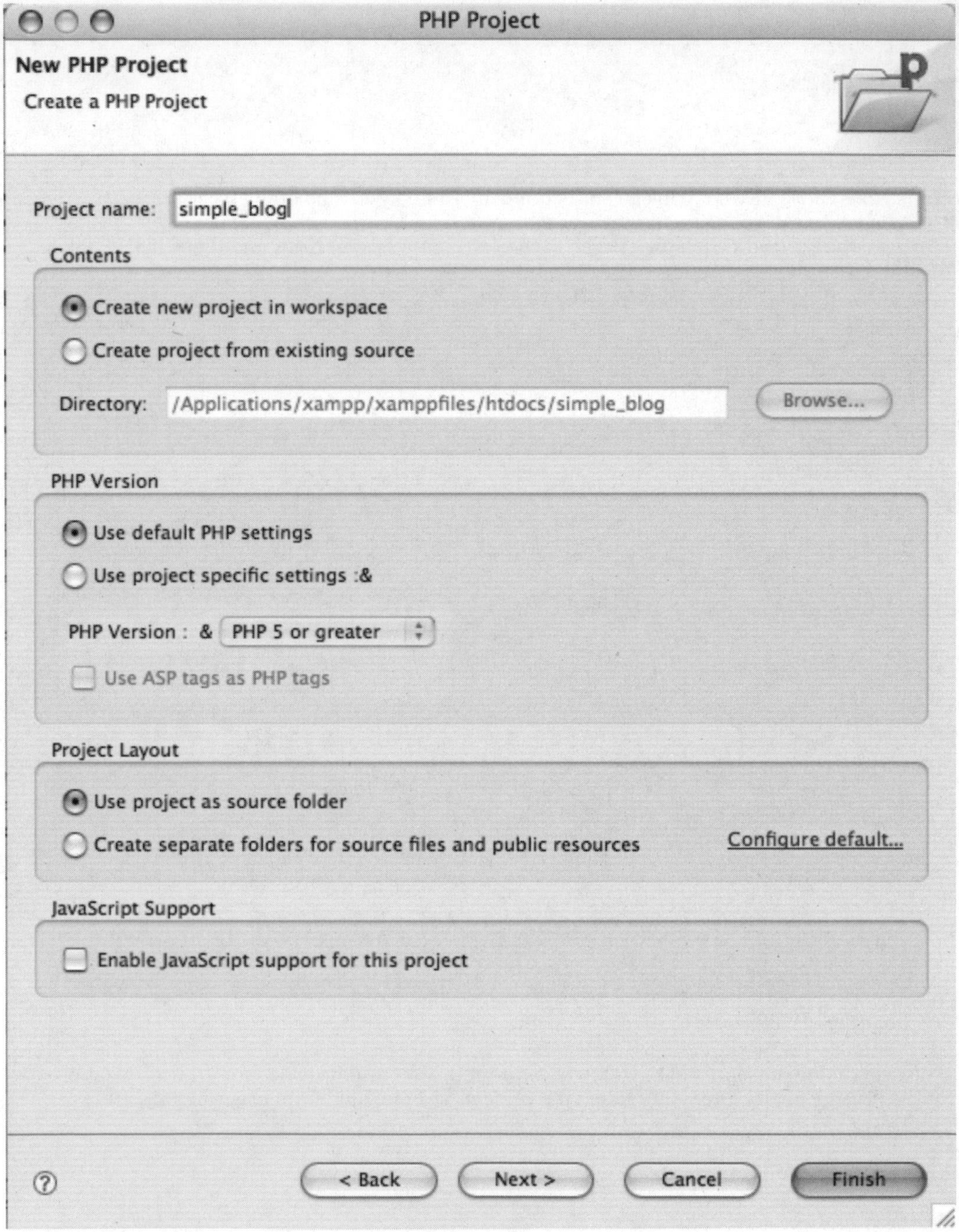

Figure 1-20. *Creating the* `simple_blog` *project*

Clicking "Finish" will bring you back to the editor; your newly created project will be listed in the left-hand panel. At this point, Eclipse lets you know that this project type is associated with the PHP perspective, and it asks whether you'd like to switch to the PHP perspective. It makes sense to do this because you're working with PHP, so select, "Yes."

Step 5: Creating a File

The final step is to create a file that you can start coding in. At first you'll be doing basic exercises to get a feel for the language, so call your first file test.php.

To create the file, right click the simple_blog project, hover over New, and then click PHP File from the resulting drop-down menu (see Figure 1-21).

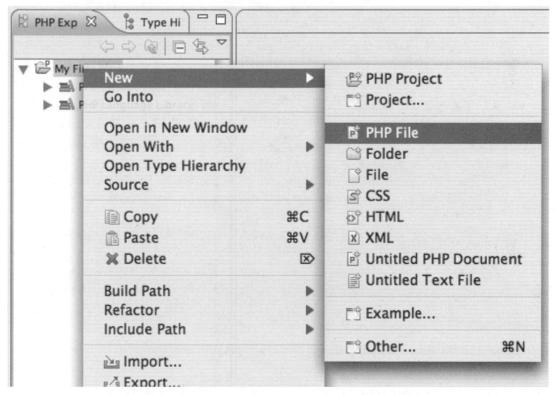

Figure 1-21. *Creating a PHP file in Eclipse*

This brings up a new dialog where you can name your file (see Figure 1-22).

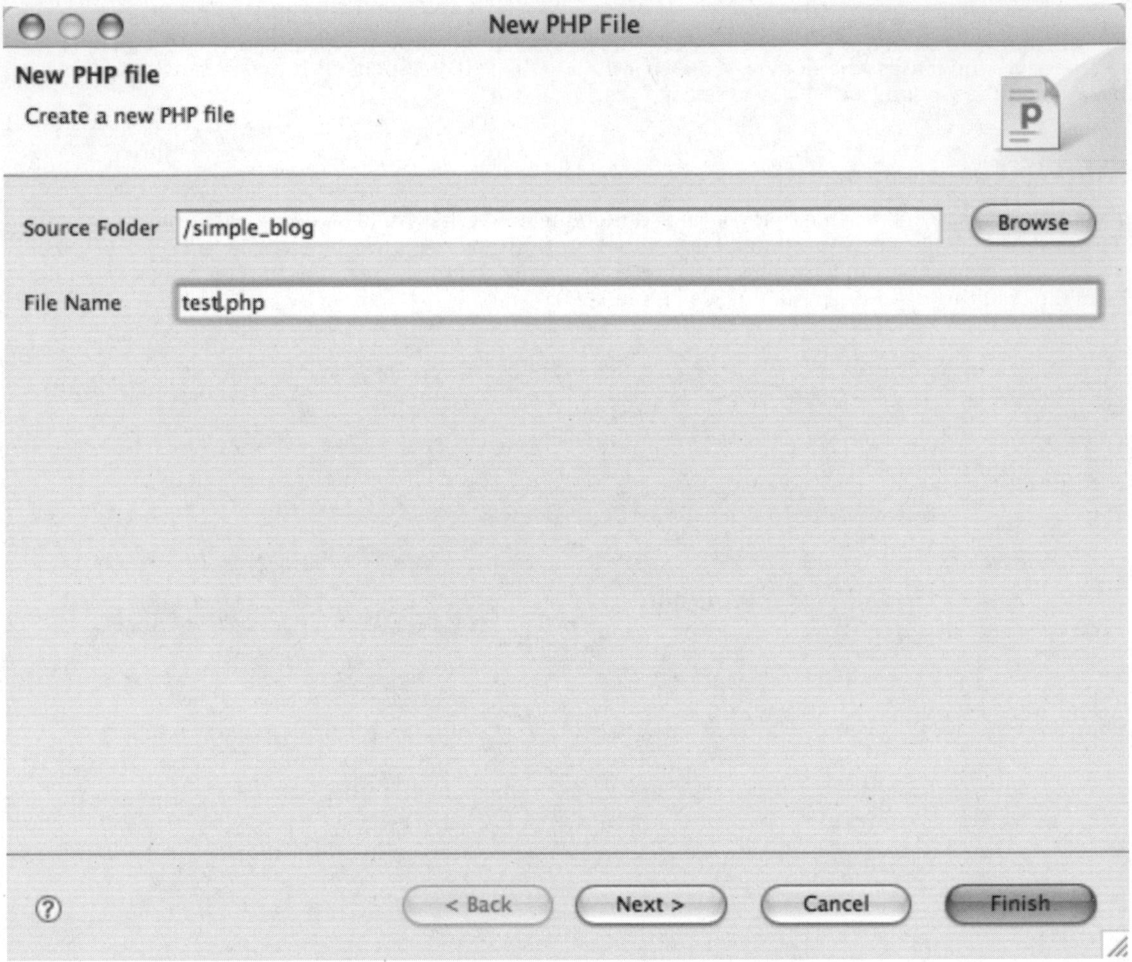

Figure 1-22. Create `test.php` *and click "Finish"*

Clicking Finish creates your first file and means you can now start coding.

Step 6: Writing Your First Script

The final step is to make sure that everything is set up correctly and ready for you to start developing your blog. You can do this by writing a short script to ensure that PHP is working in your `test.php` file. Add this code to the `test.php` file and save:

```php
<?php
    echo "Hello world!";
?>
```

Now open any browser and navigate to `http://localhost/simple_blog/test.php`; what you see should look like Figure 1-23).

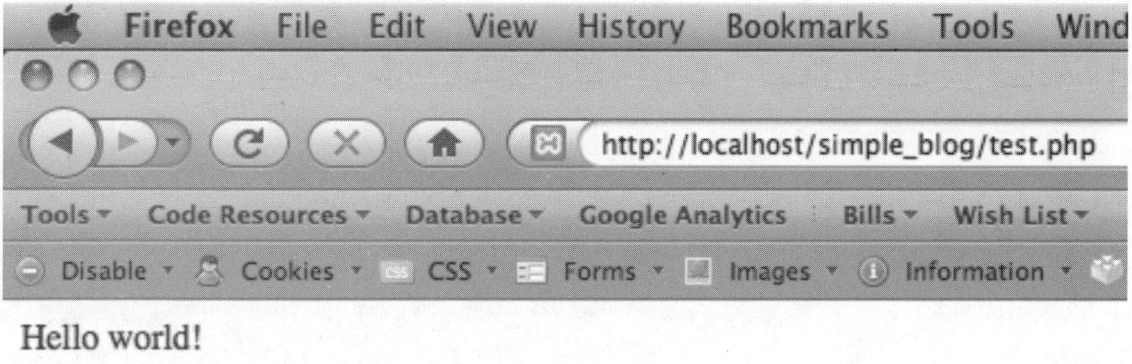

Figure 1-23. `test.php` loaded in a browser, displaying your first script!

If the above text is visible, you have installed XAMPP and Eclipse successfully, and you're ready to start building your blog.

Summary

In this chapter, you learned what PHP, MySQL, and Apache are, and what role they play in the development of dynamic web sites. You also learned a quick and easy way to install a fully functional development environment on your local computer by installing XAMPP and Eclipse PDT.

In the next chapter, you'll learn the basics of PHP, including variables, control structures, and functions. Nearly everything you learn will be tested in your new development environment, so keep `test.php` open and ready to edit.

■ ■ ■

CHAPTER 2

Understanding PHP: Language Basics

So far you've bypassed the old, cumbersome method of creating a development environment, and you're now ready to start writing code.

But where do you start? In this chapter, I'll cover the steps you need to follow to start using PHP in the creation of powerful, dynamic web applications; you'll also begin to develop the basic skills you need to create your blog.

In this chapter, you'll learn how to accomplish several tasks:

- Embed PHP in web pages

- Send data as output to the browser

- Add comments in your code

- Use variables and understand the datatypes they support

- Use operators to manipulate data

- Use control structures to add power to your scripts

By the end of this chapter, you should be comfortable writing basic PHP that will allow you to create, store, manipulate, and output data.

■Note This chapter discusses basic aspects of the PHP language, but you should keep in mind that some functions won't be covered completely. For clarification, more examples, or for concept reinforcement, visit the **PHP manual** at http://www.php.net/manual/en/ and search the function in the field where it says, "search for _____ in the function list." Alternatively, you can access information about many PHP functions by navigating to http://php.net/*function_name*. Don't forget to read the comments because many of your fellow programmers offer insight, tips, and even additional functions in their commentary.

Embedding PHP Scripts

In Chapter 1, when I talked about Apache and web servers in general, I mentioned how a server will process PHP in a file before sending that file to the browser. But you might be curious how the server knows where to look for PHP.

By default, servers look for PHP only in files that end with the `.php` extension. But a `.php` file can contain elements that aren't part of your PHP script, and searching the entire file for potential scripts is confusing and resource-intensive. To solve this issue, all PHP scripts need to be contained with *PHP delimiters.* To begin a PHP script, you include the opening delimiter `<?php` and start coding. To finish, you simply add `?>` to the end of the script. Anything outside of these delimiters will be treated as HTML or plain text.

You can see this in action by opening Eclipse and editing the `test.php` file by double-clicking the file in the project folder you created in the last chapter (full path: `/xampp/htdocs/simple_blog/test.php`) so it contains the following code:

```
<p>Static Text</p>
<?php
    echo '<p>This text was generated by PHP!</p>';
?>
<p>This text was not.</p>
```

Save the file, navigate to `http://localhost/simple_blog/test.php` in your browser, and you should see the following:

```
Static Text
This text was generated by PHP!
This text was not.
```

As you can see, the text inside the PHP delimiters was handled as a script, but the text outside was rendered as regular HTML. There is no limit to how many blocks of PHP you can include in a page, so the following snippet is completely valid:

```
<?php
    echo '<p>This is some text.</p>';
?>
<p>Some of this text is static, <?php echo 'but this sure isn't!'; ?></p>
<?php echo '<p>'; ?>
This text is enclosed in paragraph tags that were generated by PHP.
<?php echo '</p>'; ?>
```

The preceding code snippet outputs the following to the browser:

```
This is some text.
Some of this text is static, but this sure isn't!
This text is enclosed in paragraph tags that were generated by PHP.
```

Alternative Delimiters

There are a few alternative methods for delimiting your PHP scripts that you might come across from time to time, so you should be aware of them. However, it's important to note that the use of these alternative delimiters is discouraged, so you should avoid using them.

Short Tags

PHP offers a shortcut syntax known as *short tags*; these allow your scripts to be delimited with `<?` and `?>`, which is easier to type. However, the use of short tags requires that the `short_open_tag` directive be enabled, which means that scripts using short tags can create compatibility problems for applications that need to run on multiple servers that might not have the same configuration.

■**Caution** The use of short tags conflicts with XML syntax (XML declarations use the syntax `<?xml version="1.0" encoding="ISO-8859-1"?>`), so you should not use them.

There is also a shortcut syntax for outputting data quickly, which you use like this:

```
<?='Some text to output.'?>
```

The previous snippet functions identically to this longer-winded syntax:

```
<?php
    echo 'Some text to output.';
?>
```

Again, keep in mind that you should *avoid* using this syntax because of its incompatibility, both with various server configurations and XML syntax.

HTML <script> Tags and ASP-Style Delimiters

For the sake of compatibility with editing software such as Microsoft Front Page, PHP also supports the use of HTML `<script>` tags:

```
<script language="php">
    echo 'This is some text';
</script>
```

Another option provided to Front Page users was Microsoft's ASP-style delimiters:

```
<%
    echo 'This is some text';
%>
```

■**Caution** Use of the `<script>` tag is discouraged because it can cause confusion with JavaScript in files. As of PHP 6, ASP-style tags are no longer supported.

Variables and Datatypes

So far, you've learned how to output data, as well as how to use variables to a certain extent. Before going any further, let's take a moment to drill down on variables and how they work.

What Is a Variable?

A variable is a keyword or phrase that acts as an identifier for a value stored in a system's memory. This is useful because it allows us to write programs that will perform a set of actions on a variable value, which means you can change the output of the program simply by changing the variable, rather than changing the program itself.

Storing Values in a Variable

PHP lets you store nearly anything in a variable using one of the following *datatypes*:

String: Alphanumeric characters, such as sentences or names

Integer: A numeric value, expressed in whole numbers

Float: A numeric value, expressed in real numbers (decimals)

Boolean: Evaluates to TRUE or FALSE (sometimes evaluates to 1 for TRUE and 0 for FALSE)

Array: An indexed collection of data (see the "Understanding Arrays" section later in this chapter for more information on this subject)

Object: A collection of data and methods (see Chapter 4 and its section on PHP Data Objects for more information on this subject)

PHP is a loosely typed language, which means it determines the type of data being handled based on a "best guess" principle, as opposed to a strictly typed language such as C, which requires you name datatypes for every variable and function. Consider this code snippet:

```
$foo = "5"; // This is considered a string
$bar = $foo + 2; // This converts $foo to an integer (outputs 7)
```

This might seem confusing at first, but it's actually intuitive and eliminates debugging if you enclose a number in quotes accidentally.

Understanding Strings

A *string* is any series of characters enclosed in single (') or double (") quotes, or that you create using special *heredoc* or *nowdoc syntax*, which I'll cover in a moment.

Strings have a few characters that will cause problems if you do not *escape* them with a backslash (\). Escaping allows you to use characters in strings that might otherwise cause problems, such as an apostrophe in a string enclosed in single quotes:

```
$string = 'It\'s cold outside today!';
```

If you don't escape the apostrophe in *it's,* the script has no way of knowing that the apostrophe is part of the string and not the end of it—and your script would fail.

Single-Quote Syntax

Enclosing a string in single quotes is the simplest way to create a string in PHP. It doesn't expand special characters or variables, but instead delivers them as plain text to the browser.

Let's look at some examples to see how single quotes behave. Add the following into test.php to see how different data is handled:

```php
<?php

    // The <br /> adds a line break in the browser for readability
    echo 'This is a string. <br />';

    echo 'This is a string
    with line breaks. <br />';

    // Special characters, such as the newline (\n) character,
    // won't be expanded when in single quotes.
    echo 'This is a string \n with a newline character. <br />';

    echo 'This string\'s got an apostrophe. <br />';

    // A backslash doesn't need to be escaped if not escaping a
    // special character.
    echo 'This string has a backslash (\) in it. <br />';

    echo 'This string has an escaped backslash (\\) in it. <br />';

    // Variables will not be expanded in single quotes
    echo 'This $variable will not be expanded. <br />';

?>
```

The output of this code in a browser looks like this:

```
This is a string.
This is a string with line breaks.
This is a string \n with a newline character.
This string's got an apostrophe.
This string has a backslash (\) in it.
This string has an escaped backslash (\) in it.
This $variable will not be expanded.
```

■**Note** Newline characters (\n) don't render in browsers. However, they are visible in the source code of the rendered page, which you can view by choosing View Source from the View menu of your browser.

Double-Quote Syntax

Strings encased in double quotes behave similarly to strings encased in single quotes but they interpret more special characters, including expanding variables.

■**Tip** Special characters like the new line character (\n) won't affect browser output, but do affect command-line and source-code displays. Use an HTML break tag (<br />) to create a new line in the browser.

You can see the difference achieved by placing strings in double quotes by placing the following code in test.php:

```php
<?php

    echo "This is a string. <br />";

    echo "This is a string
    that spans
    multiple lines. <br />";

    // Apostrophes don't need to be escaped in double quotes
    echo "This string's got an apostrophe. <br />";
```

```php
// Double quotes will need to be escaped
echo "This string says, \"I need escaping!\" <br />";

// New line characters will be interpreted
echo "This string has \n newline \n characters. <br />";

// A backslash will be printed if a special character doesn't
// directly follow it
echo "This string contains a backslash (\). <br />";

// Variables will be expanded if not escaped
$variable = "word";
echo "This string uses a $variable. <br />";

// A variable can be interpreted as plain text by escaping the
// dollar sign with a backslash
echo "This string escapes the \$variable. <br />";

?>
```

The output of this code in a browser looks like this:

```
This is a string.
This is a string that spans multiple lines.
This string's got an apostrophe.
This string says, "I need escaping!"
This string has newline characters.
This string contains a backslash (\).
This string uses a word.
This string escapes the $variable.
```

String Concatenation

It's often necessary to join two strings together in a script. You accomplish this using the string concatenation operator, a period (.).

You join two strings together by placing a period between them:

```php
<?php
$foo = "This is a " . "string.";
echo $foo;
?>
```

This code creates the following output:

```
This is a string.
```

You can concatenate variables as well, as long as they're not of the array or object type:

```php
<?php
    $foo = "This is a ";
    $bar = "string.";
    echo $foo . $bar;
?>
```

This produces output identical to your previous script:

```
This is a string.
```

Heredoc Syntax

Another option available for handling strings is *heredoc* syntax, which begins with <<< and an identifier that can be any combination of alphanumeric characters or underscores that don't begin with a digit. You end the string by repeating the identifier on a new line, followed by a semicolon.

You can get a good idea of how heredoc syntax works by examining this example:

```
$foo = <<<EOD
This is a string created using heredoc syntax.
It can span multiple lines, use "quotes" without
escaping, and it'll allow $variables too.

Special characters are still supported \n as well.
EOD;
```

EOD (short for "end of data") is your identifier in this case, but the text you use isn't important. The most important thing to note is that the closing identifier (EOD) is on its own line with no *whitespace* (any space, tab, or newline characters) before or after it. If this isn't the case, a parse error occurs when you try to run the script.

Functionally, heredoc syntax behaves almost identically to strings encased in double quotes, except that there is no need to escape quotes in the string itself.

Nowdoc Syntax

Nowdoc syntax is functionally similar to quotes you encase in single quoted strings, and you call it in much the same way that you call heredoc syntax. The difference is that you enclose the identifier in single quotes when you open the string:

```
$foo = <<<'EOD'
```

Using nowdoc syntax tells PHP not to parse $variables or newline (\n) characters. According to the PHP manual: *Nowdocs are to single-quoted strings what heredocs are to double-quoted strings.*[1]

No variables or special characters within a nowdoc will be expanded; this makes nowdoc syntax ideal for outputting large blocks of PHP code.

■**Note** Nowdoc syntax support was added in PHP 5.3.0—this means that nowdoc syntax won't work in XAMPP out-of-the-box because PHP 5.2 is installed by default.

Understanding Integers

An *integer* is any positive or negative *whole number* (a number without a decimal value). For example, the numbers 1, -27, and 4985067 are integers, but 1.2 is not.

Because PHP is a loosely typed language, it's not necessary to declare a variable as an integer; however, if you find it necessary, you can explicitly *cast*, or force, a value as an integer using the following syntax:

```
$foo = 27; // No quotes around a whole number always means integer
$bar = (int) "3-peat"; // Evaluates to 3
$baz = (int) "seven"; // Evaluates to 0
$bat = (int) "ten 4"; // Evaluates to 0
```

■**Note** A string value will always evaluate to 0 unless it starts with a numeric value (such as "10 years").

Understanding Floating Point Numbers

Floating point numbers (also known as *floats* or *doubles*) are numbers with decimal values, or *real numbers*. This includes numbers such as 3.14, 5.33333, and 1.1.

Note that floating point numbers can produce unexpected results due to the fact that it's impossible to represent all values with a finite number of digits. A good example of this is 1/3, which evaluates to a repeating decimal (0.33333...). You should not use floating point numbers to compare equality for this reason.

Understanding Boolean Values

A *Boolean* value is the simplest type of data; it represents truth, and can contain only one of two values: TRUE or FALSE. It's important to note that the FALSE (not in quotes) Boolean value is different from the "FALSE" string value, and the same goes for TRUE. Boolean values are not case sensitive.

---

1 Quoted from the PHP Manual, "Strings," http://us.php.net/manual/en/language.types.string.php#language.
types.string.syntax.nowdoc

Booleans are very useful when determining if a condition exists. For example, you can use an if-else statement (which I'll cover in a moment) to perform different actions if a condition is TRUE:

```
if($condition===true)
{
    echo 'The condition is true!';
}
else
{
    echo 'The condition is false!';
}
```

■**Note** This example uses the comparison operator === to verify that the $condition is TRUE. I'll go over why this is important in the "Operators" section later in this chapter.

Understanding Arrays

Arrays are among the most powerful datatypes available in PHP, due to their ability to map information using a *key to value* pairing. This means that an array can store multiple pieces of information in a single variable, all indexed by key. For instance, if you have a blog entry to store in variables, you would need to do the following if you didn't use arrays:

```
<?php
    $entryTitle = "Sample Title";
    $entryDate = "April 13, 2009";
    $entryAuthor = "Jason";
    $entryBody = "Today, I wrote a blog entry.";
?>
```

This can become confusing, especially if the entry needs to be passed to a function for processing. You can use an array to simplify the entry:

```
<?php
    $entry = array(
        'title' => 'Sample Title',
        'date' => 'April 13, 2009',
        'author' => 'Jason',
        'body' => 'Today, I wrote a blog entry.'
        );
?>
```

The power of this approach resides in the fact that you now have all of that information stored in one variable, $entry. To access any part of that information, you add the key to the end of the variable in square brackets ([ ]).

```php
<?php
    echo $entry['title']; // Outputs "Sample Title"
    echo $entry['date']; // Outputs "April 13, 2009"
    echo $entry['author']; // Outputs "Jason"
    echo $entry['body']; // Outputs "Today, I wrote a blog entry."
?>
```

Arrays can also index information automatically using a numerical index that starts at 0. You access array values that have been indexed automatically using the numeric index as the key, without quotes (*e.g.*, $entry[0]). You can create an automatically indexed array by omitting the keys when you declare the array:

```php
<?php
    $entry = array('Sample Title', 'April 13, 2009', 'Jason',
        'Today, I wrote a blog entry.');

    echo $entry[0], ' by ', $entry[2];
?>
```

This snippet produces the following output in a browser:

```
Sample Title by Jason
```

■Note In programming, counts generally start at 0. This means that the first character in a string is at position 0, not position 1 as you might expect.

When using arrays in strings, you must take an additional step to avoid errors. In order to avoid an error, you must wrap the array variable and key in curly braces ({}). This is known as *complex syntax*, but not because it's complicated to use; rather, it's called complex because it allows PHP to parse complex statements within a quoted string:

```php
<?php
    $person = array('name' => 'Jason', 'age' => 23);

    echo "This person's name is {$person['name']}
        and he is {$person['age']}.";
?>
```

Another option when using arrays in double-quoted strings is to leave the single quotes off the array index:

```php
<?php
    $person = array('name' => 'Jason', 'age' => 23);

    echo "This person's name is $person[name]
        and he is $person[age].";
?>
```

■**Caution** When working with multidimensional arrays (see below), curly braces must be used. Leaving the single quotes off the array indices will behave unexpectedly.

Multidimensional Arrays

Another cool feature of arrays is their ability to nest within themselves. This creates an array within an array, or a *multidimensional array*.

Multidimensional arrays are exceptionally powerful because they allow even more information to be stored in one variable, making immense data sets conveniently portable, as you'll see when you start working with databases.

A multidimensional array of people might look something like this:

```php
<?php
    $people = array(
        array('name' => 'Jason', 'age' => 23), // $people[0]
        array('name' => 'Carly', 'age' => 18) // $people[1]
    );

    echo "{$people[0]['name']} has a sister who is
        {$people[1]['age']} years old.";
?>
```

This script produces the following output:

```
Jason has a sister who is 18 years old.
```

Multidimensional arrays can also feature multiple string literal keys:

```php
<?php
    $colors = array(
        'fruits' => array('apple' => 'red', 'plum' => 'purple'),
        'flowers' => array('rose' => 'red', 'violet' => 'blue')
    );

    // Output: An apple is red, and a violet is blue.
    echo "An apple is {$colors['fruits']['apple']}, and a
        violet is {$colors['flowers']['violet']}.";
?>
```

Sending Data to the Browser as Output

To see the data that you're processing, you need a way to send it as output. This enables you to display the contents of a variable in the browser to your users.

There are several ways to send output, but the most common methods are the commands echo(), print(), printf(), and sprintf(). There are differences in how you use each of these, but the result is the same: something is output for display in the browser.

The Different Output Commands

It's important to have a solid understanding of your options when sending output to the browser, so I'll go over the different statements available, how they work, and what special properties are associated with each.

■**Note** Whenever I introduce a language construct or function in the course of this book, I'll begin by walking you through the prototype, or breakdown, of the function's name, accepted arguments, and a return value defined by its datatype. Don't worry if you're not sure what that means yet because I'll cover all this information fully in the course of this chapter.

The print() Statement

The print() statement is the most straightforward method of generating output. Its prototype looks like this:

```
int print ( string $arg )
```

This means that print() accepts one argument, which is a *string* to be output to the browser, and returns an integer—print() always returns 1.

You can use print() by placing this code in test.php:

```php
<?php
    print("Some text.");
?>
```

This code produces the following output if you reload test.php.

```
Some text.
```

The echo() Statement

The most common method of generating output is probably the echo() statement. It differs slightly from print() in that it can accept multiple arguments. Consider this prototype:

```
void echo  ( string $arg1 [, string $... ] )
```

The echo() statement accepts one or more arguments, separated by commas, and outputs all of the arguments to the browser in succession. Unlike print(), echo() does not return a value—the void keyword in the prototype tells it not to.

Because echo() is also a language construct, the parentheses are optional and generally omitted. Add the following code to test.php:

```php
<?php echo "Hello ", "world!"; ?>
```

The preceding snippet produces this output:

```
Hello world!
```

Your two strings are added together as arguments to the echo() statement, producing one string that ends up being passed to the browser. The same approach works for variables:

```php
<?php
    $foo = "Hello ";
    $bar = "world!";
    echo $foo, $bar;
?>
```

This produces the same output as above:

```
Hello world!
```

Note Because print() is a language construct and not a function, you can use it without parentheses (*i.e.*, <?php echo 'Some text'; ?>); the clarity achieved with this syntax makes it the preferred approach for many developers. Benchmarks using echo() with arguments have generally proved slightly faster than any other method of outputting data to the browser, so I'll use this approach throughout the rest of this book.

The printf() Statement

The next statement, printf(), gives you more fine-grained control over your output, allowing you to define the format of data that will be sent to the browser. You can think of this statement as meaning "print formatted." This is especially useful when you're dealing with numbers, which I'll cover in a moment. First, take a look at the prototype for printf():

```
int printf ( string $format [, mixed $args [, mixed $... ]] )
```

Note When a function accepts a mixed type, it means that the function can accept several argument types. Generally, all datatypes except arrays and objects are acceptable. Also, arguments in square brackets in a function prototype are optional.

At this point, you can pass a formatting string to printf() along with other arguments that will fit into the format. This is a great way to verify that the data you are passing is of the proper type for the task at hand. Try the following code in test.php:

```php
<?php
    printf("PHP is %s!", "awesome");
?>
```

This snippet produces the following output:

```
PHP is awesome!
```

In the preceding code snippet, you created a formatting string ("PHP is %s!") with a *conversion specification*, which starts with a percentage sign (%) and is followed by a series of *specifiers*. In this example, you assigned a *type specifier* string, which tells the function what datatype the argument to expect.

The most practical use of printf() is with floating point numbers, such as dollar amounts. Consider the following code using echo():

```php
<?php
    $amt1 = 2.55;
    $amt2 = 3.55;
    $total = $amt1 + $amt2;

    echo 'The total cost is $', $total;
?>
```

You might expect to see this sentence when you run your code:

```
The total cost is $6.10.
```

However, what you see when you run the code is this:

```
The total cost is $6.1
```

For obvious reasons, this isn't what you want to happen if you're trying to display a price. Fortunately, this is a case where `printf()` comes in handy; simply add the following code to `test.php`:

```php
<?php
    $amt1 = 2.55;
    $amt2 = 3.55;
    $total = $amt1 + $amt2;

    printf('The total cost is $%.2f', $total);
?>
```

Saving and reloading produces the desired result:

```
The total cost is $6.10
```

The reason you get the properly formatted number in the latter case is that you've specified the type as a floating point number and told the `printf()` statement to return a decimal out to two places using your formatting string (`%.2f`). No matter what you pass as the argument, the output will be a floating point value with a decimal out to two places.

For example, you might try to placing a string into your `printf()` statement to see what happens. In `test.php`, try running the following code:

```php
<?php printf('The total cost is $%.2f', 'string'); ?>
```

When you save and reload, you see the following output:

```
The total cost is $0.00
```

This happens because PHP tries to *parse*, or process, the string called string for a value of some sort; when it doesn't find one, it evaluates to zero, and the value is taken out to two decimal places by the formatting requirements.

Some of the more common datatype specifiers supported by printf() include:

- %s: Treats the argument as and outputs a string

- %d: Treats the argument as an integer and outputs a signed decimal

- %f: Treats the argument as an integer and outputs a floating point number

---

■**Note** printf() supports a wide variety of datatypes, such as scientific notation, ASCII values, and octal numbers. You can learn more about this by visiting the PHP manual at http://www.php.net/manual/en/ and search for sprintf(). (printf() and sprintf() are very similar, so the manual only goes over type specifiers in the sprintf() entry).

The sprintf() Statement

The sprintf() statement works in the same way as the printf() statement: you provide a format with type specifiers and a set of arguments to be inserted into your formatting string. The only difference is that while printf() outputs directly to the browser, sprintf() *returns a string*.

Now is a good point to look at the prototype:

```
string sprintf  ( string $format  [, mixed $args  [, mixed $... ]] )
```

The only difference you see between sprintf() and printf() is the "string" preceding the statement. The word preceding a function tells you what type of value a function will return.

The benefit of using sprintf() in our scripts is that you're able to format only select sections of data, which saves you from having to format the entire output.

For example, try placing the following code in your test.php file:

```php
<?php
    $gpa1 = sprintf("%.1f", 4);
    $gpa2 = sprintf("%.1f", 3.7);
    echo 'Kelly had a ', $gpa1, ' GPA, and Tom had a ', $gpa2;
?>
```

When you save and reload, the output reads like this:

```
Kelly had a 4.0 GPA, and Tom had a 3.7
```

You were able to force the numbers to conform to a format necessary for them to make sense, but you weren't required to pass the entire string as a formatting string. However, if you want to format multiple variables in one call to sprintf() or printf(), you can do so easily with the following bit of code:

```php
<?php
    printf('Kelly got a %.1f GPA, and Tom got a $.1f.', 4, 3.7);
?>
```

Commenting Your Code

There are several ways to write comments in PHP, but only two are encouraged. For *inline comments*, you can use two forward slashes (//); for *block comments*, you can start with a forward slash followed by an asterisk (/*), then close with an asterisk followed by a forward slash (*/).

```php
$foo = 'some value'; // This is an inline C++ comment

    /*
     This is a block comment in C style. It allows the developer to
     go into more detail about the code.
     */
function bar() {
    return true;
}
```

Inline vs. Block Comments

There's not really a right or wrong way to comment code, but accepted practice is to use inline comments for quick descriptions, such as the purpose of a variable:

```php
<?php
    $foo = time()+7*24*60*60; // One week from now
?>
```

A block-level comment is typically used when more detail is necessary. For example, this comment might be used to describe an entire section of code:

```php
<?php
        /*
         * Determines the UNIX timestamp for one week from the current
         * timestamp. Value is stored in $one_week_from_now
         */
    $days = /;
    $one_day = 24*60*60;
    $now = time();
    $one_week_from_now = $days*$one_day+$now;
?>
```

Other Comment Styles

PHP also supports shell-style comments, which are single line comments that start with a hash mark (#). These comments are derived from command-line interfaces known as shells, which are common on UNIX operating systems. A shell-style comment looks like this:

```php
<?php
    echo 'This is some text.'; # This is a shell-style comment
?>
```

■**Caution** The use of shell-style comments is strongly discouraged because such comments don't conform to PEAR coding standards. Find more information on this topic at http://pear.php.net/manual/en/standards.comments.php.

Operators

PHP, like many other programming languages, provides a number of *operators* that allow you to manipulate data. These operators fall into several categories; this book walks you through taking advantage of the following operators:

- Arithmetic Operators: These perform basic mathematical functions
- Arithmetic Assignment Operators: These set expression values
- Comparison Operators: These determine the similarity of two values
- Error Control Operators: These special operators to suppress errors
- Incrementing/Decrementing Operators: These increase or decrease a value
- Logical Operators: These denote logical operations; examples include AND and OR
- String Operators: These manipulate strings

Arithmetic Operators

The arithmetic operators in PHP function just like the ones you used in school.

The addition operator (+) returns the sum of two values:

```
echo 2 + 2; // Outputs 4
```

The subtraction operator (-) returns the difference between two values:

```
echo 4 - 2; // Outputs 2
```

The multiplication operator (*) returns the product of two values:

```
echo 4 * 2; // Outputs 8
```

The division operator (/) returns the quotient of two values:

```
echo 8 / 2; // Outputs 4
```

■**Note** The division operator (/) returns a float value unless the two operands are integers (or strings that get converted to integers) and the numbers are evenly divisible, in which case an integer value is returned. [2]

The modulus operator (%) returns the remainder of one value divided by another:

```
echo 7 % 2; // Outputs 1
echo 8 % 2; // Outputs 0
```

Arithmetic Assignment Operators

PHP provides several assignment operators that enable you to set the value of an operand to the value of an expression. You do this with an equals sign (=), but it's important to be aware that this sign does not mean "equals" as it is commonly understood; instead, this symbol means "gets set to." For example, consider this code snippet:

```
$a = 5,
```

Read aloud, the snippet actually says, "The value of $a gets set to five."

There are also a few combined operators that allow you to declare an expression and assign its value to an operand in one quick step. These operators combine an arithmetic operator with the assignment operator:

```
<?php
```

---

2 Quoted from the PHP Manual, "Arithmetic Operators," www.php.net/manual/en/language.operators. arithmetic.php

```
$foo = 2;

$foo += 2; // New value is 4

$foo -= 1; // New value is 3

$foo *= 4; // New value is 12

$foo /= 2; // New value is 6

$foo %= 4; // New value is 2

?>
```

Note that PHP assigns by value. Thus, a variable assigned with a value copies the entire value into memory, rather than a reference to the original location of the value. In other words, assigning the value of a variable to the value of a second variable, and then changing the value of the second variable, does not affect the value of the initial variable:

```
<?php

    $foo = 2;
    $bar = $foo;

    echo $bar; // Output: 2

    $foo += 4; // New value is 6

    echo $bar; // Output: 2

?>
```

If you require the value of $foo to affect $bar after its declaration, or vice versa, then you need to *assign by reference* using an equals sign followed by an ampersand (=&). This is potentially useful for allowing a variable to be altered indirectly by a script. For instance, if you have an array that contains a person's basic information, you might assign the person's age by reference to account for a birthday.

You'll be using another output function that is extremely useful for debugging, called print_r(). This outputs a "human readable" display of the contents of variables. It is especially useful in debugging arrays:

```
<?php

    $person = array(
        'name' => 'Jason',
        'age' => 23
    );
```

```
$age =& $person['age'];

// Output the array before doing anything
print_r($person);

// Birthday! Add a year!
++$age;

// Output the array again to see the changes
print_r($person);

?>
```

Running this script produces the following output:

```
Array
(
    [name] => Jason
    [age] => 23
)
Array
(
    [name] => Jason
    [age] => 24
)
```

Comparison Operators

You use *comparison* operators to determine the similarity between values. These are especially useful in control structures, which I'll cover in just a moment.

The available comparison operators allow you to determine whether the following conditions are present between two values:

- (==): Values are equal

- (===): Values are identical

- (!= or <>): Values are not equal

- (!==): Values are not identical

- (<): Value 1 is less than value 2

- (>): Value 1 is greater than value 2

- (<=): Value 1 is less than or equal to value 2

- (>=): Value 1 is greater than or equal to value 2

■**Note**   Equal and identical are not the same thing. Identical matches both a variable's value and datatype, whereas equal matches only value. Boolean values are commonly checked with the identical comparison operator because FALSE==0 evaluates to TRUE, while FALSE===0 evaluates to FALSE. You'll use this technique several times throughout the book, so don't worry if it doesn't make perfect sense right now.

Error Control Operators

PHP offers one error control operator: the at symbol (@). This symbol temporarily sets the error reporting level of your script to 0; this prevents errors from displaying if they occur.

For example, trying to reference a nonexistent file with include_once (*e.g.*, include_once 'fake_file';) would cause an error along these lines:

```
Warning: include_once(fake_file) [function.include-once]: failed to open stream: No such file
or directory in /Applications/xampp/xamppfiles/htdocs/simple_blog/test.php on line 4

Warning: include_once() [function.include]: Failed opening 'fake_file' for inclusion
(include_path='.:/Applications/xampp/xamppfiles/lib/php') in
/Applications/xampp/xamppfiles/htdocs/simple_blog/test.php on line 4
```

That's a fairly verbose error, and you probably don't want our users to see something like that displayed on their screen. You can avoid this error by prepending the code with an at symbol:

```php
<?php

    @include_once 'fake_file';

    echo 'Text to follow the include.';

?>
```

■**Note** Placing an operator sign before a variable is called prepending; this technique enables you to perform an operation on a variable before it is instantiated. Placing an operator after the variable is called postpending; this technique instantiates a variable first, and then performs an operation on it.

The file doesn't exist, and an error is generated, but the at symbol prevents the error from displaying and produces the following result:

```
Text to follow the include.
```

■**Caution** You should avoid using an error suppression operator whenever possible because it can adversely affect performance in your scripts. Alternative methods for catching errors exist, and I'll go into more details about those later on in the book.

Incrementing/Decrementing Operators

In some scripts, it becomes necessary to add or subtract one from a value quickly. PHP provides an easy way to do this with its *incrementing* and *decrementing operators*.

To add one to a value, add two plus signs (++) before or after the variable. To subtract one, add two minus signs (--)—remember that placing the (++) or (--) operators before a variable increments or decrements the variable before it is instantiated, while placing these operators after a variable increments or decrements the variable after it is instantiated. Adding signs in front of the variable is called *prepending*, which means the variable is incremented or decremented before it is instantiated:

```php
<?php

    $foo = 5;
    ++$foo; // New value is 6
    $foo++; // New value is 7

    --$foo; // New value is 6
    $foo--; // New value is 5

    $bar = 4;

    // Echo a prepended value
    echo ++$bar; // Output is 5, new value is 5

    // Echo a postpended value
    echo $bar++; // Output is 5, new value is 6

?>
```

Logical Operators

It is difficult to cover the *logical operators* available in PHP without using control structures to illustrate how they work, so let's jump a little ahead and use the if statement to demonstrate how to use them.

Logical operators allow you to determine whether two conditions are true or not. This is very useful when using conditional statements to dictate what happens in a program. PHP's available operators include:

- AND or &&: Returns true if both expressions are true

- OR or ||: Returns true if at least one expression is true

- XOR: Returns true if one expression is true, but not the other

- !: Returns true if the expression is not true

You can place the following code in test.php for a practical demonstration of how these operators work:

```php
<?php

    $foo = true;
    $bar = false;

    // Print the statement if $foo AND $bar are true
    if($foo && $bar) {
        echo 'Both $foo and $bar are true. <br />';
    }

    // Print the statement if $foo OR $bar is true
    if($foo || $bar) {
        echo 'At least one of the variables is true. <br />';
    }

    // Print the statement if $foo OR $bar is true, but not both
    if($foo xor $bar) {
        echo 'One variable is true, and one is false. <br />';
    }

    // Print the statement if $bar is NOT true
    if(!$bar) {
        echo '$bar is false. <br />';
    }

?>
```

Loading `http://localhost/simple_blog/test.php` should produce the following output:

```
At least one of the variables is true.
One variable is true, and one is false.
$bar is false.
```

Now, set `$bar = true` and reload. The output should now read:

```
Both $foo and $bar are true.
At least one of the variables is true.
```

■**Note** For an explanation of how the `if` statement works, see the section on *Control Structures* later in this chapter.

String Operators

There are two *string operators* available in PHP: the concatenation operator (`.`) and the concatenating assignment operator (`.=`). The concatenation operator combines two strings into one by joining the end of the string to the left of the operator to the beginning of the string on the right of the operator. The concatenating assignment operator adds a string to the end of an existing variable:

```php
<?php

    $foo = "Hello";

    $bar = $foo . " world! <br />";

    echo $bar; // Output: Hello world!

    $bar .= " And again!";

    echo $bar; // Output: Hello world! And again!

?>
```

Control Structures

To add power and convenience to your scripts, PHP supports a number of conditional statements, loops, and other *control structures* that allow us to manipulate data easily throughout your code.

The control structures supported by PHP are:

- `if`
- `else`
- `elseif/else if`
- `while`
- `do-while`
- `for`
- `foreach`
- `break`
- `continue`
- `switch`
- `return`
- `require`
- `include`
- `require_once`
- `include_once`
- `goto`

if, else, and else if

The most basic control structure is the `if` statement. It defines a block of code between curly braces (`{}`) that is to be executed *only if* a condition is met:

```php
<?php

    $foo = 5;

    if($foo < 10) {
        echo "The condition was met. <br />";
    }

?>
```

In this program, nothing is output if `$foo` doesn't meet your condition. In some cases, this is an unacceptable result, so you would need to use an `else` statement to provide an alternative value to output if the condition isn't met:

```php
<?php

    $foo = 15;

    if($foo < 10) {
        echo "The condition was met. <br />";
    } else {
        echo "The condition was not met. <br />";
    }

?>
```

If you have a value that failed the if condition, but you aren't ready to pass it to the else statement yet, you can add an elseif statement to be evaluated. You place this new statement between the if and else blocks; it executes only if the first condition isn't met, but the second is:

```php
<?php

if($age < 18) {
    echo "Not old enough to vote or drink! <br />";
} else if ($age < 21) {
    echo "Old enough to vote, but not to drink. <br />";
} else {     // If we get here, $age is >= 21
    echo "Old enough to vote and drink! <br />";
}

?>
```

while and do-while

The while loop allows you to repeat a block of code continuously for as long as a condition is TRUE. This allows you to cycle through data sets without needing to know how many *exist*; all that matters is the number of datasets you want to use at a maximum.

In this example, you use a counter variable ($i) that stores the count, incrementing this at the end of each loop cycle. When the counter reaches three, the condition is no longer true, so the loop ends. Place this code in test.php:

```php
<?php
    $i = 0;
    while($i<3) {
        echo "Count is at $i. <br />";
        ++$i;
    }
?>
```

Loading this script in a browser produces the following output:

```
Count is at 0.
Count is at 1.
Count is at 2.
```

■**Note** Keep in mind that the loop will not execute if the condition isn't met. In the previous example, no output would be generated if $i were set to 4.

A more practical example is looping through an array to generate output based on the stored values. You can add the following code to test.php to output a list of bands:

```php
<?php

    $bands = array("Minus the Bear", "The Decemberists",
        "Neko Case", "Bon Iver", "Now It's Overhead");

    $i = 0;
    $n = count($bands); // Stores the number of values in the array
    while($i < $n) {
        echo $bands[$i], "<br />";
        ++$i;
    }

?>
```

This loop produces the following output when loaded in a browser:

```
Minus the Bear
The Decemberists
Neko Case
Bon Iver
Now It's Overhead
```

You need to use a do-while loop if you want to set up a loop that executes *at least once*, then continues if the condition is met:

```php
<?php
    $i = 10;
```

```php
do {
    echo "The count is at $i.\n";
    ++$i;
} while($i<5);

// Outputs "The count is at 10."
// even though $i doesn't meet the condition.
?>
```

for

One of the most versatile statements in PHP programming is the for loop, which accepts three expressions: expression one is evaluated once at the beginning of the loop, unconditionally; expression two is evaluated at the beginning of each iteration of the loop, and the loop continues only if the expression evaluates to true; expression three is evaluated at the end of each iteration.

Each expression can have more than one part, with each part separated by a comma. You separate the three main expressions using semicolons:

```php
<?php
    for($i=0; $i<3; ++$i) {
        echo "The count is at $i.\n";
    }

    // Output:
    // The count is at 0.
    // The count is at 1.
    // The count is at 2.
?>
```

At this point, you might find it helpful to revisit the previous code example where you created a list of bands. This code produces output identical to the while loop you used previously, while also cleaning up the code a bit:

```php
<?php

    $bands = array("Minus the Bear", "The Decemberists",
        "Neko Case", "Bon Iver", "Now It's Overhead");

    for($i=0, $n=count($bands); $i<$n; ++$i) {
        echo $bands[$i], "<br />";
    }

?>
```

foreach

The foreach loop provides a powerful option for cases where you deal with arrays. Continuing with the code example that outputs a list of bands, you can use foreach to cycle quickly through the array elements:

```php
<?php

    $bands = array("Minus the Bear", "The Decemberists",
        "Neko Case", "Bon Iver", "Now It's Overhead");

    foreach($bands as $band) {
        echo $band, "<br />";
    }

?>
```

The foreach loop lets you iterate through an array and treat each array element as an individual variable; this makes for very readable code.

If the array is associative, you also have the option to separate the array key as a variable. This proves useful in some cases. For example, add the following code in test.php:

```php
<?php

    $person = array(
        'name' => 'Jason',
        'age' => 23,
        'passion' => 'craft beer'
    );

    foreach($person as $key => $value) {
        echo "His $key is $value. <br />";
    }

?>
```

The preceding snippet produces the following output when you load it into a browser:

```
His name is Jason.
His age is 23.
His passion is craft beer.
```

If you're dealing with multidimensional arrays, you can nest your foreach statements to access the different keys and values. Simply add the following code to test.php:

```php
<?php
```

```php
    $people = array(
        'Jason' => array(
            'gender' => 'male',
            'hair' => 'brown'
        ),
        'Carly' => array(
            'gender' => 'female',
            'hair' => 'blonde'
        )
    );

    foreach($people as $name => $person) {
        foreach($person as $key => $value) {
            echo "$name's $key is $value. <br />";
        }
    }

?>
```

This code produces the following output:

```
Jason's gender is male.
Jason's hair is brown.
Carly's gender is female.
Carly's hair is blonde.
```

break

In any loop, the break statement causes the loop to end. In the case of nested loops, a numeric argument can be passed to tell the break statement how many loops to run before breaking out of the loop:

```php
<?php

    while($i<10) {
        if($i == 7) {
            break; // Exit the while loop
        }
    }
```

```php
    foreach($values as $val) {
        switch($val) {
            case 'bad_value':
                break 2; // Exit the switch and the foreach
            case 'good_value':
                // Do something...
        }
    }

?>
```

switch

If a multitude of conditions exist, you can use the switch control structure to create different responses for different conditions—much as you can for an if statement. However, switch works much better in situations where you have more than one or two conditions.

A switch accepts an expression, then sets up *cases*. Each case is functionally equivalent to an if statement; this means that if the expression passed to the switch matches the case, then the code within the case is executed. You must separate each case with a break statement or else your code will continue to execute, producing unexpected results.

To see switch in action, you can write a quick script that determines what day it is and outputs a different response based on the result. This script uses a function called date() that allows you to format the current date (or any date, using the optional second parameter for a *timestamp*, which I'll cover in the next chapter).

Insert the following code into test.php:

```php
<?php

$day = date('w');

switch($day)
{
    case '0':
        echo "It's Sunday!";
        break;
    case '1':
        echo "It's Monday!";
        break;
    case '2':
        echo "It's Tuesday!";
        break;
    case '3':
        echo "It's Wednesday!";
        break;
```

```
    case '4':
        echo "It's Thursday!";
        break;
    case '5':
        echo "Woohoo! It's Friday!";
        break;
    case '6':
        echo "It's Saturday!";
        break;
    default:
        echo "That's no day I recognize...";
        break;
}

?>
```

Depending on the day you run this script, you get output that follows this example when you load test.php in a browser:

```
It's Wednesday!
```

continue

The continue statement works similarly to break, with one essential difference: it ends only the *current iteration*. After a continue statement, the loop starts over at the condition evaluation.

This is useful in instances where you want to perform actions only on data in a loop that meets a certain criteria, such producing only even values:

```
<?php

    for($i=0; $i<=10; ++$i) {
        /*
         * If the modulus of $i and 2 is not zero (which evaluates
         * to false), we continue
         */
        if($i%2) {
            continue;
        }
        echo $i, " ";
    }

?>
```

Running this loop creates the following output:

```
0 2 4 6 8 10
```

return

The `return` statement in PHP is most useful in functions. When reached within a function, `return` immediately stops the execution of the function and passes its argument as the value of the function call. I'll cover the `return` statement in the section of this chapter named, "User-Defined Functions."

If you use the `return` statement outside of a function, the statement ends the execution of the script. Like `echo` and `print`, `return` is a construct of the PHP language, so no parentheses are required when you use it.

include, include_once, require, and require_once

A great feature provided by PHP is the ability to load a script from an external file; this makes it much easier to organize your code in larger projects.

PHP provides four constructs you can use to load an external script: `include`, `include_once`, `require`, and `require_once`.

The PHP manual recommends that developers use `include_once` and `require_once` because these constructs first check whether the file has already been loaded before either will load a given script. This saves resources and can increase the performance of your applications.

Now let's take a look at an exercise that illustrates the power of loading external scripts. Fire up Eclipse and press Ctrl+click or right-click your `simple_blog` project folder, hover over "New…" and select "File…" from the drop-down menu. Name the new file `extras.php` and add the following code to the blank document that opens:

```php
<?php
    $foo = "green";
    $bar = "red";
?>
```

Save the file, then go back to our `test.php` file and write the following code:

```php
<?php
    include_once 'extras.php';

    echo 'Variable $foo has a value of ', $foo, "<br />\n";
    echo 'Variable $bar has a value of ', $bar, "<br />\n";
?>
```

Save, then navigate to http://localhost/simple_blog/test.php in a browser to see the results:

```
Variable $foo has a value of green
Variable $bar has a value of red
```

By including the extras.php file you created using include_once, you are able to access the information stored in the file. This proves especially useful when you're working with a large set of functions, which allows common functions to be stored in a file that is included in other areas of your site, rather than requiring that you copy-and-paste those functions into each file. Adopting this approach reduces the size of your applications and can play a part in optimizing your application's performance.

This next short example illustrates how using include_once can reduce the load on your server; begin by adding this code toe extras.php:

```php
<?php

$var += 1;

?>
```

Next, add this code to test.php:

```php
<?php

$var = 0;

include 'extras.php';

echo $var, "<br />";

include 'extras.php';

echo $var, "<br />";

?>
```

This code produces the following output when loaded into a browser:

```
1
2
```

Now, change `test.php` so it uses `include_once` instead of `include`:

```php
<?php

$var = 0;

include_once 'extras.php';

echo $var, "<br />";

include_once 'extras.php';

echo $var, "<br />";

?>
```

Next, load `test.php` in a browser to see the result:

```
1
1
```

The file is loaded only once, the script executes only once. This reduces the load on the server, which in turn reduces the execution time of your scripts.

goto

PHP 5.3.0 introduced the goto statement, which enables you to skip ahead to a new section of code:

```php
<?php

    if ($i==7) {
        goto foo;
    }

    echo "This will be jumped if \$i is equal to 7.";

    foo:
    echo "This should be printed.";

?>
```

■**Note** goto is a controversial addition to the language, not least because many developers feel it will have negative effects on code legibility. Also be aware that XAMPP is running PHP 5.2 by default, so goto will not work in the default testing environment.

User-Defined

Perhaps the most powerful feature of PHP is the ability to define and execute functions from within your code. A function is a named block of code that you declare within your scripts that you can call at a later time. Functions can accept any number of arguments and can return a value using the return statement.

The basic format of a function requires that you first identify the function using the function *reserved word* in front of a string that serves as the function's name. This string can contain any alphanumeric characters and underscores, but it must not start with a number. You enclose any arguments you want in parentheses after the function name. Note that you still must include the parentheses even if the function doesn't require that you pass any arguments.

■**Note** Reserved words are special terms that cannot be used for function names. These include the word function, control structure names, and several other terms which will be noted as they come up. You can find a full list of reserved words at http://us2.php.net/manual/en/reserved.php.

Begin by declaring your first function in test.php:

```php
<?php

    function sayHello()
    {
        echo "Hello world!";
    }

    // Execute the function
    sayHello();

?>
```

The function produces the following output when you call it:

```
Hello world!
```

To add arguments, you place variables inside the function declaration's parentheses, separated by commas. You can use these arguments within the function to determine the function's return value:

```php
<?php

    function meet($name)
    {
        echo "Hello, my name is $name. Nice to meet you! <br />";
    }

    meet("Jason");

?>
```

For example, calling meet("Jason") produces the following output:

```
Hello, my name is Jason. Nice to meet you!
```

Returning Values from Functions

Most of the time, you won't want to immediately the result of a function call immediately. To store the result in a variable, you use the return statement discussed earlier. Add the following code to test.php:

```php
<?php

/*
 * Based on the time passed to the function in military (24 hour)
 * time, returns a greeting
 */
function greet($time)
{
    if($time<12)
    {
        return "Good morning!";
    }
    elseif($time<18)
    {
        return "Good afternoon!";
    }
```

```
    else
    {
        return "Good evening!";
    }
}

$greeting = greet(14);

echo "$greeting How are you?";

?>
```

PHP stores the result of greet()in the $greeting variable, which you can use later to display a time-sensitive greeting to the user. When you set 14 (2 PM) as your parameter and run this script in your browser, you get the following output:

```
Good afternoon! How are you?
```

Summary

At this point, you should be comfortable placing PHP scripts into our web pages, adding comments them to help clarify their purpose, using variables to manipulate data, and using operators and control structures to traverse and manipulate data. You should also know how to write a function and call it from within our scripts.

In the next chapter, you'll learn how to send data from one page to another in your web applications, and you'll start building the basics of your blog!

■ ■ ■

CHAPTER 3

Passing Information with PHP

Now that you're comfortable with the basics of PHP, you're ready to go over how information is moved from page to page. You'll need this for nearly every aspect of the blog, from writing new posts to allowing users to comment.

In this chapter, you'll learn the following:

- What superglobal arrays are in PHP and how to use them

- How to send data using HTML forms using the POST method

- How to send data in the URL using the GET method

- How to store data in SESSIONS for use across multiple pages

- How to create and store COOKIES for returning users

Passing data is what separates dynamic web pages from static ones; by customizing an experience based on the user's choices, you're able to add an entirely new level of value to a web site.

Superglobal Arrays

PHP offers several types of *superglobal arrays* to developers, each with a different useful purpose. A superglobal array (refer back to Chapter 2 for more information on arrays) is a special variable that are always available in scripts, regardless of the current scope of the script (see the *Variable Scope* section later in this chapter). PHP includes several superglobals:

- $GLOBALS: Variables available in the global scope

- $_SERVER: Information about the server

- $_GET: Data passed using the HTTP GET method

- $_POST: Data passed using the HTTP POST method

- $_REQUEST: Data passed via an HTTP request

- $_FILES: Data passed by an HTML file input

- $_SESSION: Current session data specific to the user

- $_COOKIE: Data stored on the user's browser as a cookie

Variable Scope

In programming, *scope* refers to the context you declare a variable in. Most variables in PHP have a single scope: *global*. Using this scope means that a variable is available in the script that declares it, as well as in any script that is included after the variable is declared or in any script that includes the file in which the variable is declared.

For example, try opening test.php again and experimenting with variable scope:

```php
<?php

    $foo = "some value";

    include_once 'extras.php'; // $foo is available in extras.php

    $bar = "another value"; // $bar is not available in extras.php

    echo "test.php: Foo is $foo, and bar is $bar. <br />";

?>
```

Now open up extras.php and insert the following code:

```php
<?php

    echo "extras.php: Foo is $foo, and bar is $bar. <br />";

?>
```

When you load http://localhost/simple_blog/test.php in your browser, you get the following output:

```
extras.php: Foo is some value, and bar is .
test.php: Foo is some value, and bar is another value.
```

■**Note** When error_reporting(E_ALL) is active, a notice will display, letting you know that $bar is an undefined variable. Error reporting is a great way to make sure all the bases are covered in your scripts. When developing an application, best practice dictates that you should use error_reporting(E_ALL), which means all errors and notices are displayed. You don't want our users to see nasty error codes in your production scripts, however, so you should use error_reporting(0) to turn off errors in your finished application.

Scope changes a bit when you start using functions, because variables declared within a function have *local scope*, meaning they're only available within the function that declares them. Additionally, variables declared in the global scope are only available if they are explicitly declared as global inside the function.

You're now ready to see how error_reporting(E_ALL) affects your scripts. In test.php, write the following code:

```php
<?php

    error_reporting(E_ALL);

    $foo = "I'm outside the function!";

    function test()
    {
        return $foo;
    }

    echo test(); // A notice is issued that $foo is undefined

?>
```

$foo is undefined if you run your test() function, which issues a notice. You can clear this up by declaring $foo as global within your test() function; this means that $foo in local scope will now refer to the variable $foo in global scope:

```php
<?php

    $foo = "I'm outside the function!";

    function test()
    {
        global $foo; // Declare $foo as a global variable
        return $foo;
    }

    echo test();

?>
```

Visiting test.php executes test(), you can see the result in this output:

```
I'm outside the function!
```

A variable declared within a function is not available outside that function unless it is specified as the function's return value. For instance, consider the following code:

```php
<?php
    error_reporting(E_ALL);

    function test()
    {
        $foo =  "Declared inside the function. <br />";
        $bar = "Also declared inside the function. <br />";

        return $bar;
    }

    $baz = test();

    /*
     * Notices are issued that $foo and $bar are undefined
     */
    echo $foo, $bar, $baz;

?>
```

This code gives the following results:

```
Notice: Undefined variable: foo in /Applications/xampp/xamppfiles/htdocs/simple_blog/↵
test.php on line 19

Notice: Undefined variable: bar in /Applications/xampp/xamppfiles/htdocs/simple_blog/↵
test.php on line 19
Also declared inside the function.
```

You need to declare two variables within a function and return both; next, you use an array and the list() function to access the values easily.

```php
<?php

    function test()
    {
        $foo = "Value One";
        $bar = "Value Two";

        return array($foo, $bar);
    }
```

```
    /*
     * The list() function allows us to assign a variable
     * to each array index as a comma-separated list
     */
    list($one, $two) = test();

    echo $one, "<br />", $two, "<br />";

?>
```

Running this code produces the desired output:

```
Value One
Value Two
```

Using list() is a way to declare multiple variables in one line; for example this line declares the variables $one and $two:

```
list($one, $two) = test();
```

The following handful of lines accomplishes the same thing:

```
$array = test();

$one = $array[0];
$two = $array[1];
```

■**Note** Only numerically indexed arrays will work when using list(). Using an array with text-based keys issues a notice that indicates you have undefined array indexes.

$GLOBALS

PHP provides another option for accessing variables in the global scope: the $GLOBALS superglobal array. All variables in the global scope are loaded into the $GLOBALS array, enabling you to access them using the variable name as the array key.

You can try out this array in test.php:

```
<?php

    $foo = "Some value.";

    function test()
```

```
    {
        echo $GLOBALS['foo'];
    }

    test();

?>
```

This code produces the following output:

```
Some value.
```

Tip It is generally a good practice to avoid using globals wherever possible. The preferred method of accessing global variables inside functions is to pass them as arguments. This makes your scripts more readable, which simplifies maintenance over the long term.

$_SERVER

The $_SERVER superglobal stores information about the server and the current script. It also has features that allow you to access the IP address of a site visitor, what site referred the visitor to this script, and many other useful pieces of information. I won't cover all of the capabilities of $_SERVER here, so be sure to check the PHP manual to learn more about this feature.

One of the most useful pieces of information available in the $_SERVER superglobal is the name of the host site, which is stored in HTTP_HOST. The host site's name is useful because it allows you to create a simple template that you can use across different projects without requiring that you change any of your code.

For instance, you can use the following code snippet to welcome a visitor to your site:

```
<?php

    echo "<h1> Welcome to $_SERVER[HTTP_HOST]! </h1>";

?>
```

Running this code in test.php produces this output:

```
Welcome to localhost!
```

Loading the exact same snippet on a live web site produces this output:

```
Welcome to yoursite.com!
```

As you continue forward with creating your simple blog, you'll discover a few uses for HTTP_HOST in your scripts.

Other useful pieces of information are available as well, shown below (see comments for a description of what each piece means).

Note the use of print_r() at the bottom of the script. This is a great way to debug code, especially arrays, because it outputs a "human-readable" display of a variable's contents. You can see this at work when you load your test script in test.php:

```php
<?php

    /*
     * Note that <pre> tags and newline characters (\n) are used
     * for the sake of legibility
     */

    // Path to the current file (i.e. '/simple_blog/test.php')
    echo $_SERVER['PHP_SELF'], "\n\n";

    // Information about the user's browser
    echo $_SERVER['HTTP_USER_AGENT'], "\n\n";

    // Address of the page that referred the user (if any)
    echo $_SERVER['HTTP_REFERER'], "\n\n";

    // IP address from which the user is viewing the script
    echo $_SERVER['REMOTE_ADDR'], "\n\n";

    // Human-readable export of the contents of $_SERVER
    print_r($_SERVER);

?>
```

Loading test.php in your browser displays output something like the following:

/simple_blog/test.php

Mozilla/5.0 (Macintosh; U; Intel Mac OS X 10.5; en-US; rv:1.9.0.10) Gecko/2009042315
Firefox/3.0.10

Notice: Undefined index: HTTP_REFERER in
/Applications/XAMPP/xamppfiles/htdocs/simple_blog/test.php on line **19**

::1

Array
(
    [UNIQUE_ID] => ShwUrQoAAQYAAAE4T@OAAAAA
    [HTTP_HOST] => localhost
    [HTTP_USER_AGENT] => Mozilla/5.0 (Macintosh; U; Intel Mac OS X 10.5; en-US;↵
rv:1.9.0.10) Gecko/2009042315 Firefox/3.0.10
    [HTTP_ACCEPT] => text/html,application/xhtml+xml,application/xml;q=0.9,*/*;q=0.8
    [HTTP_ACCEPT_LANGUAGE] => en-us,en;q=0.5
    [HTTP_ACCEPT_ENCODING] => gzip,deflate
    [HTTP_ACCEPT_CHARSET] => ISO-8859-1,utf-8;q=0.7,*;q=0.7
    [HTTP_KEEP_ALIVE] => 300
    [HTTP_CONNECTION] => keep-alive
    [HTTP_COOKIE] =>

    [HTTP_CACHE_CONTROL] => max-age=0
    [PATH] => /usr/bin:/bin:/usr/sbin:/sbin
    [SERVER_SIGNATURE] =>

    [SERVER_SOFTWARE] => Apache/2.2.11 (Unix) DAV/2 mod_ssl/2.2.11 OpenSSL/0.9.7l ↵
PHP/5.2.9 mod_perl/2.0.4 Perl/v5.10.0
    [SERVER_NAME] => localhost
    [SERVER_ADDR] => ::1
    [SERVER_PORT] => 80
    [REMOTE_ADDR] => ::1
    [DOCUMENT_ROOT] => /Applications/XAMPP/xamppfiles/htdocs
    [SERVER_ADMIN] => you@example.com
    [SCRIPT_FILENAME] => /Applications/XAMPP/xamppfiles/htdocs/simple_blog/test.php
    [REMOTE_PORT] => 49310

```
[GATEWAY_INTERFACE] => CGI/1.1
[SERVER_PROTOCOL] => HTTP/1.1
[REQUEST_METHOD] => GET
[QUERY_STRING] =>
[REQUEST_URI] => /simple_blog/test.php
[SCRIPT_NAME] => /simple_blog/test.php
[PHP_SELF] => /simple_blog/test.php
[REQUEST_TIME] => 1243354285
[argv] => Array
    (
    )

[argc] => 0
)
```

Be sure to check whether HTTP_REFERER, is set before you use it. Otherwise, HTTP_REFERER is undefined if the visitor was not referred by another site a notice will be issued that. This code provides an easy way to tell whether it is set:

```php
if(isset($_SERVER['HTTP_REFERER']))
{
    echo $_SERVER['HTTP_REFERER'];
}
else
{
    echo "No referer set!";
}
```

$_GET

One of the two most common methods of passing data between pages is the GET method. GET data is passed through a *query string* in the URL, which looks something like this:

```
http://example.com?var1=somevalue&var2=othervalue
```

The query string begins with a question mark (?) and then names a variable (var1 in the preceding example). The next part of the query string is an equals sign (=), followed by a value. You can add more variables by appending an ampersand (&) to the end of the first value, then declaring another variable name (var2 in the preceding example), followed by an equals sign and a value. Note that you do not enclose the values in the query string in quotes; this can cause problems when you use values that have spaces and/or special characters.

URL Encoding

Fortunately, PHP includes the urlencode() function, which you can use to get values ready to be passed in a URL. You use this function in tandem with urldecode(); together, the two functions enable you to pass complex values through the URL. Add this code to test.php to learn how URL encoding works:

```php
<?php

    error_reporting(E_ALL);

    $foo = "This is a complex value & it needs to be URL-encoded.";

    // Output the original string
    echo $foo, "<br /><br />";

    // URL encode the string
    $bar = urlencode($foo)

    // Output the URL-encoded string
    echo $bar, "<br /><br />";

    // Decode the string and output
    echo urldecode($bar);

?>
```

Loading test.php in a browser produces the following result:

```
This is a complex value & it needs to be URL-encoded.
This+is+a+complex+value+%26+it+needs+to+be+URL-encoded.
This is a complex value & it needs to be URL-encoded.
```

Accessing URL Variables

You use the $_GET superglobal array to access the variables in the query string. You can access the variables in this array with the variable name as the array key. For instance, you can use this code to access your variables from the URL example at the beginning of this section:

```php
<?php

    echo "var1: ", $_GET['var1'], "<br />";
    echo "var2: ", $_GET['var2'], "<br />";

?>
```

To test this snippet of code, navigate to this URL: `http://localhost/simple_blog/test.php?var1=somevalue&var2=anothervalue`. Running this code produces the following output:

```
var1: somevalue
var2: anothervalue
```

The $_GET superglobal allows you to determine what information displays on a page, depending on the values you pass in the URL. For example, you can use this code if you want to allow a user to view either a brief description of your site *or* your contact information:

```html
<ul id="menu">
    <li> <a href="test.php">Home</a> </li>
    <li> <a href="test.php?page=about">About Us</a> </li>
    <li> <a href="test.php?page=contact">Contact Us</a> </li>
</ul>

<?php

    /*
     * Very basic security measure to ensure that
     * the page variable has been passed, enabling you to
     * ward off very basic mischief using htmlentities()
     */
    if(isset($_GET['page'])) {
        $page = htmlentities($_GET['page']);
    } else {
        $page = NULL;
    }


    switch($page) {

        case 'about':
            echo "
        <h1> About Us </h1>
            <p> We are rockin' web developers! </p>";
            break;

        case 'contact':
            echo "
                <h1> Contact Us </h1>
                    <p> Email us at
```

```
                        <a href=\"mailto:info@example.com\">
                        info@example.com
                            </a>
                </p>";
            break;

        /*
         * Create a default page in case no variable is passed
         */
        default:
            echo "
                <h1> Select a Page! </h1>
                <p>
                    Choose a page from above

                    to learn more about us!
                </p>";
                break;
    }

?>
```

Loading the page displays a screen similar to what you see in Figure 3-1.

Figure 3-1. *The default page if no $_GET variable is supplied*

After clicking the "About Us" link at the top, the page will reload (see Figure 3-2).

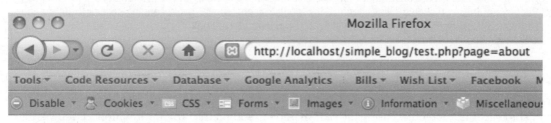

- Home
- About Us
- Contact Us

About Us

We are rockin' web developers!

Figure 3-2. *The About Us page is loaded when the* `page=about` *query string is passed in the URL*

Click the Contact Us link to bring up a page similar to what you see in Figure 3-3.

- Home
- About Us
- Contact Us

Contact Us

Email us at info@example.com

Figure 3-3. *The Contact Us page is loaded when* `page=contact`

Caution $_GET variables are useful, but they also allow malicious users to pass information directly into your script. Because of this, you should always sanitize the input. You should also avoid sending sensitive information via a GET request. Basic security precautions will be covered later in this book.

$_POST

PHP provides a second method for sending data: POST. Submitting most web forms (such as a contact form or site registration) requires using the POST method to submit the form information for processing.

Structurally, POST requests are very similar to GET requests, and you access their values in the same way: you use the $_POST superglobal and append the variable name as the array key.

In most cases, a POST value is passed by a web form that you build in HTML. For example, take a look at this registration form:

```
<form action="test.php" method="post">
    <input type="text" name="username" />
    <input type="text" name="email" />
    <input type="submit" value="Register!" />
</form>
```

The name attribute tells you the array key to use to access the information submitted with the form. For example, you use the $_POST['username'] variable in your script to access the "username" field.

Open test.php to build a simple form-handling script:

```
<?php

    /*
     * Checks if the form was submitted
     */
    if($_SERVER['REQUEST_METHOD'] == 'POST') {
        // Displays the submitted information
        echo "Thanks for registering! <br />",
        "Username: ", htmlentities($_POST['username']), "<br />",
        "Email: ", htmlentities($_POST['email']), "<br />";
    } else {
    // If the form was not submitted, displays the form

?>
```

```
<form action="test.php" method="post">
    <label for="username">Username:</label>
    <input type="text" name="username" />
    <label for="email">Email:</label>
    <input type="text" name="email" />
    <input type="submit" value="Register!" />
</form>

<?php } // End else statement ?>
```

When you load `http://localhost/simple_blog/test.php`, the script checks whether any data has been submitted via the POST method. If so, the script thanks the user for registering and the displays the selected username and supplied email address. If nothing is submitted via POST, the script displays the registration form (see Figure 3-4).

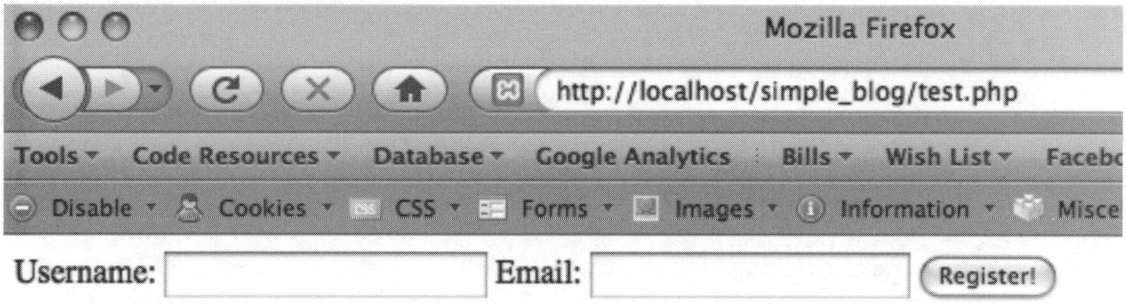

Figure 3-4. *Your registration form*

Set the action attribute set to `test.php`; doing so prompts the form to send the request to the script when the form is submitted. This enables you to both accept user input and process it within the same script.

Use the `$_SERVER` superglobal to check the `REQUEST_METHOD` value for information on whether a POST request has been made. If so, you perform basic escaping of the input (using `htmlentities()`) to filter the input.

Entering a name and email address causes your confirmation message to display (see Figure 3-5).

Figure 3-5. *This confirmation message is displayed after you use your registration form*

$_REQUEST

The $_REQUEST superglobal is an array that contains the contents of the $_GET, $_POST, and $_COOKIE superglobals. If you modify your form in test.php to submit to test.php?submit=true with a username and email text input, you can access all the submitted data using the following code:

```php
<?php

    // Checks if the form was submitted
    if($_SERVER['REQUEST_METHOD'] == 'POST') {

        // Output the contents of $_REQUEST
        foreach($_REQUEST as $key => $val) {
            echo $key, " : ", $val, "<br />";
        }

    } else {
    // If the form was not submitted, displays the form HTML

?>

<form action="test.php?submit=true" method="post">
    <label for="username">Username:</label>
    <input type="text" name="username" />
    <label for="email">Email:</label>
    <input type="text" name="email" />
    <input type="submit" name="submit" value="Register!" />
</form>

<?php } // End else statement ?>
```

This script's output looks something like this:

```
submit : true
username : Test
email : test@example.com
```

The precedence of values is important in this case. Declaring an index in $_COOKIE, $_POST, and $_GET with the same name could cause confusion for new developers. $_REQUEST causes $_COOKIE to override both $_POST and $_GET. If $_COOKIE does not contain the variable name, $_POST will override $_GET. For example, if you set the action attribute to test.php?username=agetvariable, you won't see any change in the username value because $_POST will override $_GET, even if the username field is left blank.

$_FILES

Another feature of HTML forms is the ability to allow users to upload files. In an application such as the blog, you need to be able to accept images to include with your entries. In order to access an uploaded file, you need to use the $_FILES superglobal.

$_FILES works a little differently from $_POST and $_GET in that each file creates an array of related elements that provide information about the uploaded file. The provided information includes:

- name: The file name

- type: The file type (e.g. image/jpeg)

- tmp_name: The temporary location of the uploaded file

- error: An error code corresponding to error type (0 if no errors found)

- size: The file size in bytes (e.g. 9347012)

You store each file uploaded as a multidimensional array in the $_FILES superglobal, which you access using first the field name as the array key and then the name of the desired field value (*i.e.,* $_FILES['upload1']['name']).

You can experiment with $_FILES by creating a file upload field in test.php. Remember to add enctype="multipart/form-data" to the <form> tag to allow file uploads:

```php
<?php

    // Checks if the form was submitted
    if($_SERVER['REQUEST_METHOD'] == 'POST') {

        // Checks if a file was uploaded without errors
        if(isset($_FILES['photo'])
        && is_uploaded_file($_FILES['photo']['tmp_name']))
```

```php
        && $_FILES['photo']['error']==UPLOAD_ERR_OK) {

            // Outputs the contents of $_FILES
            foreach($_FILES['photo'] as $key => $value) {
                echo "$key : $value <br />";
            }
        } else {
            echo "No file uploaded!";
        }
    } else {
    // If the form was not submitted, displays the form HTML

?>

<form action="test.php" method="post"
        enctype="multipart/form-data">
    <label for="photo">User Photo:</label>
    <input type="file" name="photo" />
    <input type="submit" value="Upload a Photo" />
</form>

<?php } // End else statement ?>
```

Running this script in test.php displays the screen shown in Figure 3-6.

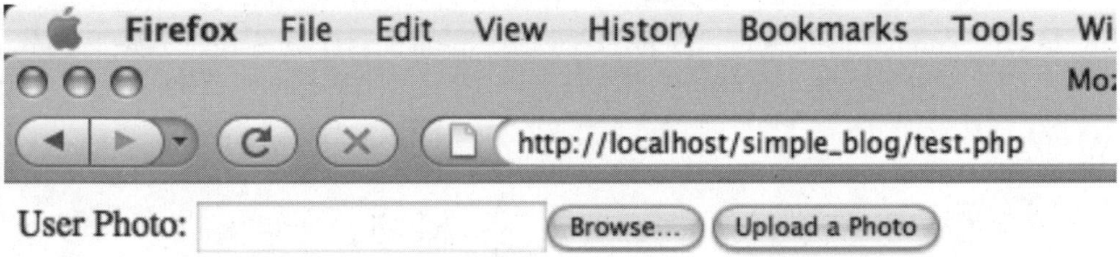

Figure 3-6. *Creating a file upload form*

Uploading a file creates output similar to the following:

```
name : sample_image.jpg
type : image/jpeg
tmp_name : /private/var/tmp/phpU6q76q
error : 0
size : 226452
```

Using an uploaded file is a little trickier—Chapter 8 explains how you do this in significantly more detail. However, you can add this script to test.php to see a very basic example of using an uploaded file:

```php
<?php

    // Checks if the form was submitted
    if($_SERVER['REQUEST_METHOD'] == 'POST') {

        // Checks if a file was uploaded without errors
        if(isset($_FILES['photo'])
        && is_uploaded_file($_FILES['photo']['tmp_name'])

        && $_FILES['photo']['error']==UPLOAD_ERR_OK) {

            // Checks if the file is a JPG image
            if($_FILES['photo']['type']=='image/jpeg') {
                $tmp_img = $_FILES['photo']['tmp_name'];

                // Creates an image resource
                $image = imagecreatefromjpeg($tmp_img);

                // Tells the browser what type of file
                header('Content-Type: image/jpeg');

                // Outputs the file to the browser
                imagejpeg($image, '', 90);

                // Frees the memory used for the file
                imagedestroy($image);
            } else {
                echo "Uploaded file was not a JPG image.";
            }
        } else {
            echo "No photo uploaded!";
        }
    } else {
    // If the form was not submitted, displays the form HTML

?>
```

```
<form action="test.php" method="post"

        enctype="multipart/form-data">
    <label for="photo">User Photo:</label>
    <input type="file" name="photo" />
    <input type="submit" value="Upload a Photo" />
</form>

<?php } // End else statement ?>
```

Once a user selects a JPG file and clicks the "Upload a Photo" option, your script implements a series of actions:

1. It verifies that the form was submitted using the POST method

    a. If not, it displays the form and no further processing is performed

    b. If so, it proceeds to Step 2

2. It checks whether a file was uploaded and that the file has no errors

    a. If both conditions are not met, the script kicks out an error message

    b. If both conditions are met, it proceeds to Step 3

3. It verifies that the uploaded file is a JPG image

    a. If not, the script generates an error message

    b. If so, it proceeds to Step 4

4. It uses imagecreatefromjpeg() to create an image resource from the temporary file

5. It sends a content-type header to the browser, so the image is handled properly

6. It generates the image using imagejpeg()

7. It uses imagedestroy() to free the memory consumed by the image resource

After the file is uploaded, the script displays the image in the browser (see Figure 3-7).

Figure 3-7. The image displayed by `test.php` after uploading and processing

---

■**Note** You can find a more in-depth explanation of PHP's image-handling functions in Chapter 8.

$_SESSION

In cases where you need to store a value for a user's entire visit, the $_SESSION superglobal provides a practical, easy solution. When a $_SESSION variable is declared, it remains in memory until it is explicitly unset, the session times out (the default time-out value is 180 minutes), or the browser is closed.

One common use of $_SESSION variables is to store a user's login status. You can build on your simple registration form to create a session for a user that has already registered.

Your script will accomplish the following tasks:

1. Display a registration form

2. Thank user for registering after she does so

3. Tell the user she has already registered on consequent page loads

You must initiate session data before you can use session variables; you do this by calling session_start() at the top of your script.

■**Note** If you call session_start() more than once, PHP generates a notice and additional session_start() calls will be ignored. Also, you should call session_start() at the very beginning of any script you use it in, before you send any output to the browser. Failure to do so will also generate a notice and prevents the session from starting. Finally, the script that starts the session must be the first thing in the file, so make sure you place the opening <?php on line 1 of the file.

You can implement a $_SESSION variable by inserting the following code in test.php:

```php
<?php

    // Initialize session data
    session_start();

    /*
     * If the user is already registered, display a
     * message letting them know.
     */
    if(isset($_SESSION['username'])) {
        echo "You're already registered as $_SESSION[username].";
    }

    // Checks if the form was submitted
    else if($_SERVER['REQUEST_METHOD'] == 'POST') {

        /*
         * If both the username and email fields were filled
         * out, save the username in a session variable and
         * output a thank you message to the browser. To
         * eliminate leading and trailing whitespace, we use the
         * trim() function.
         */
        if(!empty(trim($_POST['username']))
        && !empty(trim($_POST['email']))) {
```

```php
            // Store escaped $_POST values in variables
            $uname = htmlentities($_POST['username']);
            $email = htmlentities($_POST['email']);

            $_SESSION['username'] = $uname;

            echo "Thanks for registering! <br />",
                "Username: $uname <br />",
                "Email: $email <br />";
        }

        /*
         * If the user did not fill out both fields, display
         * a message letting them know that both fields are
         * required for registration.
         */
        else {
            echo "Please fill out both fields! <br />";
        }
    }

    // If the form was not submitted, displays the form HTML
    else {

?>

<form action="test.php?username=overwritten" method="post">
    <label for="username">Username:</label>
    <input type="text" name="username" />
    <label for="email">Email:</label>
    <input type="text" name="email" />
    <input type="submit" value="Register!" />
</form>

<?php } // End else statement ?>
```

You should see your registration form after you load test.php in your browser, and your script will display the following message after you fill in the fields:

```
Thanks for registering!
Username: Test User
Email: test@example.com
```

Reloading the page should display this message:

```
You're already registered as Test User.
```

You use unset() to destroy a $_SESSION variable. Removing the username session variable and showing the registration form again is as simple as inserting the following code:

```
unset($_SESSION['username']);
```

Using session_destroy()

PHP provides a function called session_destroy(), the name of which can be somewhat misleading. When you call this function, a session will be destroyed the next time the page loads. However, the session variables remain available with the same script. Insert this code in test.php to see this behavior in action:

```php
<?php

error_reporting(E_ALL);

session_start();

// Create a session variable
$_SESSION['test'] = "A value.";

// Destroy the session
session_destroy();

// Attempt to output the session variable (output: A value.)
echo $_SESSION['test'];

// Unset the variable specifically
unset($_SESSION['test']);

// Attempt to output the session variable (generates a notice)
echo $_SESSION['test'];

?>
```

Loading this script in a browser generates the following output:

```
A value.
Notice: Undefined index: test in /Applications/XAMPP/xamppfiles/htdocs/simple_blog/test.php on
line 20
```

This behavior can be confusing, so you should specifically unset() session variables that need you want destroyed before the end of the script to avoid unexpected behavior.

$_COOKIE

Cookies behave similarly to sessions, but they allow you to store information on a user's machine for a longer period of time. Information stored in cookies remains available even after the user closes her browser, assuming that the expiration date on the cookie is set far enough in the future.

You can use cookies to make a user's repeat visits more pleasant by retaining pertinent, non-sensitive data. This can include settings that customize the user's experience on your site, perform repetitive tasks automatically, or allow a user to stay logged in and avoid the extra step of logging in each time she visits.

In PHP, you use the $_COOKIE superglobal to access cookie values. However, setting a cookie requires that you use the setcookie() function. Open test.php again and set a cookie that contains your username and greet you whenever you load the page.

■**Note** This snippet uses the time() function. The returned value from time() is the number of seconds since the Unix Epoch[1], which is commonly used in programming to determine dates and intervals.

```php
<?php

    /*
     * If the user is returning to this page
     * after previously registering, use the
     * cookie to welcome them back.
     */
    if(isset($_COOKIE['username'])) {
        echo "Welcome back, ",
            htmlentities($_COOKIE['username']),
            "! <br />";
    }

    /*
     * If the user is new and submits the
     * registration form, set a cookie with
     * their username and display a thank
     * you message.
     */
```

---

1. The Unix Epoch was midnight Coordinated Universal Time (UTC) of January 1, 1970. It serves as a measuring stick for determining time when dealing with UNIX systems.

```php
    else if($_SERVER['REQUEST_METHOD']=='POST'
            && !empty($_POST['username'])) {

        // Sanitize the input and store in a variable
        $uname = htmlentities($_POST['username']);

        // Set a cookie that expires in one week
        $expires = time()+7*24*60*60;
        setcookie('username', $uname, $expires, '/');

        // Output a thank you message
        echo "Thanks for registering, $uname! <br />";
    }

    /*
     * If the user has neither previously registered
     * or filled out the registration form, show the
     * registration form.
     */
    else {

?>

<form method="post">
    <label for="username">Username:</label>
    <input type="text" name="username" />
    <input type="submit" value="Register" />
</form>

<?php } // End else statement ?>
```

As in this book's earlier examples, a user will see the registration form the first time he navigates to test.php. After filling out and submitting the form, he will see the following message, assuming he entered the username, "Jason":

Thanks for registering, Jason!

Subsequent visits will load the $_COOKIE variable and display this message to the user:

Welcome back, Jason!

■**Note** Browsers allow users to refuse cookies, so it's a good idea not to use them for vital parts of your application. When testing a new application that uses cookies, you should turn cookies off in your browser and make sure that a user can still get the benefit of your application without them.

Summary

At the end of this chapter, you should feel comfortable using superglobal arrays to access data sent from one page to the next. You should also know the difference between sessions and cookies, as well as how to use superglobal arrays to access the values stored in them.

In the next chapter, I'll introduce you to MySQL and explain how to interact with database tables to store, retrieve, modify, and delete data, which form a core part of the blog's functionality.

CHAPTER 4

■ ■ ■

Working with Databases

Modern web sites are incredibly powerful, and much of this power derives from their ability to store information. Storing information allows developers to create highly customizable interactions between their software and its users, ranging from entry-based blogs and commenting systems to high-powered banking applications that handle sensitive transactions securely.

In this chapter, I'll cover the basics of MySQL, a powerful, open-source database. Subjects I'll cover include:

- The basics of MySQL data storage

- Manipulating data in MySQL tables

- Your options in PHP for interacting with MySQL databases

- Table structure, usage, and a crash-course in planning

This is the last chapter that covers the theory of building PHP applications; in Chapter 5, I'll begin covering the practical aspects of building a blog!

The Basics of MySQL Data Storage

MySQL is a *relational database management system*, which lets you store data in multiple tables, where each table contains a set of named columns and each row consists of a data entry into the table. Tables will often contain information about other table entries, which allows developers to group relevant information into smaller groups to ease a script's load on the server, as well as simplifying data retrieval.

For example, take a look at how you might store information about musical artists (see Tables 4-1 and 4-2).

Table 4-1. *The* artists *Table*

artist_id	artist_name
1	Bon Iver
2	Feist

Table 4-2. *The albums Table*

album_id	artist_id	album_name
1	1	For Emma, Forever Ago
2	1	Blood Bank - EP3
3	2	Let It Die
4	2	The Reminder

The first table, `artists`, includes two fields. The first field, `artist_id`, stores a unique numerical identifier for the artists. The second column, `artist_name`, stores the artist's name.

The second table, `albums`, stores a unique identifier for each album in the `album_id` column and the album name in the—you guessed it!—`album_name` column. The `album` table includes a third column, `artist_id`, that relates the `artists` and `albums` tables. This column stores the unique artist identifier that corresponds to the artist that recorded the album.

Manipulating Data in MySQL Tables

You can manipulate the data in a MySQL table via several types of MySQL statements. In this section, you will learn the MySQL statements that perform the following actions:

- Create a database
- Create a table in the database
- Insert data into the table
- Retrieve the data from the table
- Modify the data in the table
- Delete the data from the table

You'll test these commands using the phpMyAdmin control panel provided by XAMPP. Open a browser and navigate to `http://localhost/phpmyadmin` to access the control panel (see Figure 4-1).

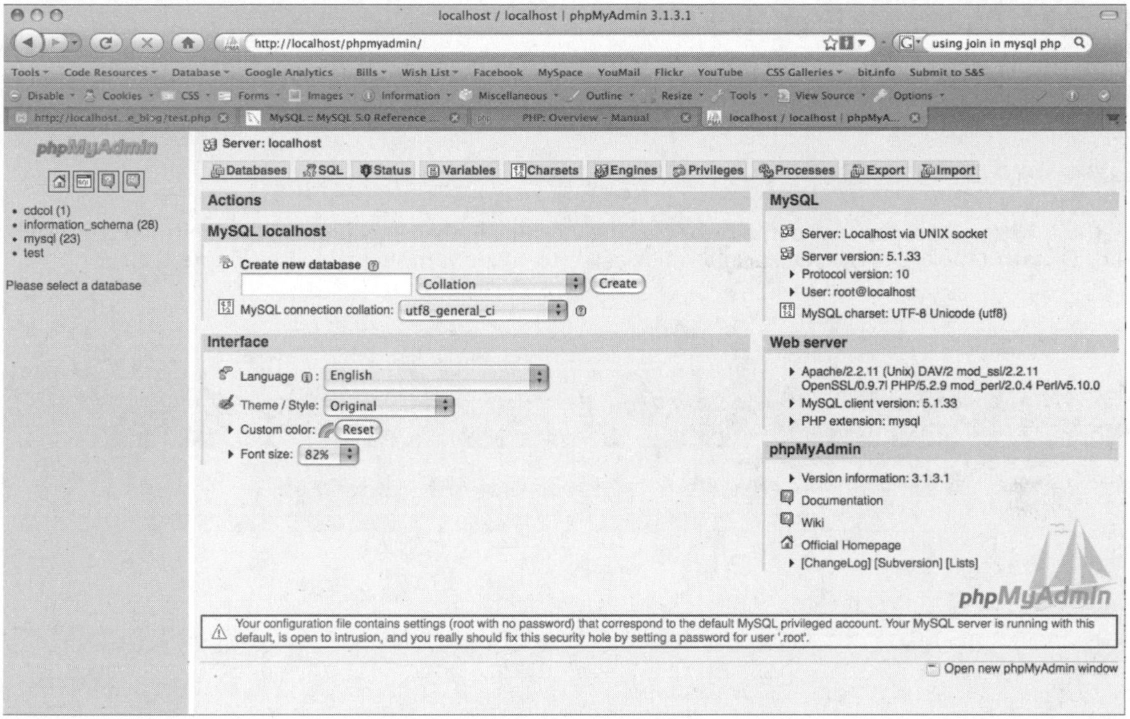

Figure 4-1. *The home page of phpMyAdmin on XAMPP*

Creating and Deleting Databases

The best way to get a feel for creating databases is to create one for testing. By default, XAMPP creates a database called test. In the interests of learning, go ahead and delete this database, and then recreate it.

Deleting Databases Using DROP

MySQL uses the word DROP to indicate that a database or table should be removed. After you start the DROP clause, you need to indicate whether you're removing a database or a table, which you indicate by name, then the name of the database or table (in this case, test).

Your complete command should look like this:

```
DROP DATABASE test
```

Click the SQL tab at the top of the screen and enter the preceding command, then click the Go button beneath the SQL field to execute the command and remove the table. Because you're deleting information, an alert pops up asking you to confirm whether you really want to drop the table.

Creating Databases Using CREATE

Next, you need to recreate the test database. MySQL uses the word CREATE to indicate that a table or database is being created. Then, as with the DROP command, you specify a DATABASE and the name of the database: test. Enter this command in the SQL tab, then click the Go button to execute it:

```
CREATE DATABASE test
```

Next, access the test database by clicking its name in the left column of the control panel. Click the SQL tab at the top of the screen, and you're ready to create your first table (see Figure 4-2).

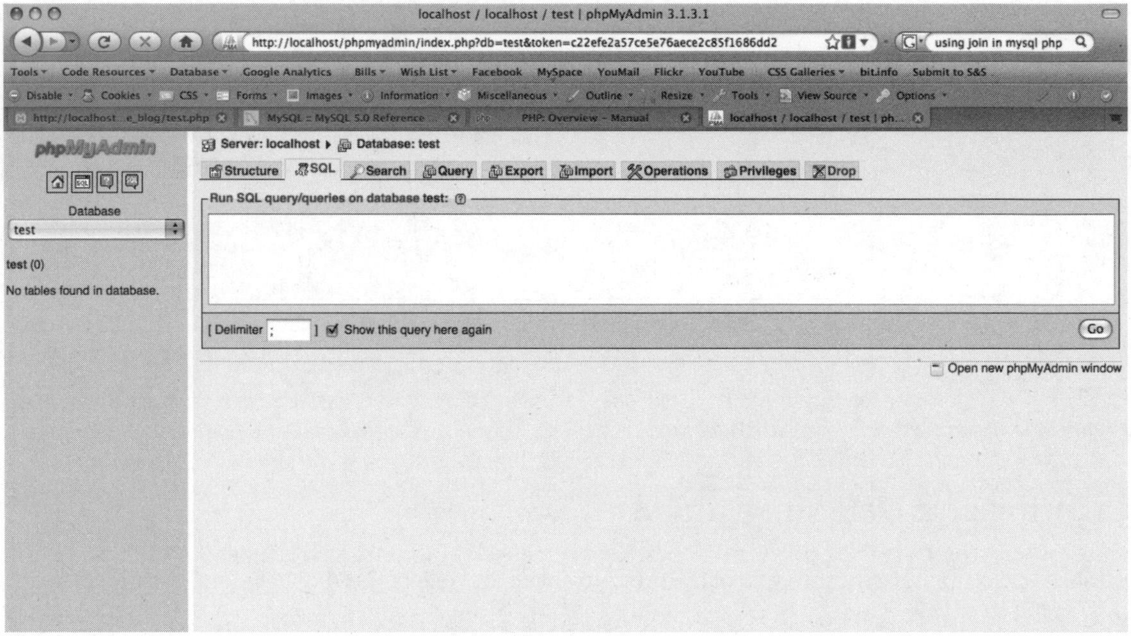

Figure 4-2. The SQL tab inside the test table on phpMyAdmin

The CREATE TABLE Statement

Of course, the first thing you need to do to start working with MySQL is to create your first table.

MySQL syntax is very simple because it generally mimics natural speech patterns. In the text field, add the following statement:

```
CREATE TABLE IF NOT EXISTS artists
(
artist_id       INT PRIMARY KEY AUTO_INCREMENT,
artist_name     VARCHAR(150)
)
```

This code creates the artists table from the previous example about musicians. The created tables will be empty, but all the columns will be in place.

The statement starts out with the words CREATE TABLE, which tells MySQL to do exactly that. You append the optional IF NOT EXISTS to ensure you don't overwrite a table if it has already been created, then add the name of the table to be created (artists).

The tricky part is defining the columns within the table. To start, you enclose the column names in parentheses after the name of the table, starting with the first column name:

(artist_id)

To identify the type of information you want to store in this column, you follow the column name with a type identifier:

(INT [see Data Types in MySQL])

This snippet instructs MySQL to store only integer values in this column.

The PRIMARY KEY (see the "Understanding PRIMARY KEY" section later in this chapter) and AUTO_INCREMENT (see the "Understanding AUTO_INCREMENT" section later in this chapter) keywords enable you to make this field update automatically with a unique ID, or *index* (see the "Indexes in MySQL" section later in this chapter).

You create the artist_name column with data type VARCHAR and specify a maximum length of 150 characters. VARCHAR is a variable-length string that can contain anywhere from 0 to 65,535 bytes. You must specify a length with columns of the VARCHAR type, or you get an error.

■**Note** MySQL supports both VARCHAR and CHAR type columns. The primary difference between the two is that CHAR columns are right padded with spaces to fill the specified length, whereas VARCHAR columns are not. For example, if the specified field length were 8, the word "data" would be stored as 'data' in a VARCHAR and as 'data   ' in a CHAR column.

Clicking the Go button beneath the text field creates the artists table. You need to repeat the process and create the albums table, which you accomplish using the following code:

```
CREATE TABLE IF NOT EXISTS albums
(
album_id INT PRIMARY KEY auto_increment,
artist_id INT,
album_name VARCHAR(150)
)
```

Again, click the Go button beneath the text field, then click the Structure tab at the top of the field to verify that your tables have been created (see Figure 4-3).

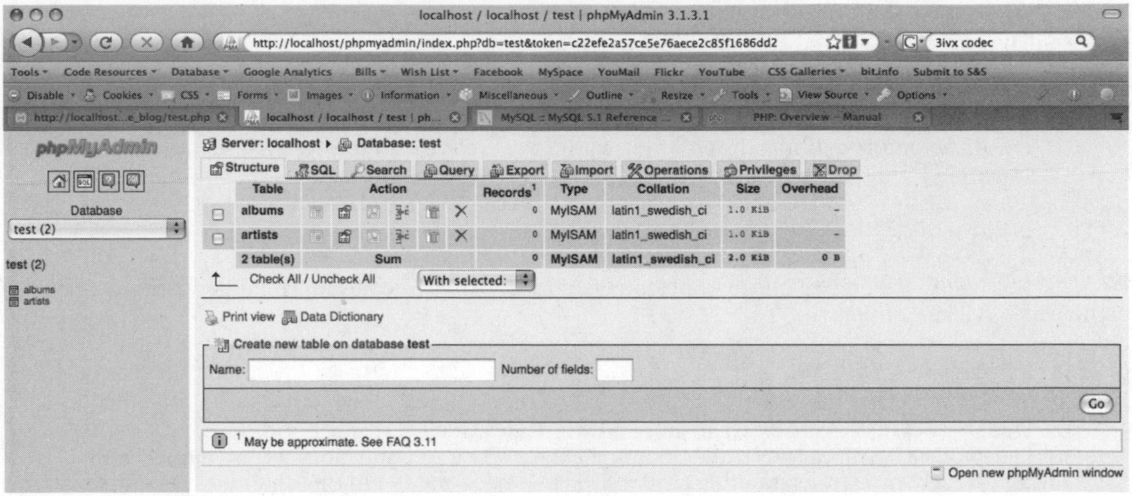

Figure 4-3. The albums and artists tables created in phpMyAdmin

Data Types in MySQL

MySQL supports numerous data types. The types you will use most often include:

- INT: an integer value

- FLOAT: a floating point number

- VARCHAR: a short string value

- TEXT: a large string value that is treated as a character string (it's best suited for blog entries)

- BLOB: a binary large object that is treated as a binary string (it can store images and similar numbers)

- DATETIME: a date value (formatted YYYY-MM-DD HH:MM:SS)

Understanding PRIMARY KEY

A column assigned with the PRIMARY KEY identifier should contain a value that uniquely identifies each value throughout the table. Because you're using numerical IDs for each artist, you know that there won't be any overlap in the artist_id column.

The use of primary keys in MySQL tables is mandatory because the data isn't really useful if you can't identify entries uniquely.

Understanding AUTO_INCREMENT

Using a unique numerical identifier for individual entries is incredibly useful, so MySQL includes an easy way to create unique identifiers called AUTO_INCREMENT. A column flagged with AUTO_INCREMENT generates identifiers in sequence automatically as entries are created, starting at 1.

Indexes in MySQL

When you look up data in a MySQL table, queries can start to back up, depending on the number of rows contained within the table. Imagine a site like CNN.com, where hundreds of thousands of people might be looking up one of the site's articles at any given moment; if each query had to go through every piece of data in every row of the table, sites like this would slow to a crawl under the stress of daily use.

Fortunately, MySQL provides a way to speed up queries by allowing you to create one or more *index* columns, which are sorted snippets of a table's data that enable much faster searching.

In the artists table, it makes a lot of sense to use the artist_id as an index. Declaring this column as the PRIMARY KEY means you've already created an index on it. However, in the albums table, the artist_id column is not an index, so searching for an artist's recordings could take much longer than you want it to if you had thousands of artists in your database.

To create an index, you'll need to ALTER the albums table. Next, you add the index by using the ADD INDEX clause with the column to index enclosed in parentheses. The complete command looks like this:

```
ALTER TABLE albums ADD INDEX (artist_id)
```

The proper use of MySQL indexes can add a huge performance boost to SELECT queries. It should be noted, however, that each index creates a separate column that must be updated every time data is added. This means it can take longer to add data to an indexed column than for an unindexed column.

The INSERT Statement

With your tables created, you're ready to start storing data. The first step is to store artist information in the artists table. Each entry must be entered separately, so you start with the first artist, Bon Iver:

```
INSERT INTO artists (artist_name) VALUES ('Bon Iver')
```

The INSERT INTO phrase tells MySQL that you're adding information. The next steps are to determine what table you want to add information into (artists) and then specify the column(s) you're adding values into (artist_name), which you enclose in parentheses.

With your table name and columns selected, you can insert data using the word VALUES, followed by the data you wish to insert, enclosed in parentheses:

```
("Bon Iver")
```

You follow the same format to add the next artist:

```
INSERT INTO artists (artist_name) VALUES ('Feist')
```

If you select the artists table from the left-hand column of phpMyAdmin and click the Browse tab, you see that even though you specified only the artist_name column, the artist_id column was filled out for you automatically (see Figure 4-4).

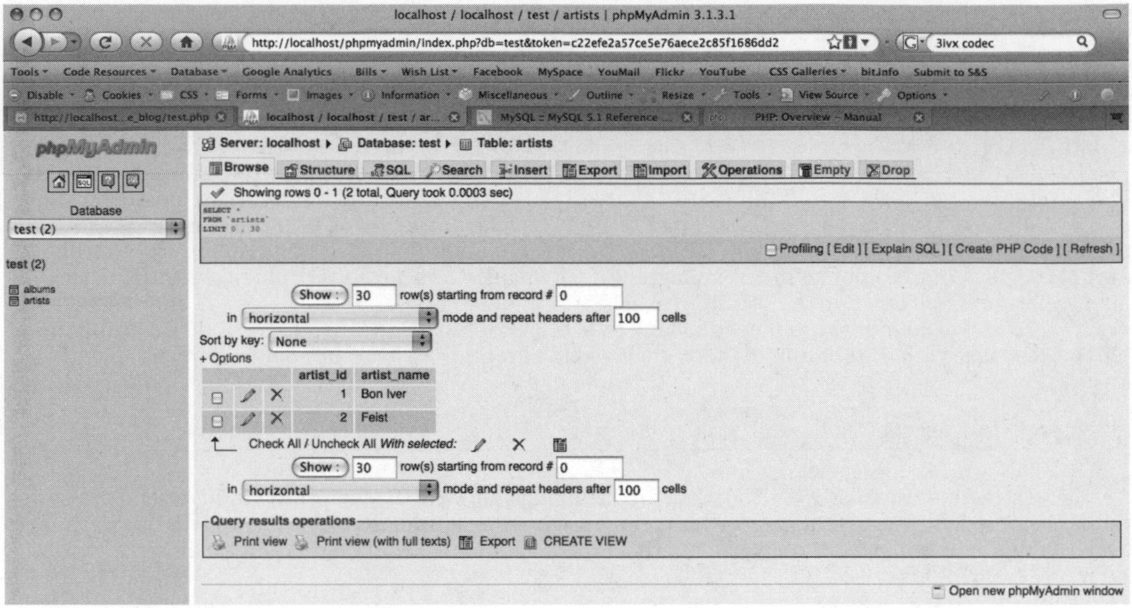

Figure 4-4. *The* artists *table populated with two entries*

To populate the albums table, you specify two columns to enter data into, then execute four statements simultaneously, separating them with a semicolon. Enter the following into the SQL text field and click the Go button:

```
INSERT INTO albums (artist_id, album_name)
VALUES ('1', 'For Emma, Forever Ago'),
('1', 'Blood Bank - EP'),
('2', 'Let It Die'),
('2', 'The Reminder')
```

Instead of executing four different commands to insert the albums, as you did in the preceding example, you can use what is called an *extended insert* to add all four albums at once. This works by enclosing each entry in parentheses, separated by commas.

Now, if you select the albums table from the left column and browse its contents, you see the four entries, as well as the automatically assigned album_id values (see Figure 4-5).

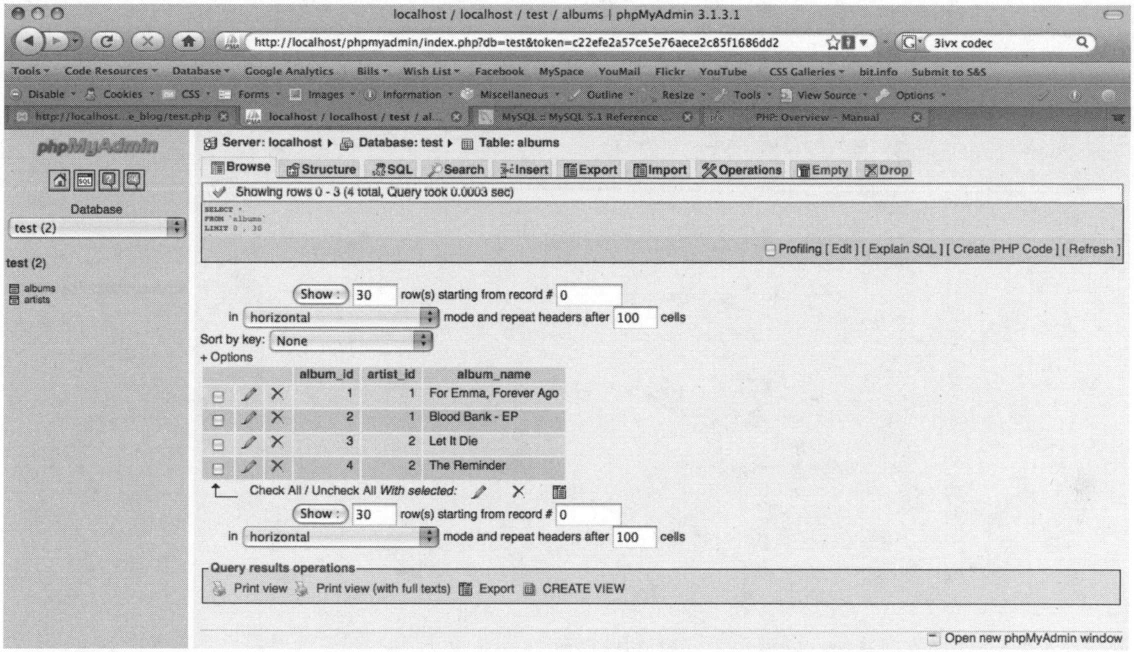

Figure 4-5. *The albums table populated with four entries*

The SELECT Statement

Now that you're comfortable inserting data into your tables, you need to figure out how to retrieve it for use with your scripts.

You do this using the SELECT statement, followed by the column name(s) you want to retrieve. You specify the table you want to query using the format FROM table_name. For example, you can get all album names from the albums table by clicking the SQL tab and inserting the following line of code:

```
SELECT album_name FROM albums
```

The result of this query when you execute it in the SQL tab of phpMyAdmin: the four album names (see Figure 4-6).

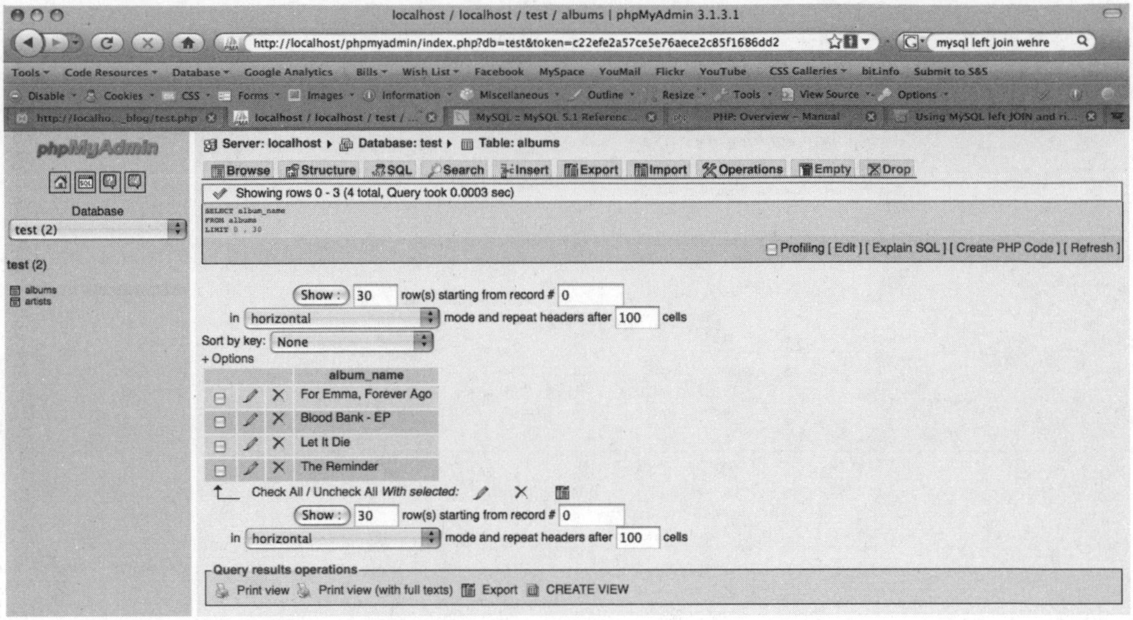

Figure 4-6. *The result of a query for all* `album_name` *column values*

You're also provided with options to modify the results, which enables you to make sure results match certain conditions before they are returned. The `WHERE` clause is the most common query modifier. For example, if you want to retrieve only album titles by Bon Iver, you can use a `WHERE` clause to ensure that returned entries match Bon Iver's `artist_id` of 1.

```
SELECT album_name FROM albums WHERE artist_id = 1
```

Telling your query to match only the `artist_id` of 1 displays only the albums by Bon Iver (see Figure 4-7).

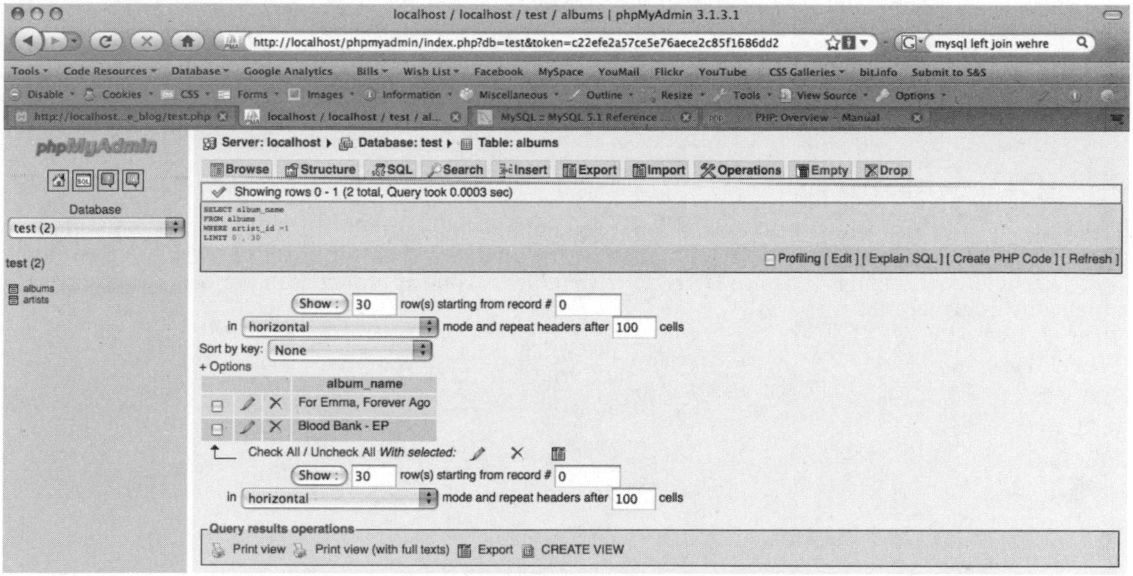

Figure 4-7. Album names returned from rows that contain the `artist_id` *of 1*

■**Note** There are many other modifiers available you can use in SELECT statements. Refer to the MySQL manual for more information on what they are and how they work. Any further modifiers used throughout this book will be introduced in their appropriate contexts as they come up.

The UPDATE Statement

At some points in your scripts, you will need to change information in an entry. To do this, you use the UPDATE statement. For example, if you were to decide to append the release year to Feist's album, "Let It Die," you could do so with the following statement:

```
UPDATE albums
SET album_name = 'Let It Die (2005)'
WHERE album_name = 'Let It Die'
```

You begin by telling MySQL that you're going to update a row using the UPDATE statement and indicating which table name (albums) you want to update. Next, you identify the column(s) to update using the word SET, followed by the column name (album_name) and the value you wish to update the field with:

```
("Let It Die (2005)")
```

Finally, you add a WHERE clause to ensure that only entries that match conditions you set (in this case, album_name = 'Let It Die') are updated.

■**Caution** When updating rows, it's important to use the WHERE clause to limit the rows being updated. Omitting the WHERE clause in an update statement will result in all table rows being updated.

The JOIN Statement

Sometimes it's necessary to select information from multiple tables. In the current example, you might have only an artist's ID but need to select both the artist's name and the albums that artist has recorded.

That information is separated between two tables, so one approach is to perform two queries to retrieve the information:

```
SELECT artist_name
FROM artists
WHERE artist_id = 1;
SELECT album_name
FROM albums
WHERE artist_id = 1;
```

Or you can use the JOIN statement to select from both tables at once. For example, look closely at you do this first, then I'll go over how it works:

```
SELECT artist_name, album_name
FROM artists
JOIN albums
USING (artist_id)
WHERE artist_id = 1
```

First, you specify that you want to retrieve both the artist_name and album_name columns, which are stored in the artists and albums tables, respectively. This might seem wrong at first, because you're selecting from the artists table, which would throw an error if not for the JOIN clause.

The JOIN clause enables you to specify a second table to use in the query (albums in this case). This means that the two tables will be combined into one table temporarily, which enables you to retrieve both the artist_name and the album_name columns with a single query.

However, you must tell MySQL how the two tables are related before this will work. The artist_id column exists in both tables, so you're going to use it to tie the two tables together. You accomplish this with the USING (artist_id) clause.

Finally, you add a WHERE clause, as when using a normal SELECT query. In plain English, this preceding query reads, "Retrieve the artist_name and album_name columns where the artist_id field has a value of 1 from the artists and albums tables."

Executing this query in the SQL tab of http://localhost/phpmyadmin returns the following results:

```
Artist_name      album_name
Bon Iver         For Emma, Forever Ago
Bon Iver         Blood Bank - EP
```

The DELETE Statement

If it becomes necessary to remove an entry, you do so using the DELETE statement. For example, assume you want to remove Feist's "The Reminder" from your list altogether:

```
DELETE FROM albums
WHERE album_name = 'The Reminder'
LIMIT 1
```

You start the statement with the DELETE FROM statement, then identify the table you want to remove an entry from (albums). Next, you create a WHERE clause to create the condition you want to match before you delete an entry (album_name = 'The Reminder'). And, just to be sure you don't accidentally delete your entire table, you add LIMIT 1 to the query, which means that only one entry will be deleted, even if more than one entry matches the conditions.

When you click the Go button, phpMyAdmin pops up a confirmation box and asks you if you're sure you want to complete the command. This is your last chance to verify that your command has no errors, such as a missing WHERE clause. This confirmation box pops up only when deleting information.

Opening a Connection

You need a method through which your PHP scripts can connect to MySQL in order to interact with the database. You can establish this connection in any of several approaches:

- PHP's MySQL Extension
- PHP's MySQLi Extension
- PHP Data Objects (PDO)

■**Caution** Due to potential security weaknesses in the MySQL Extension, developers are strongly encouraged to use PDO or MySQLi when using MySQL 4.1.3 or later.

PHP's MySQL Extension

The MySQL Extension is the original extension provided by PHP that allows developers to create PHP applications that interact with MySQL databases earlier than version 4.1.3.

The MySQL Extension uses a *procedural interface*, which means that each action is an individual function (see the code sample that follows). You can use the artists table described earlier as a basis for writing a PHP script that retrieve all the artists' names. Open test.php in Eclipse and enter the following code:

```php
<?php
    // Open a MySQL connection
    $link = mysql_connect('localhost', 'root', '');
    if(!$link) {
        die('Connection failed: ' . mysql_error());
    }
```

```php
    // Select the database to work with
    $db = mysql_select_db('test');
    if(!$db) {
        die('Selected database unavailable: ' . mysql_error());
    }

    // Create and execute a MySQL query
    $sql = "SELECT artist_name FROM artists";
    $result = mysql_query($sql);

    // Loop through the returned data and output it
    while($row = mysql_fetch_array($result)) {
        printf("Artist: %s<br />", $row['artist_name']);
    }

    // Free the memory associated with the query
    mysql_free_result($result);

    // Close the connection
    mysql_close($link);
?>
```

Navigating to http://localhost/simple_blog/test.php in your browser yields the following result:

```
Artist: Bon Iver
Artist: Feist
```

As the immediately preceding example illustrates, each step in the process has a function assigned to it:

mysql_connect(): Accepts the host, username, and password for a MySQL connection. You must call this function before any interaction with the database can take place.

die(): This is an alias for the exit() command. It stops execution of a script after displaying an optional message (passed as the function argument).

mysql_error(): If an error occurs in the MySQL database, this function displays that error; this is helpful for debugging.

mysql_select_db(): Selects the database that the script will interact with.

mysql_query(): Executes a query to the database. This query can create, modify, return, or delete table rows, as well as perform many other tasks.

mysql_fetch_array(): Converts the MySQL resource returned by mysql_query() into an array.

mysql_free_result():Frees the memory used by mysql_query() to maximize script performance.

mysql_close(): Closes the connection opened by mysql_connect().

The MySQL extension doesn't support prepared statements (see the "Using Prepared Statements" section later in this chapter), so it is susceptible to SQL injection, a potentially devastating security issue in web applications. Malicious users can use SQL injection to extract sensitive information from a database, or even go so far as to erase all the information in a given database.

You can minimize this risk by *sanitizing* all information that you want to insert into the database. The MySQL extension provides a function for escaping data called `mysql_real_escape_string()`, which escapes (inserts a backslash before) special characters. Additional functions for sanitizing data, such as `htmlentities()` and `strip_tags()`, are available. However, some risks exist even if you implement these safeguards.

The MySQLi Extension

The MySQL manual recommends that developers using MySQL 4.1.3 or later use the MySQLi extension. There are many benefits to using MySQLi over the original MySQL extension, including MySQLi's:

- Support for both object-oriented and procedural programming methods
- Support for multiple statements
- Enhanced debugging capabilities
- Support for prepared statements

Using Prepared Statements

The MySQLi and PDO extensions provide an extremely useful feature in *prepared statements*.

In a nutshell, prepared statements enable you to separate the data used in a SQL command from the command itself. If you fail to separate these, a malicious user could potentially tamper with your commands. Using a prepared statement means that all submitted data is completely escaped, which eliminates the possibility of SQL injection. You can read more about this subject in Harrison Fisk's article on prepared statements at `http://dev.mysql.com/tech-resources/articles/4.1/prepared-statements.html`.

A prepared statement works similarly to a regular MySQL statement, except that it uses a placeholder (a question mark [?]) to represent data. You can make the best use of prepared statements when use your user input in a query.

For instance, if you have a form on your site that asks what a user's favorite color is, you could use that input in a MySQL query via the $_POST superglobal:

```
$sql = "SELECT info FROM colors WHERE color = '$_POST[fav_color]'";
```

However, you aren't performing any sanitization of this input, so a malicious user could potentially exploit your form or harm your site using SQL injection. To avoid this, you can rewrite the preceding statement as a prepared statement:

```
$sql = "SELECT info FROM colors WHERE color = ?";
```

The question mark acts as a placeholder, and it signifies to MySQL that anything passed to this query is to be used only as a parameter for the current statement. This prevents a malicious user from tricking MySQL into giving away information or damaging the database.

Using MySQLi

To use MySQLi, you establish a connection using an object-oriented interface. I'll cover how to take advantage of object-oriented programming (OOP) in the next chapter, as well as discuss the pros and cons of OOP versus procedural programming.

The primary difference between OOP and procedural code is that an object can store information, freeing you from having to pass variables explicitly from function to function.

■**Note** MySQLi also provides a procedural interface to developers. See the PHP manual entry on MySQLi for more information.

To familiarize yourself with MySQLi, you can rewrite the preceding example using MySQLi. Modify test.php so it contains the following:

```php
<?php
    // Open a MySQL connection
    $link = new mysqli('localhost', 'root', '', 'test');
    if(!$link) {
        die('Connection failed: ' . $link->error());
    }

    // Create and execute a MySQL query
    $sql = "SELECT artist_name FROM artists";
    $result = $link->query($sql);

    // Loop through the returned data and output it
    while($row = $result->fetch_assoc()) {
        printf("Artist: %s<br />", $row['artist_name']);
    }

    // Free the memory associated with the query
    $result->close();

    // Close the connection
    $link->close();
?>
```

Navigating to http://localhost/simple_blog/test.php in your browser yields the following result:

```
Artist: Bon Iver
Artist: Feist
```

MySQLi works similarly to the MySQL extension, with one key exception: instead of providing individual functions, developers using MySQLi have access to *methods*, or functions contained within the MySQLi object. In the preceding code snippet, you instantiate your MySQLi object in the variable $link and establish a connection with your host, username, password, and a database name.

To execute a query, you call the query() method and pass the variable containing your MySQL statement. You call a method in OOP using the variable that contains the object, followed by an arrow (->) and the name of the method you want to call. For example, this line from the previous code example illustrates how to call a method in OOP:

```
$result = $link->query($sql);
```

The query() method returns a mysqli_result object, which has methods that allow you to access the information returned by the query.

To access each returned entry in order, you set up a loop that uses the result of calling this line:

```
$result->fetch_assoc();
```

Next, you kick out the returned data, then destroy the returned data set by calling the close() method on the $result object. Also, you close the MySQLi connection by calling the close() method on $link, as well.

Using Prepared Statements with MySQLi

What really sets MySQLi apart from the MySQL extension is its ability to use prepared statements. If you want to allow a user to select an artist that she wants to see albums from, you can create a form that looks something like this:

```
<form method="post">
    <label for="artist">Select an Artist:</label>
    <select name="artist">
        <option value="1">Bon Iver</option>
        <option value="2">Feist</option>
    </select>
    <input type="submit" />
</form>
```

When the user selects an artist, the artist's unique ID is passed to the processing script in the $_POST['artist'] variable (review Chapter 3 for a refresher on $_POST), which allows you to change your query based on user input.

In test.php, you can build a quick script that displays album names based on user input:

```
<?php
    if($_SERVER['REQUEST_METHOD']=='POST')
    {
        // Open a MySQL connection
        $link = new mysqli('localhost', 'root', '', 'test');
```

```php
        if(!$link) {
            die('Connection failed: ' . $mysqli->error());
        }

        // Create and execute a MySQL query
        $sql = "SELECT album_name FROM albums WHERE artist_id=?";
        if($stmt = $link->prepare($sql))
        {
            $stmt->bind_param('i', $_POST['artist']);
            $stmt->execute();
            $stmt->bind_result($album);
            while($stmt->fetch()) {
                printf("Album: %s<br />", $album);
            }
            $stmt->close();
        }

        // Close the connection
        $link->close();
    }
    else {
?>

<form method="post">
    <label for="artist">Select an Artist:</label>
    <select name="artist">
        <option value="1">Bon Iver</option>
        <option value="2">Feist</option>
    </select>
    <input type="submit" />
</form>

<?php } // End else ?>
```

When a user submits the form, a new MySQLi object is created, and a query is created with a placeholder for the artist_id in the WHERE clause. You can then call the prepare( ) method on your MySQLi object ($link->prepare($sql)) and pass the query as a parameter.

With your statement ($stmt) prepared, you need to tell MySQL how to handle the user input and insert it into the query. This is called *binding parameters* to the query, and you accomplish this by calling the bind_param( ) method on the newly created $stmt, which is a MySQLi_STMT object.

Binding parameters requires a couple steps: begin by passing the type of the parameter, then pass the parameter value.

MySQLi supports four data types:

- i: Integer (any whole number value)

- s: String (any combination of characters)

- d: Double (any floating point number)

- b: Blob (data is sent in packets that is used for storing images or other binary data)

You're passing the artist's ID, so you set the parameter type to i, then pass the value of $_POST['artist'].

With the parameters bound, you can execute the statement using the execute() method.

After the query is executed, you need to specify variables to contain the returned results, which you accomplish using the bind_result() method. For each column you've requested, you need to provide a variable to contain it. In this example, you need to store the album name, which you accomplish by supplying the $album variable.

Your script now knows where to store returned values, so you can set up a loop to run while results still exist (as returned by the fetch() method). Inside the loop, you output each album name.

Finally, you destroy your resultset and close the connection by calling the close() method on both your MySQLi_STMT and MySQLi objects; this frees the memory used by the query.

If you load your script by navigating to http://localhost/simple_blog/test.php and select Bon Iver from the list, you see the following output:

```
Album: For Emma, Forever Ago
Album: Blood Bank – EP
```

PHP Data Objects (PDO)

PHP Data Objects, or PDO, is similar to MySQLi in that it is an object-oriented approach to handling queries that supports prepared statements.

The main difference between MySQLi and PDO is that PDO is a *database-access abstraction layer*. This means that PDO supports multiple database languages and provides a uniform set of methods for handling most database interactions.

This is a great advantage for applications that need to support multiple database types, such as PostgreSQL, Firebird, or Oracle. Changing from one database type to another generally requires that you rewrite only a small amount of code, which enables developers to change your existing drivers for PDO and continue with business as usual.

The downside to PDO is that some of the advanced features of MySQL are unavailable, such as support for multiple statements. Another potential issue when using PDO is that it relies on the OOP features of PHP5, which means that servers running PHP4 won't be able to run scripts using PDO. This is becoming less of an issue over time because few servers lack access to PHP5; however, it's still something you need to take into consideration when choosing your database access method.

Rewriting Your Example in PDO

You can use PDO to rewrite your prepared statement. In test.php, modify the code as follows:

```php
<?php
    if($_SERVER['REQUEST_METHOD']=='POST')
    {
        // Open a MySQL connection
        $dbinfo = 'mysql:host=localhost;dbname=test';
```

```php
        $user = 'root';
        $pass = '';
        $link = new PDO($dbinfo, $user, $pass);


        // Create and execute a MySQL query
        $sql = "SELECT album_name
                FROM albums
                WHERE artist_id=?";
        $stmt = $link->prepare($sql);
        if($stmt->execute(array($_POST['artist'])))
        {
            while($row = $stmt->fetch()) {
                printf("Album: %s<br />", $row['album_name']);
            }
            $stmt->closeCursor();
        }
    }
    else {
?>

<form method="post">
    <label for="artist">Select an Artist:</label>
    <select name="artist">
        <option value="1">Bon Iver</option>
        <option value="2">Feist</option>
    </select>
    <input type="submit" />
</form>

<?php } // End else ?>
```

The first step, opening the database connection, is a little different from the other two methods you've learned about so far. This difference stems from the fact that PDO can support multiple database types, which means you need to specify a driver to create the right type of connection.

First, you create a variable called $dbinfo that tells PDO to initiate itself using the MySQL driver for the host localhost host and the test database. Next, you create two more variables, $user and $pass, to contain your database username and password.

After you pen your connection, you form your query with a placeholder, pass it to the prepare() method, and then pass the query to be prepared. This returns a PDOStatement object that you save in the $stmt variable.

Next, you call the execute() method with an array containing the user-supplied artist ID, $_POST['artist']. This is equivalent to calling both bind_param() and execute() with the MySQLi extension.

After the statement has executed, you set up a loop to run while results still exist. Each result is sent to the browser, and you free the memory using the closeCursor() method.

Running this script by loading `http://localhost/simple_blog/test.php` produces the following:

```
Album: For Emma, Forever Ago
Album: Blood Bank - EP
```

■**Note** PDO is highly versatile, so I rely on it for most of this book's examples. Feel free to substitute another method, but be advised that code that interacts with the database will look differently if you do.

Table Structure and a Crash Course in Planning

As your PHP applications become more complicated, your app's performance will start to play a key role in development. MySQL is a potential performance killer in applications, creating bottlenecks that prevent scripts from executing as quickly as you want them to.

Part of your role as a developer is to know the risks involved with MySQL queries and eliminate as many performance issues as possible. The most common risks I'll show you how to address in this chapter include:

- Poor planning of database tables
- Requests for unnecessary data (using the shortcut selector [*])

■**Note** Database architecture and optimization is a huge task; it's actually a career in and of itself. This book covers only the basics of this subject; however, knowing about the potential performance problems associated with your databases is important because you might not always have a database architect available to you.

Planning Database Tables

Database tables are fairly simple, but interconnected tables can be a hindrance to your scripts' performance if you don't plan them properly. For example, a list of blog entries (entries) and a list of a web site's pages (pages) might look something like this (see Tables 4-3 and 4-4).

Table 4-3. *The entries Table*

title	textSample
Entry	This is some text.
Entry Title	This is more text.
Example Title	A third entry.

Table 4-4. *The pages Table*

page_name	type
Blog	Multi
About	Static
Contact	Form

You might use another table (entry_pages) to link the entries to the page you want to display them on (see Table 4-5).

Table 4-5. *The entry_pages Table*

page	entry
Blog	Sample Entry
Blog	Entry Title
About	Example Title

Unfortunately, you're storing redundant data in this case, which is both unnecessary and potentially harmful to your application's performance. If you know you're on the blog page, you can use two queries to retrieve the entry data:

```php
<?php
    // Initiate the PDO object
    $dbinfo = 'mysql:dbname=test;host=localhost';
    $user = 'root';
    $pass = '';
    try {
        $db = new PDO($dbinfo, $user, $pass);
    } catch(PDOException $e) {
        echo 'Connection failed: ', $e->getMessage();
    }

    // Creates the first query
    $sql = "SELECT entry
        FROM entry_pages
        WHERE page='Blog'";
```

```
    // Initialize the $entries variable in case there's no saved data
    $entries = NULL;

    // Retrieves the entries from the table
    foreach($db->query($sql) as $row) {
        $sql2 = "SELECT text
            FROM entries
            WHERE title='$row[entry]'";
        foreach($db->query($sql) as $row2) {
            $entries[] = array($row['title'], $row2['entry']);
        }
    }

    // Display the output
    print_r($entries);
?>
```

This code returns the following:

```
Array
(
    [0] => Array
        (
            [0] => Sample Entry
            [1] => This is some text.
        )

    [1] => Array
        (
            [0] => Entry Title
            [1] => This is more text.
        )

)
```

■**Note** For the preceding code to work, you need to create the entry_pages table and populate it with the data described in Table 4-5.

However, this approach is extremely inefficient because you're retrieving redundant data from the entry_pages and entries tables.

One way to avoid this problem is to add an additional column to tables containing an ID for each row that will automatically increment as rows are added. This allows for less redundancy in data storage. For example, assume you want to revisit your pages and entries by adding an ID column (see Tables 4-6 and 4-7).

Table 4-6. *The Revised pages Table*

id	page_name	type
1	Blog	Multi
2	About	Static
3	Contact	Form

Table 4-7. *The Revised entries Table*

id	page_id	title	text
1	1	Sample Entry	This is some text.
2	1	Entry Title	This is more text.
3	2	Example Entry	This is a third entry.

Adding an ID column enables you to eliminate entry_pages altogether, which leaves you with an easy way to cross-reference your tables. This means you can rewrite your script to retrieve entries for a particular page far more efficiently:

```php
<?php
    $dbinfo = 'mysql:dbname=test;host=localhost';
    $user = 'root';
    $pass = '';

    try {
        $db = new PDO($dbinfo, $user, $pass);
    } catch(PDOException $e) {
        echo 'Connection failed: ', $e->getMessage();
    }

    $sql = "SELECT title, text
            FROM entries
            WHERE page_id=1";
    foreach($db->query($sql) as $row) {
        $entries[] = array($row['title'], $row['text']);
    }

    print_r($entries);
?>
```

This code returns an identical result to your previous example, but takes only half as long to execute because it executes only one query instead of the original two.

■**Note** Database design is a highly specialized area of programming. You can learn more this subject by picking up a copy of *Beginning Database Design: From Novice to Professional* by Clare Churcher (Apress, 2007).

The Shortcut Selector (*)

MySQL provides a shortcut selector (`SELECT *`) that enables developers to select all data contained within a table. At first glance, this seems like a convenient way to retrieve data from our tables easily. However, the shortcut selector poses a threat to the performance of your scripts by requesting data that isn't needed, which consumes memory unnecessarily.

To avoid wasting resources, it's considered best practice to request all information required by your scripts explicitly. For example, you shouldn't use this approach if you can help it:

```
SELECT * FROM entries
```

Instead, you should write code that goes something like this:

```
SELECT title, text, author FROM entries
```

This ensures that information you won't need for a particular script isn't loaded and thus saves memory. This approach has the added benefit of simplifying your code maintenance because you won't have to remember which columns are returned from table if the code needs to be updated in the future—that information is readily available.

Summary

In this chapter, you've learned the basics of MySQL statements, as well as how to interact with the database from your PHP scripts.

In the next chapter, you'll learn how to begin building your blog by creating a basic entry manager that will allows you to create, modify, and delete entries, as well as display them on a public page.

Recommended Reading

You might find the following links useful for drilling down in more detail on several of the topics covered in this chapter.

- *The MySQL Extension*: http://us2.php.net/manual/en/book.mysql.php

- *The MySQLi Extension*: http://us3.php.net/mysqli

- *PHP Data Objects (PDO)*: http://us.php.net/manual/en/book.pdo.php

PART 2

■ ■ ■

Building Your Blog

Now that you have a grasp of the basics of PHP development, including how it works and interacts with a MySQL database, you're ready to create your blog. In this section, you will learn how to create and process a form that saves blog entries to the database. You'll also learn how to allow multiple pages with your entry manager, as well as how to edit entries and add photos.

CHAPTER 5

■ ■ ■

Building the Entry Manager

At this point, you know enough to start building your blog! In this chapter, I'll walk you through how to build the backbone of your blogging application. The pieces you'll build include:

- A form to accept entry input
- A script to handle input from the form
- A script to save the entry in the database
- A script to retrieve the entry from the database
- An HTML document to display the retrieved information

By the end of this chapter, you will have a very basic, but fully functional blogging system.

Planning the Entry Database Table

One of the most important steps with any new application is the planning of the tables that will hold data. This has a huge impact on the ease of *scaling* our application later. Scaling is the expansion of an application to handle more information and/or users, and it can be a tremendous pain if we don't look ahead when starting a new project.

At first, your blog needs to store several types of entry information to function:

- Unique ID
- Entry title
- Entry text
- Date created

Using a unique ID for each entry in the entry table enables you to access the information contained with just a number. This is extremely helpful for data access, especially if this dataset changes in the future (if you add an "imageURL" column to the table, for example).

The first step is to determine the fields you will need for the entries table. Your table needs to define what type of information is stored in each column, so let's take a quick look at the information each column needs to store:

- id: *A unique number identifying the entry.* This will be a positive integer, and it makes sense for this number to increment automatically because that ensures the number is unique. You will also use this as the primary method for accessing an entry, so it will double as the primary key for the table.

- title: An alphanumeric string that should be relatively short. You'll limit the string to 150 characters.

- entry: *An alphanumeric string of indeterminate length.* You won't limit the length of this field (within reason).

- created: *The timestamp generated automatically at the original creation date of the entry.* You'll use this to sort your entries chronologically, as well as for letting tour users know when an entry was posted originally.

Now it's time to create the database. Do this by navigating to `http://localhost/phpmyadmin/` and creating a database called `simple_blog` using the "Create new database" field on the homepage (see Figure 5-1).

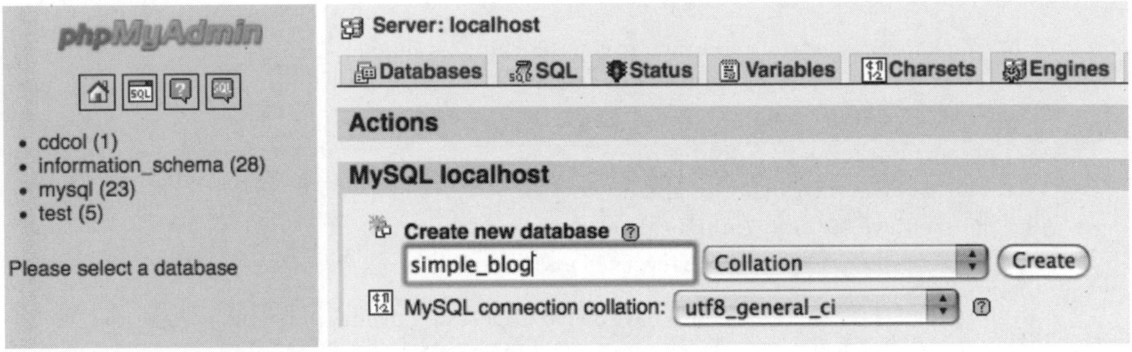

Figure 5-1. Creating a new database in phpMyAdmin

The new database is created after you click "Create." Next, you're shown a confirmation message and given options for interacting with your new database (see Figure 5-2).

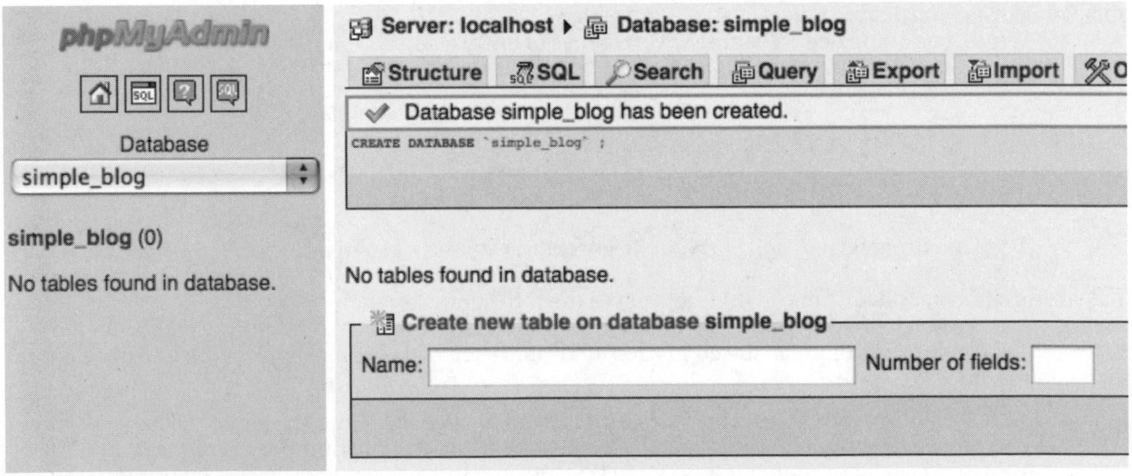

Figure 5-2. The simple_blog database confirmation screen and options

126

The next step is to write the code that creates your entries table:

```
CREATE TABLE entries
(
    id      INT PRIMARY KEY AUTO_INCREMENT,
    title   VARCHAR(150),
    entry   TEXT,
    created TIMESTAMP DEFAULT CURRENT_TIMESTAMP
)
```

To create the entries table, click the SQL tab at the top of the page and enter the command that creates your table (see Figure 5-3).

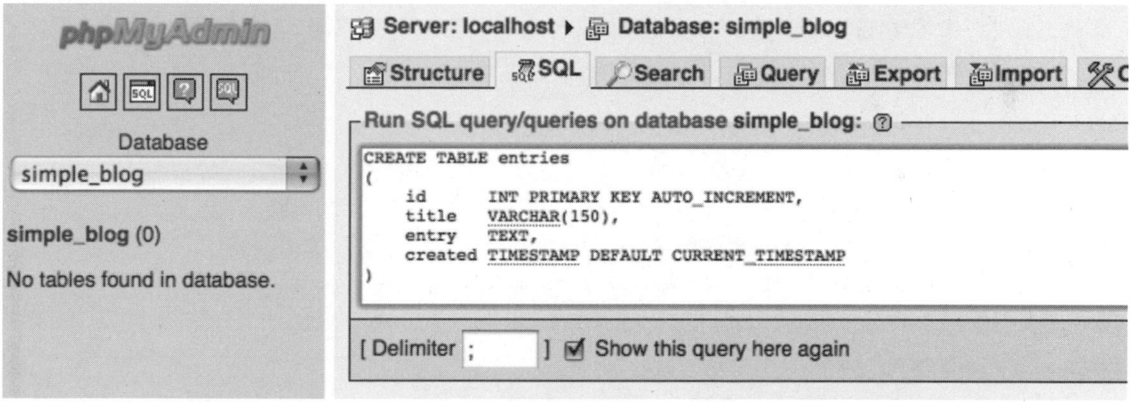

Figure 5-3. *Creating the* entries *table in phpMyAdmin*

After you click the Go button at the bottom right of the SQL text field, the entries table shows up in the left-hand column of the screen. You can see a table's structure by clicking the table you're interested in (see Figure 5-4).

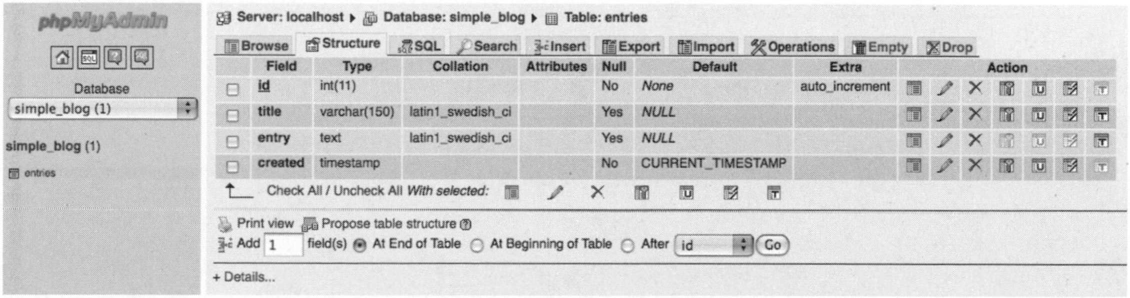

Figure 5-4. *The structure of the* entries *table in phpMyAdmin*

At this point, you have created the entries table, and you're ready to create your input form.

Creating the Entry Input Form

Storing entries in your database requires that you allow site administrators to enter data via a web form. Before you can do this, you need to identify which fields the form must include.

Two of your fields are populated automatically when an entry is created: the id field will generate an automatically incremented number to identify the entry, and the created field automatically stores the timestamp for the entry's creation date. All you need to include are fields to enter the title and entry fields.

Your title field has a maximum length of 150 characters, so you use an input tag with a maxlength attribute for this. The entry field can be as long as you want it to, so create a textarea tag.

In Eclipse, create a new file in the simple_blog project called admin.php; this file should end up saved in the xampp folder at /xampp/htdocs/simple_blog/admin.php).

In the new file, add the following HTML:

```
<!DOCTYPE html
    PUBLIC "-//W3C//DTD XHTML 1.0 Strict//EN"
    "http://www.w3.org/TR/xhtml1/DTD/xhtml1-strict.dtd">

<html xmlns="http://www.w3.org/1999/xhtml" xml:lang="en" lang="en">

<head>
    <meta http-equiv="Content-Type"
        content="text/html;charset=utf-8" />
    <title> Simple Blog </title>
</head>

<body>
    <h1> Simple Blog Application </h1>

    <form method="post" action="inc/update.inc.php">
        <fieldset>
            <legend>New Entry Submission</legend>
            <label>Title
                <input type="text" name="title" maxlength="150" />
            </label>
            <label>Entry
                <textarea name="entry" cols="45" rows="10"></textarea>
            </label>
            <input type="submit" name="submit" value="Save Entry" />
            <input type="submit" name="submit" value="Cancel" />
        </fieldset>
    </form>
</body>

</html>
```

You can view the form you've created by navigating to `http://localhost/simple_blog/`
`admin.php` in your browser (see Figure 5-5).

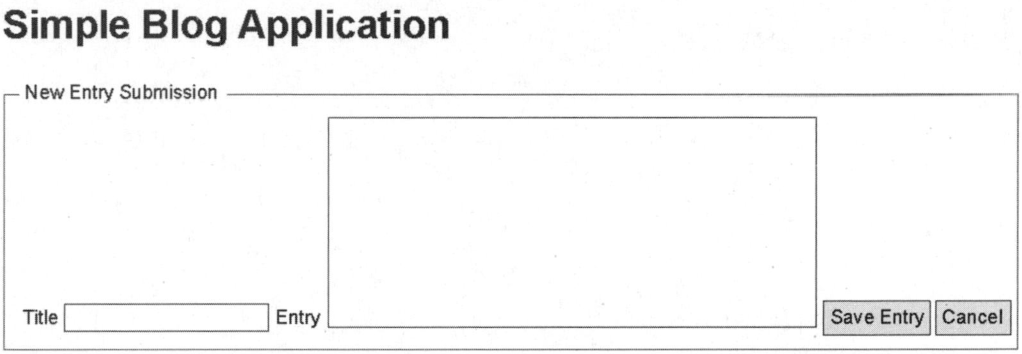

Simple Blog Application

Figure 5-5. *The entry creation form*

This is not a book about *Cascading Style Sheets* (CSS), a language used to describe the
presentation of HTML- and XML-based documents, but you'll take advantage of CSS to make your form
easy-to-use. Begin by creating a new folder in the `simple_blog` project called `css`. Next, create a file
called `default.css` in the `css` folder (full path: `/xampp/htdocs/simple_blog/css/default.css`), then add
the following style information to your new file:

```
h1 {
    width:380px;
    margin:0 auto 20px;
    padding:0;
    font-family:helvetica, sans-serif;
}
ul#menu {
        width:350px;
        margin:0 auto;
        padding:0;
        list-style:none;
}
ul#menu > li {
        display:inline;
}
ul#menu > li > a {
        padding:6px;
        color:#FFF;
        background:#333;
        font-family:helvetica, sans-serif;
        text-decoration:none;
}
```

```css
#control_panel, #entries, fieldset {
    width:350px;
    margin:0 auto;
    padding:10px;
    font-family:helvetica, sans-serif;
}
#control_panel {
    width:350px;
    margin:20px auto 0;
    padding:4px;
    font-size:80%;
    text-align:center;
    background:#DDD;
    border-top:1px dotted #000;
    border-bottom:1px dotted #000;
}
input, textarea {
    font-size:95%;
    font-family:helvetica, sans-serif;
    display:block;
    width:340px;
    margin:0 auto 10px;
    padding:4px;
    border:1px solid #333;
}
input[type=submit] {
    display:inline;
    width:auto;
}
input[type=hidden] {
        display:none;
}
.backlink {
    border:0;
    text-align:right;
}
#comment-form > fieldset {
  width:330px;
  border:1px solid #000;
}
#comment-form input[type=text],
#comment-form textarea {
  width:320px;
}
```

```css
.error {
  color:#F00;
  text-align:center;
  font-weight:bold;
  margin:5px 0 15px;
}
.comment {
  padding:0 0 10px;
}
.comment > span,
.comment > .admin {
  display:block;
  font-size:80%;
  margin:0 0 10px;
  padding:4px;
  text-align:right;
  background:#DDD;
  border-bottom:1px dotted #000;
}
.comment > .admin {
  background:transparent;
  border:0;
}
.comment > span > strong {
  float:left;
}
```

I won't go into the specifics of how this works, but this code will provide styling information for all the components I'll be building in this book. To apply these styles to your form, you need to link to the CSS file in the head section of admin.php. Do this by adding the code highlighted in bold to admin.php:

```html
<head>
    <meta http-equiv="Content-Type"
        content="text/html;charset=utf-8" />
    <link rel="stylesheet" href="/css/default.css" type="text/css" />
    <title> Simple Blog </title>
</head>
```

Once you save the linked stylesheet in admin.php, you can reload admin.php to see the cleaned up form (see Figure 5-6).

■**Note** You can learn more about CSS by checking out the book, *Beginning CSS Web Development: From Novice to Professional*, by Simon Collison (Apress, 2006).

Simple Blog Application

Figure 5-6. The input-manager form styled with CSS

Create a Script to Process the Form Input

Your entry form is set to submit entered values using the POST method to a file located at inc/update.inc.php. The next step is to create the file that will accept the input from the form and save entries to the database.

First, you need to create the inc folder. You create a folder for this script because it won't be accessed directly by a browser.

■**Tip** To keep our project organized, you can separate scripts that process information from scripts that display it. This makes maintenance a little easier because it groups similar files.

In your simple_blog project, create the inc folder, then create a file called update.inc.php. This script will have logic that determines whether input should be saved; it will also have the ability to save entries to the entries table.

■**Tip** Be sure to save files that aren't accessed directly by the browser with a different file extension, such as .inc.php; this helps you identify files that should not be public easily.

It is critical that you plan your script that processes form input properly; a good way to do that is to break the process into small, discrete steps:

1. Verify that information was submitted via the POST method
2. Verify that the Save Entry button was pressed
3. Verify that both the title and entry form fields were filled out
4. Connect to the database
5. Formulate a MySQL query to store the entry data
6. Sanitize the input and store it in the entries table
7. Obtain the unique ID for the newly created entry
8. Send the user to the newly created entry

Performing the Initial Verification

You can combine the first three steps into one conditional statement. All conditions are required, so you can use the && operator to require that all conditions are true. The conditional statement looks like this:

```php
<?php

if($_SERVER['REQUEST_METHOD']=='POST'
    && $_POST['submit']=='Save Entry'
    && !empty($_POST['title'])
    && !empty($_POST['entry']))
{
    // Continue processing information . . .
}

// If both conditions aren't met, sends the user back to the main page
else
{
    header('Location: ../admin.php');
    exit;
}

?>
```

You use the $_SERVER superglobal to determine whether the script was accessed using the POST method. Making this check helps you ensure that the page wasn't accessed by mistake. You use the $_POST superglobal to access the value of the button pressed to submit the form. If the pressed button wasn't the "Save Entry" button, the form isn't submitted. This makes it possible for the Cancel button to send the user back to the main page without saving any of the input from the form. Finally, you use the $_POST superglobal to verify that the user filled out the title and entry fields of the form; performing this check helps you ensure that you don't store any incomplete entries in the database.

If any of these conditions isn't met, the user is sent back to the main page, and your script performs no further processing. This means that any information submitted won't be saved to the database.

Connect to the Database

If all conditions were met, the script can proceed to Step 4, where you save the information to your database. You need to open a connection to the database before you can save to it; you open the connection using PHP Data Objects (PDO).

Keeping Database Credentials Separate

It's a good habit to keep database credentials and other site-wide information separate from the rest of your scripts. The reason: This allows you to change an entire project's configuration quickly and easily by altering a single file.

You might wonder why skipping this step could matter. Imagine that you build a project that has dozens of scripts, all of which need to contact the database for some reason or another. Now imagine that the database is moved to a new server, and the login credentials need to be updated. If you did not keep site-wide information separate from the rest of your scripts in this scenario, you would be required to open every single file in your project to swap in the new login information—this would be a tedious and potentially time-consuming task.

If, however, you store all the login credentials and other scripts that access the database in one file, you're able to move the site to a new database by altering a single file.

You store your database credentials in a file you create and store in the inc folder called db.inc.php (full path: /xampp/htdocs/simple_blog/inc/db.inc.php). You can define the credentials as constants with the following code:

```php
<?php

define('DB_INFO', 'mysql:host=localhost;dbname=simple_blog');
define('DB_USER', 'root');
define('DB_PASS', '');

?>
```

All that remains is to include db.inc.php in any file that needs database access, and you have access to your credentials.

Connecting to the Database in update.inc.php

Next, add the bolded lines to update.inc.php to include your credentials and open a connection to the database:

```php
<?php

if($_SERVER['REQUEST_METHOD']=='POST'
    && $_POST['submit']=='Save Entry')
{
    // Include database credentials and connect to the database
    include_once 'db.inc.php';
    $db = new PDO(DB_INFO, DB_USER, DB_PASS);

    // Continue processing data...
}

// If both conditions aren't met, send the user back to the main page
else
{
    header('Location: ../admin.php');
    exit;
}

?>
```

Save the Entry to the Database

When you're sure that all the necessary conditions have been met and a connection to the database is open, you're ready to proceed with Steps 5 and 6: formulating a MySQL query to store the entry data and then sanitizing the input and storing it in the entries table. To accomplish these tasks, you need to create a prepared statement. Begin by creating a query template, which you use to save the title and entry fields entered to the title and entry columns in the entries table. The query looks like this:

```
INSERT INTO entries (title, entry) VALUES (?, ?)
```

You store this query in a variable that you pass to PDO's prepare() method. With your query prepared, you can execute the statement using the supplied form information, confident that the input is being escaped properly.

Add the code in bold to update.inc.php:

```php
<?php

if($_SERVER['REQUEST_METHOD']=='POST'
    && $_POST['submit']=='Save Entry')
{
    // Include database credentials and connect to the database
    include_once 'db.inc.php';
    $db = new PDO(DB_INFO, DB_USER, DB_PASS);
```

```
    // Save the entry into the database
    $sql = "INSERT INTO entries (title, entry) VALUES (?, ?)";
    $stmt = $db->prepare($sql);
    $stmt->execute(array($title, $entry));
    $stmt->closeCursor();

    // Continue processing data...
}

// If both conditions aren't met, sends the user back to the main page
else
{
    header('Location: ../admin.php');
    exit;
}


?>
```

The execute() method saves the information into the entries table. Finally, call the closeCursor() method to end the query.

Retrieve the Entry's Unique ID and Display the Entry to the User

You've saved your new entry successfully; the final pair of steps is to obtain the unique ID of the new entry and enable the user to view his new entry.

To accomplish this, you need the ID generated for the entry you just saved. Fortunately, MySQL provides a built-in function for tackling the first part of this; you can use the LAST_INSERT_ID() function to structure a query that retrieves the unique ID of the new entry:

```
SELECT LAST_INSERT_ID()
```

When you access the results of the query using the fetch() method, you're given an array in which the first index (0) contains the ID of the last entry inserted into the database.

Once you have the ID, you want to send the user to the publicly displayed page that contains his entry, which you call index.php. To do this, you need to insert the id of the entry you want to display in a URL:

```
http://localhost/simple_blog/index.php?id=1
```

You can shorten the URL like this:

```
http://localhost/simple_blog/?id=1
```

■**Tip** This script uses *relative paths* to access the publicly displayed site. This approach allows the scripts to exist in any directory, as long as they remain in the same relationship to each other within the file structure. The relative path ../ means, in plain English: "Go up one folder." In this case, the relative path takes you out of the inc folder and back into the simple_blog folder.

Now add the following code to update.inc.php to retrieve the entry's ID and direct the user to the entry's public display:

```php
<?php

if($_SERVER['REQUEST_METHOD']=='POST'
    && $_POST['submit']=='Save Entry')
{
    // Include database credentials and connect to the database
    include_once 'db.inc.php';
    $db = new PDO(DB_INFO, DB_USER, DB_PASS);

    // Save the entry into the database
    $sql = "INSERT INTO entries (title, entry) VALUES (?, ?)";
    $stmt = $db->prepare($sql);
    $stmt->execute(array($_POST['title'], $_POST['entry']));
    $stmt->closeCursor();

    // Get the ID of the entry we just saved
    $id_obj = $db->query("SELECT LAST_INSERT_ID()");
    $id = $id_obj->fetch();
    $id_obj->closeCursor();

    // Send the user to the new entry
    header('Location: ../admin.php?id='.$id[0]);
    exit;
}

// If both conditions aren't met, sends the user back to the main page
else
{
    header('Location: ../admin.php');
    exit;
}

?>
```

■Note You haven't created index.php yet, so this code redirects to admin.php. You'll change this when you create index.php in the next step.

No matter how the script is accessed, the user will receive a resolution: either the script executes successfully and the user is shown her new entry, or the script takes her back out to the main display and nothing is saved.

You can test the new system by adding three dummy entries to the system:

- Title: *First Entry*; Entry: *This is some text.*

- Title: *Second Entry*; Entry: *More text and a <a href="#">link</a>.*

- Title: *Third Entry*; Entry: *A third entry in the database.*

These entries will give you some test data to work with when you move on to the next step, which is to build the script that retrieves entries from the database and displays them.

Displaying the Saved Entries

As I stated earlier, you will call your script to display the entries index.php, and you will store it in the root of the simple_blog project (full path: /xampp/htdocs/simple_blog/index.php). Your first step is to put together the structure of the page that will display the information.

Add the following HTML to index.php:

```
<!DOCTYPE html
    PUBLIC "-//W3C//DTD XHTML 1.0 Strict//EN"
    "http://www.w3.org/TR/xhtml1/DTD/xhtml1-strict.dtd">

<html xmlns="http://www.w3.org/1999/xhtml" xml:lang="en" lang="en">

<head>
    <meta http-equiv="Content-Type"
        content="text/html;charset=utf-8" />
    <link rel="stylesheet" href="/css/default.css" type="text/css" />
    <title> Simple Blog </title>
</head>

<body>

    <h1> Simple Blog Application </h1>

    <div id="entries">
```

```php
<?php

    // Format the entries from the database

?>
        <p class="backlink">
            <a href="/admin.php">Post a New Entry</a>
        </p>

    </div>

</body>

</html>
```

This code creates a valid HTML page, complete with a link to the CSS file you created earlier this chapter. It also creates a page heading ("Simple Blog Application"), a container for the entries, and a link to admin.php, which you can use to create additional entries.

Planning Our Scripts

You want your script to scale to your future needs, so now is a good time to explore best practices, organizational techniques, and other ways to eliminate unnecessary rewrites as you modify your code going forward. This might seem like a bit of a departure from the simple blogging application, but taking a moment to learn how to separate your code properly now can save you a lot of time in the future (as you'll see in upcoming chapters).

Separation of Logic in Programming

When you write scripts, it's important to know what your script is doing and why. This helps you separate different parts of your script into smaller chunks with specific purposes, which simplifies the organization, maintenance, and readability of your applicatoin's code.

To separate your code, you need to identify the different categories that scripts can fall into. In general, there are three main types of coding logic:

- Database logic
- Business logic
- Presentation logic

Database Logic

Database logic refers to any code that connects to the database, whether that code creates, modifies, or retrieves data.

Business Logic

Business logic is a much broader area of coding, and it includes any script that *processes* data. Business logic typically exists between the database and presentation logic, and it serves to modify the data in some capacity that doesn't involve specific output properties. For example, you might use business logic to replace words in some text, convert a timestamp to a date, and so on.

Business logic represents a large area of coding, so it can be tough to describe it precisely. However, it's generally safe to assume that if a given bit of code doesn't access the database or generate the presentation (such as HTML markup), it's probably performing business logic.

Presentation Logic

Presentation logic is the part of a script that displays output to a user. This code can include generating HTML markup, XML output, or any other format that allows a user to access the information a script is working with.

Organizational Philosophies and Programming Patterns

There isn't a hard and fast "right way" to separate logic in an application, and the methods a developer chooses for a given project are determined largely by her preferences. However, there are several popular *programming patterns*, or general philosophies, you can choose from when deciding how to structure an application.

A couple of the more popular patterns are the Multitier Architecture pattern and the Model-View-Controller (MVC) pattern—you can learn more about the MVC pattern at http://en.wikipedia.org/wiki/Model-View-Controller. The simple blog application relies on the Multitier Architecture pattern—you can more about the basics of this pattern in a great article on Wikipedia at http://en.wikipedia.org/wiki/Multitier_architecture.

Mapping Your Functions to Output Saved Entries

Planning the necessary steps of your script can help you identify the different types of logic involved, enabling you to group different steps into their respective functional categories.

Your script needs to allow users to see a list of entry titles if no entry is selected; it also needs to let users see a full entry if an entry ID is supplied. To accomplish this, your script needs to accomplish several tasks:

- Connect to the database

- Retrieve all entry titles and IDs if no entry ID was supplied

- Retrieve an entry title and entry if an ID was supplied

- Sanitize the data to prepare it for display

- Present a list of linked entry titles if no entry ID was supplied

- Present the entry title and entry if an ID was supplied

If you look at what each step is doing, you can assign each step to a *database, business,* or *presentation* layer. For example, a simple breakdown of tasks might look like this:

Database layer

- Connect to the database

- Retrieve all entry titles and IDs if no entry ID was supplied

- Retrieve an entry title and entry if an ID was supplied

Business layer

- Sanitize the data to prepare it for display

Presentation layer

- Present a list of linked entry titles if no entry ID was supplied

- Present the entry title and entry if an ID was supplied

A good way to approach this problem is to separate your tasks into a database function called retrieveEntries(), a business function called sanitizeData(), and the presentation logic, which you will store in index.php.

You can reinforce these logical separations by defining your database and business functions in a separate file, which you'll call functions.inc.php and create in the inc folder. This makes your functions accessible to other pages in your application, should that become necessary in the future.

Writing the Database Functions

Begin by creating the file that will contain your functions. In the inc folder, create a new file called functions.inc.php (full path: /xampp/htdocs/simple_blog/inc/functions.inc.php).

In your new file, define tour database function, retrieveEntries(). This function accepts two parameters: your database connection and an optional parameter for the entry ID. Your defined function should look like this:

```php
<?php

function retrieveEntries($db, $id=NULL)
{
    // Get entries from database
}

?>
```

You declare the default value for $id to be NULL; doing this means you can omit it without causing an error. Before you design your database query, you must determine whether an entry ID was passed; if so, you need to retrieve different information. The default value is NULL, so you simply need to check whether $id is NULL. Do this by adding the code in bold to retrieveEntries():

```php
<?php

function retrieveEntries($db, $id=NULL)
{
    /*
     * If an entry ID was supplied, load the associated entry
     */
    if(isset($id))
    {
        // Load specified entry
    }

    /*
     * If no entry ID was supplied, load all entry titles
     */
    else
    {
        // Load all entry titles
    }

    // Return loaded data
}

?>
```

Your next step is to write a script that executes if no entry ID is supplied. Your database query needs to retrieve two pieces of information from the entries table: the id and title fields. You need to store this information so it can be returned from the retrieve_entries() function and used by your business and presentation layers. A function can only return one variable, so you need to store the entry information in an array.

The query to retrieve the necessary information looks like this:

```
SELECT id, title
FROM entries
ORDER BY created DESC
```

There aren't any user-supplied parameters in the query, so you don't need to prepare the statement. This means you can execute the query immediately and loop through the results, storing the id and title in a multidimensional array.

Add the lines in bold to functions.inc.php:

```php
<?php

function retrieveEntries($db, $id=NULL)
{
    /*
     * If an entry ID was supplied, load the associated entry
     */
    if(isset($id))
    {
        // Load specified entry
    }

    /*
     * If no entry ID was supplied, load all entry titles
     */
    else
    {
        $sql = "SELECT id, title
                FROM entries
                ORDER BY created DESC";
        // Loop through returned results and store as an array
        foreach($db->query($sql) as $row) {
            $e[] = array(
                'id' => $row['id'],
                'title' => $row['title']
            );
        }

        // Set the fulldisp flag for multiple entries
        $fulldisp = 0;
    }

    // Return loaded data
}

?>
```

If no entry ID is supplied, your script now loads all entry titles and IDs into an array called $e; your script also sets a flag called $fulldisp to 0, which tells your presentation layer that the supplied information is *not* for full display.

As a safeguard, you should set some default values in the event that no entries come back from the entries table. To do this, you check whether the $e variable is an array. If it isn't, you know that no entries were returned, and you can create a default entry in $e and set the $fulldisp flag to 1, which signifies that your default entry should be displayed as a full entry.

Again, add the code highlighted in bold code to functions.inc.php:

```php
<?php

function retrieveEntries($db, $id=NULL)
{
    /*
     * If an entry ID was supplied, load the associated entry
     */
    if(isset($id))
    {
        // Load specified entry
    }

    /*
     * If no entry ID was supplied, load all entry titles
     */
    else
    {
        $sql = "SELECT id, title
                FROM entries
                ORDER BY created DESC";

        // Loop through returned results and store as an array
        foreach($db->query($sql) as $row) {
            $e[] = array(
                'id' => $row['id'],
                'title' => $row['title']
            );
        }

        // Set the fulldisp flag for multiple entries
        $fulldisp = 0;

        /*
         * If no entries were returned, display a default
         * message and set the fulldisp flag to display a
         * single entry
         */
```

```
        if(!is_array($e))
        {
            $fulldisp = 1;
            $e = array(
                'title' => 'No Entries Yet',
                'entry' => '<a href="/admin.php">Post an entry!</a>'
            );
        }
    }


    // Return loaded data
}

?>
```

You can now run your function safely without an error, so long as no entry ID is supplied. Next, you need to modify the script so it retrieves an entry if an ID is supplied.

This code needs to use the supplied ID in a query to retrieve the associated entry title and entry fields. As before, you store the returned data in an array called $e.

Add the code in bold to functions.inc.php:

```
<?php

function retrieveEntries($db, $id=NULL)
{
    /*
     * If an entry ID was supplied, load the associated entry
     */
    if(isset($id))
    {
        $sql = "SELECT title, entry
                FROM entries
                WHERE id=?
                LIMIT 1";
        $stmt = $db->prepare($sql);
        $stmt->execute(array($_GET['id']));

        // Save the returned entry array
        $e = $stmt->fetch();

        // Set the fulldisp flag for a single entry
        $fulldisp = 1;
    }
```

```
    /*
     * If no entry ID was supplied, load all entry titles
     */
    else
    {
        $sql = "SELECT id, title
                FROM entries
                ORDER BY created DESC";

        // Loop through returned results and store as an array
        foreach($db->query($sql) as $row) {
            $e[] = array(
                'id' => $row['id'],
                'title' => $row['title']
            );
        }

        // Set the fulldisp flag for multiple entries
        $fulldisp = 0;

        /*
         * If no entries were returned, display a default
         * message and set the fulldisp flag to display a
         * single entry
         */
        if(!is_array($e))
        {
            $fulldisp = 1;
            $e = array(
                'title' => 'No Entries Yet',
                'entry' => '<a href="/admin.php">Post an entry!</a>'
            );
        }
    }

    // Return loaded data
}

?>
```

At this point, your function has two variables: $e and $fulldisp. Both variables must be returned from the function for further processing; however, a function can return only one value, so you need to somehow combine these variables into a single variable.

You do this using a function called array_push(), which adds a value to the end of an array. Using this function, you can add the value of $fulldisp to the end of $e and return $e.

You can accomplish this by adding the code in bold to functions.inc.php:

```php
<?php

function retrieveEntries($db, $id=NULL)
{
    /*
     * If an entry ID was supplied, load the associated entry
     */
    if(isset($id))
    {
        $sql = "SELECT title, entry
                FROM entries
                WHERE id=?
                LIMIT 1";
        $stmt = $db->prepare($sql);
        $stmt->execute(array($_GET['id']));

        // Save the returned entry array
        $e = $stmt->fetch();

        // Set the fulldisp flag for a single entry
        $fulldisp = 1;
    }

    /*
     * If no entry ID was supplied, load all entry titles
     */
    else
    {
        $sql = "SELECT id, title
                FROM entries
                ORDER BY created DESC";

        // Loop through returned results and store as an array
        foreach($db->query($sql) as $row) {
            $e[] = array(
                'id' => $row['id'],
                'title' => $row['title']
            );
        }

        // Set the fulldisp flag for multiple entries
        $fulldisp = 0;
```

```
        /*
         * If no entries were returned, display a default
         * message and set the fulldisp flag to display a
         * single entry
         */
        if(!is_array($e))
        {
            $fulldisp = 1;
            $e = array(
                'title' => 'No Entries Yet',
                'entry' => '<a href="/admin.php">Post an entry!</a>'
            );
        }
    }

    // Add the $fulldisp flag to the end of the array
    array_push($e, $fulldisp);

    return $e;
}

?>
```

Writing the Business Function

At this point in your application, the business layer is pretty simple. All you need to do at this point is escape your output to avoid potential issues. You can accomplish this by writing a function called sanitizeData(), which you declare right below retrieveEntries() in functions.inc.php.

This function accepts one parameter, $data, and performs basic sanitization using the strip_tags() function. Sanitizing the function removes all HTML from a string unless a tag is specifically *whitelisted*, or placed in a collection of allowed tags, in strip_tags() second parameter.

The data you pass to sanitizeData() is potentially a mixture of both array and string data, so you need to check whether $data is an array before you process any data—doing this can help you avoid any parsing errors.

If $data isn't an array, you use strip_tags() to eliminate all HTML tags except the <a> tag; this enables your entries to contain links.

If $data *is* an array, you use the array_map() function to call sanitizeData() *recursively* on each element in the array.

Recursive Functions

In some cases, it becomes necessary to call a function from within itself. This technique is known as a recursive function call, and it has a number of useful applications. In this instance, you use recursion to ensure that every element in an array is sanitized, no matter how deep your array goes. In other words, the first element contains an array where its first element is another array, and so on. Recursion allows your function to be called repeatedly until you reach the bottom of the array.

Sanitizing the Data

The next step is to declare sanitizeData() and write the code to perform the recursive technique just described. Add this code to functions.inc.php, just below retrieveEntries():

```php
function sanitizeData($data)
{
    // If $data is not an array, run strip_tags()
    if(!is_array($data))
    {
        // Remove all tags except <a> tags
        return strip_tags($data, "<a>");
    }

    // If $data is an array, process each element
    else
    {
        // Call sanitizeData recursively for each array element
        return array_map('sanitizeData', $data);
    }
}
```

Writing the Presentation Code

Your last step in this phase of creating the blog is to use the information retrieved and formatted by your database and business layers to generate HTML markup and display the entries.

You will write this code in index.php inline with the HTML markup. The reason for this approach: This code is strictly for inserting your processed data into HTML markup.

Begin by including both db.inc.php and functions.inc.php in index.php. At the very top of index.php, add the following code:

```php
<?php

    /*
     * Include the necessary files
     */
    include_once 'inc/functions.inc.php';
    include_once 'inc/db.inc.php';

?>
```

Next, you need to open a connection to the database. You also need to check whether an entry ID was passed in the URL.

■**Note** Passing entry IDs in the URL (*i.e.*, `http://localhost/simple_blog/?id=1` is a popular and straightforward way of using one page to display different entries. You accomplish this in PHP using the `$_GET` superglobal.

Now add the bold lines to `index.php`:

```php
<?php

    /*
     * Include the necessary files
     */
    include_once 'inc/functions.inc.php';
    include_once 'inc/db.inc.php';

    // Open a database connection
    $db = new PDO(DB_INFO, DB_USER, DB_PASS);

    // Determine if an entry ID was passed in the URL
    $id = (isset($_GET['id'])) ? (int) $_GET['id'] : NULL;

?>
```

So far, you've determined whether an ID is set using the ternary operator, which allows you to compress an `if` statement into one line. Translated into plain English, the previous code snippet would read like this: "if `$_GET['id']` is set to some value, save its value as an integer in `$id`, or else set the value of `$id` to NULL."

Next, you need to load the entries from the database. Do this by calling your `retrieveEntries()` function and passing it your database connection (`$db`) and the ID you collected (`$id`) as parameters. Now add the lines in bold to `index.php`:

```php
<?php

    /*
     * Include the necessary files
     */
    include_once 'inc/functions.inc.php';
    include_once 'inc/db.inc.php';

    // Open a database connection
    $db = new PDO(DB_INFO, DB_USER, DB_PASS);
```

```
// Determine if an entry ID was passed in the URL
$id = (isset($_GET['id'])) ? (int) $_GET['id'] : NULL;

// Load the entries
$e = retrieveEntries($db, $id);

?>
```

The appropriate entries for the page are stored in the $e array and are ready to be displayed. You know that the last element of the array contains a flag telling you whether a full entry is stored, so your next step is to pop the last element off the array and store it in a variable ($fulldisp) that you'll use in just a moment.

Also, you need to sanitize the entry data, which we do by calling sanitizeData() and passing $e as the parameter. Next, add the lines in bold to index.php:

```
<?php

    /*
     * Include the necessary files
     */
    include_once 'inc/functions.inc.php';
    include_once 'inc/db.inc.php';

    // Open a database connection
    $db = new PDO(DB_INFO, DB_USER, DB_PASS);

    // Determine if an entry ID was passed in the URL
    $id = (isset($_GET['id'])) ? (int) $_GET['id'] : NULL;

    // Load the entries
    $e = retrieveEntries($db, $id);

    // Get the fulldisp flag and remove it from the array
    $fulldisp = array_pop($e);

    // Sanitize the entry data
    $e = sanitizeData($e);

?>
```

At this point, you have a flag to let you know whether you're displaying a full entry or a list of entry titles ($fulldisp), as well as an array of information to insert into HTML markup ($e).

To create the output, you need to determine whether the flag is set to 1, which would signify a full entry. If so, you insert the entry title into an <h2> tag and place the entry in a <p> tag.

In index.php, in the middle of the page below `<div id="entries">`, add the following lines of bold code:

```
    <div id="entries">

<?php

// If the full display flag is set, show the entry
if($fulldisp==1)
{

?>

        <h2> <?php echo $e['title'] ?> </h2>
        <p> <?php echo $e['entry'] ?> </p>
        <p class="backlink">
            <a href="./">Back to Latest Entries</a>
        </p>

<?php

} // End the if statement

?>

        <p class="backlink">
            <a href="/admin.php">Post a New Entry</a>
        </p>

    </div>
```

Navigating to the http://localhost/simple_blog/?id=1 address enables you to see the first entry (see Figure 5-7).

Simple Blog Application

First Entry

This is some text.

Back to Latest Entries

Post a New Entry

Figure 5-7. The first entry loaded using a variable passed in the URL

Next, you need to determine how you should display your list of entry titles. Ideally, you want to show the title as a link that takes the user to view the full entry.

This list of links is displayed if the $fulldisp flag is set to 0, so add an else to the conditional statement that checks whether $fulldisp is set to 1. Inside the else statement, you need to create a loop to process each paired ID and title together.

Just after the if statement, add the bold lines of code to index.php:

```php
<?php

} // End the if statement

// If the full display flag is 0, format linked entry titles
else
{
    // Loop through each entry
    foreach($e as $entry) {

?>

        <p>
            <a href="?id=<?php echo $entry['id'] ?>">
                <?php echo $entry['title'] ?>

            </a>
        </p>
```

```php
<?php

    } // End the foreach loop
} // End the else

?>

        <p class="backlink">
            <a href="/admin.php">Post a New Entry</a>
        </p>

    </div>
```

Now, navigate to `http://localhost/simple_blog/`, and you should see the title of each entry listed as a link(see Figure 5-8). Clicking any of the links takes you to the associated entry.

Figure 5-8. *The title of each entry is listed as a link*

Fix the Redirect

Now that index.php exists, you want to be taken to your new entries after they are submitted. To do this, you need to change the address of the header() calls to take the user to index.php. Change the code in bold in update.inc.php to make this happen:

```php
<?php

if($_SERVER['REQUEST_METHOD']=='POST'
    && $_POST['submit']=='Save Entry')
{
    // Include database credentials and connect to the database
    include_once 'db.inc.php';
    $db = new PDO(DB_INFO, DB_USER, DB_PASS);

    // Save the entry into the database
    $sql = "INSERT INTO entries (title, entry) VALUES (?, ?)";
    $stmt = $db->prepare($sql);
    $stmt->execute(array($_POST['title'], $_POST['entry']));
    $stmt->closeCursor();

    // Get the ID of the entry we just saved
    $id_obj = $db->query("SELECT LAST_INSERT_ID()");
    $id = $id_obj->fetch();
    $id_obj->closeCursor();

    // Send the user to the new entry
    header('Location: ../?id='.$id[0]);
    exit;
}

// If both conditions aren't met, sends the user back to the main page
else
{
    header('Location: ../');
    exit;
}

?>
```

Summary

You have now created a blog in the basic sense! Basic techniques you learned in this chapter included:

- How to use a web form to create and save entries in the database

- How to retrieve and display entries based on variables passed in the URL

As you continue on, you'll add several cool features to the blog, including a formatted date, authoring information, and images. In the next chapter, you'll learn how to make your blog support multiple pages, which in turn will enable you to build an "About the Author" page.

■ ■ ■

CHAPTER 6

Adding Support for Multiple Pages

So far you've created an extremely basic blog. But what good is a blog if a user can't find out more about its author?

In this chapter, you'll learn how to modify your application to support multiple pages, so you can add an "About the Author" page. To do this requires that you learn how to accomplish each of the following steps:

- Add a page column to the entries table

- Modify functions to use a page as part of the WHERE clause in your MySQL query

- Add a hidden input to the form on admin.php to store the page

- Modify update.inc.php to save page associations in the database

- Use an .htaccess file to create friendly URLs

- Add a menu

- Modify display options for the "About the Author" and "Blog" pages

By the end of this chapter, your blog will have two pages: one will support multiple entries, while the other will support only a single entry.

Add a page Column to the entries Table

Your first task is learning to identify what entries belong on what page. Essentially, you need to add a page identifier. This could be a number or a string. Your application is pretty simple, so you can just use the name of the page as your identifier.

To add this to your entries, you need to get back into your database controls, located at http://localhost/phpmyadmin. Open the simple_blog database, then the entries table. You need to add a column called page to the entries table, which will hold the name of the page to which each entry belongs.

This column cannot be blank, or the entries will get lost. To avoid this, you can set the column to NOT NULL and provide a default value. Most entries will end up on the blog page, so set the default to "blog." Finally, for organizational purposes, you want to put the column right after the id column; you can accomplish this in your query by using AFTER id.

Additionally, you can speed up your queries by adding an index to the page column. This is as simple as appending ADD INDEX (page) to the end of the query, separated by a comma. The full query looks like this:

```
ALTER TABLE entries
ADD page VARCHAR(75) NOT NULL DEFAULT 'blog'
AFTER id,
ADD INDEX (page)
```

Now execute the preceding query in the SQL tab of `http://localhost/phpmyadmin`. When the query finishes, click the Browse tab to verify that the page column has been created and that all the pages have been identified as blogs.

Modify Your Functions to Accept Page Parameters

Now that your entries have a page associated with them, you can start using the page as a *filter* to retrieve only the data that matches your current page. This is really similar to the way you used the id column to filter your query to only return one entry. By using the page, you filter the query to only return entries for one page.

Accepting Page Information in the URL

First—and this is very important—you need to somehow pass a page variable to your script. You do this in the same way that you previously passed an entry ID to the script, using the URL and the `$_GET` superglobal.

For example, you navigate to the following address to look at the blog page:

```
http://localhost/simple_blog/?page=blog
```

Navigating to an entry within the blog requires that you use a URL similar to the following:

```
http://localhost/simple_blog/?page=blog&id=2
```

To use the preceding URL format, you need to modify `index.php` to use the page variable passed in the URL, then modify `functions.inc.php` to accept the page variable and use it in your database query.

Begin by opening `index.php` (full path: `/xampp/htdocs/simple_blog/index.php`) and adding the code in bold to the top of the script:

```php
<?php
    /*
     * Include the necessary files
     */
    include_once 'inc/functions.inc.php';
    include_once 'inc/db.inc.php';

    // Open a database connection
    $db = new PDO(DB_INFO, DB_USER, DB_PASS);
```

```
    /*
     * Figure out what page is being requested (default is blog)
     * Perform basic sanitization on the variable as well
     */
    if(isset($_GET['page']))
    {
        $page = htmlentities(strip_tags($_GET['page']));
    }
    else
    {
        $page = 'blog';
    }

    // Determine if an entry ID was passed in the URL
    $id = (isset($_GET['id'])) ? (int) $_GET['id'] : NULL;

    // Load the entries
    $e = retrieveEntries($db, $page, $id);

    // Get the fulldisp flag and remove it from the array
    $fulldisp = array_pop($e);

    // Sanitize the entry data
    $e = sanitizeData($e);
?>
```

Here you add a line that collects the page variable from the $_GET superglobal array, then assigns its value (or a default value, which you've set to "blog") to a variable called $page.

Next, you add the $page variable as an argument in your call to retrieveEntries($db, **$page,** $id); so that you can use the information in retrieving entry data.

For now, you're finished in index.php. Next, you need to modify your retrieveEntries() function.

Using the Page Information to Filter Entries

The first thing you need to do is to alter retrieveEntries() to accept the $page parameter you've just added. Open functions.inc.php and alter the function definition to read as follows:

```
function retrieveEntries($db, $page, $url=NULL)
{
```

The page is being sent to your entry retrieval function, so you can use the information to filter your query and return only results relevant to the page being viewed. You accomplish this using a WHERE clause.

Originally, your query for retrieving entries when no entry ID was supplied looked like this:

```
SELECT id, title, entry
FROM entries
ORDER BY created DESC
```

Adding the WHERE clause means you can no longer simply execute the query because you're now relying on user-supplied data, which is potentially dangerous. To keep your script secure, you need to use a prepared statement. Your query uses a placeholder for the page variable and looks something like this:

```
SELECT id, page, title, entry
FROM entries
WHERE page=?
ORDER BY created DESC
```

Now you can retrieve only the entries that correspond to the page being viewed. The next step is to update your query in functions.inc.php (full path: /xampp/htdocs/simple_blog/inc/functions.inc.php). This snippet starts at line 25 in the file; add the changes highlighted in bold:

```
/*
 * If no entry ID was supplied, load all entry titles for the page
 */
else
{
    $sql = "SELECT id, page, title, entry
            FROM entries
            WHERE page=?
            ORDER BY created DESC";
    $stmt = $db->prepare($sql);
    $stmt->execute(array($page));

    $e = NULL; // Declare the variable to avoid errors
```

In this snippet, you create a prepared statement out of the query you wrote previously, then execute the statement using the $page variable you passed to retrieveEntries() from index.php.

This code also adds a line declaring the $e variable as NULL. This part serves as a precautionary measure against empty result sets, which would otherwise result in an error notice if no entries exist for the specified page.

■**Tip** It's a good habit to get into to always declare a variable as NULL if there's the potential for a query or loop to come back empty. This means any variable defined in a conditional statement or used to store the result of a database query should contain a NULL value before the query or loop is executed.

You changed the method you use to execute the query, so now you need to modify the way you store the result set. Add the following code in bold where indicated in `functions.inc.php`, immediately beneath the script you just altered, starting at `line 39`:

```
// Loop through returned results and store as an array
while($row = $stmt->fetch()) {
    $e[] = $row;
}
```

Once this code is in place, each result array is stored as an array element in $e; this means that your script will now work. Save `functions.inc.php` and navigate to `http://localhost/simple_blog/?page=blog` in a browser. At this point, you should see the previews of the blog entry (see Figure 6-1).

Figure 6-1. *The blog previews page loaded with URL variables*

The blog is the default page, so previews will also load without the page variable. To see the power of what you've just built, navigate to a page that doesn't exist yet: your "About the Author" page. Navigate to `http://localhost/simple_blog/?page=about` in a browser, and you should see your default "No Entries" message (see Figure 6-2).

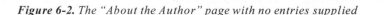

Figure 6-2. *The "About the Author" page with no entries supplied*

Here you face with a slight problem: you have a "Back to Latest Entries" link on your "About the Author" page. This could prove misleading because it might give your users the impression that there are more entries about the author.

Additionally, the "Post a New Entry" link appears on this page. You want only one entry to appear on the "About the Author" page, so you don't want this link to appear here.

To correct this, you must modify index.php with a conditional statement that displays the "Back to Latest Entries" and "Post a New Entry" links only on the "Blog" page. Accomplish this by opening index.php and adding the code in bold to the body of the document:

```
<!DOCTYPE html
    PUBLIC "-//W3C//DTD XHTML 1.0 Strict//EN"
    "http://www.w3.org/TR/xhtml1/DTD/xhtml1-strict.dtd">

<html xmlns="http://www.w3.org/1999/xhtml" xml:lang="en" lang="en">

<head>
    <meta http-equiv="Content-Type"
        content="text/html;charset=utf-8" />
    <link rel="stylesheet" href="css/default.css" type="text/css" />
    <title> Simple Blog </title>
</head>
```

```php
<body>

    <h1> Simple Blog Application </h1>

    <div id="entries">

<?php

// If the full display flag is set, show the entry
if($fulldisp==1)
{

?>

        <h2> <?php echo $e['title'] ?> </h2>
        <p> <?php echo $e['entry'] ?> </p>
        <?php if($page=='blog'): ?>
        <p class="backlink">
            <a href="./">Back to Latest Entries</a>
        </p>
        <?php endif; ?>

<?php

} // End the if statement

// If the full display flag is 0, format linked entry titles
else
{
    // Loop through each entry
    foreach($e as $entry) {

?>

        <p>
            <a href="?id=<?php echo $entry['id'] ?>">
                <?php echo $entry['title'] ?>

            </a>
        </p>

<?php

    } // End the foreach loop
} // End the else

?>
```

```
    <p class="backlink">
    <?php if($page=='blog'): ?>
        <a href="/simple_blog/admin/<?php echo $page ?>">
            Post a New Entry
        </a>
    <?php endif; ?>
    </p>

</div>

</body>

</html>
```

Now you don't see the potentially misleading links when you load
http://localhost/simple_blog/?page=about (see Figure 6-3).

Figure 6-3. *The "About the Author" page without potentially misleading links*

The next step is to create an entry for the "About the Author" page. However, you need to
update your admin.php script before you can create this entry.

Modifying admin.php to Save Page Associations

Saving the page an entry is associated with is as easy as adding another input to your form. However, there are a couple reasons you don't want to require the user to fill out the page an entry belongs on. First, it's inconvenient for the user; second, it increases the risk of typos or confusion.

Fortunately, HTML forms allow you to insert *hidden inputs*, which contain a value that is passed in the $_POST superglobal, but isn't displayed to the user. In your admin.php script (full path: /xampp/htdocs/simple_blog/admin.php), add a hidden input to your form by inserting the lines in bold:

```php
<?php
if(isset($_GET['page']))
{
    $page = htmlentities(strip_tags($_GET['page']));
}
else
{
    $page = 'blog';
}
?>
<!DOCTYPE html
    PUBLIC "-//W3C//DTD XHTML 1.0 Strict//EN"
    "http://www.w3.org/TR/xhtml1/DTD/xhtml1-strict.dtd">

<html xmlns="http://www.w3.org/1999/xhtml" xml:lang="en" lang="en">

<head>
    <meta http-equiv="Content-Type"
        content="text/html;charset=utf-8" />
    <link rel="stylesheet"
        href="/simple_blog/css/default.css" type="text/css" />
    <title> Simple Blog </title>
</head>

<body>
    <h1> Simple Blog Application </h1>

    <form method="post" action="/simple_blog/inc/update.inc.php">
        <fieldset>
            <legend>New Entry Submission</legend>
            <label>Title
                <input type="text" name="title" maxlength="150" />
            </label>
            <label>Entry
                <textarea name="entry" cols="45" rows="10"></textarea>
            </label>
```

```
        <input type="hidden" name="page"
            value="<?php echo $page ?>" />
        <input type="submit" name="submit" value="Save Entry" />
        <input type="submit" name="submit" value="Cancel" />
    </fieldset>
  </form>
</body>

</html>
```

In the first line of this script, you retrieve the page variable, which will be passed in the URL. To make sure a variable was passed, you use the *ternary operator* (a shortcut syntax for the if else statement) to check whether $_GET['page'] is set. If so, you perform basic sanitization by removing any HTML tags from the string, then encoding any special characters that could cause problems in your script. If not, you provide a default page, blog, to avoid any unexpected behavior.

Then, in the form itself, you insert a hidden input with the name of "page" and a value that contains the sanitized value from the URL.

This means that creating an entry with an associated page requires that you access admin.php using a path that includes a page variable:

http://localhost/simple_blog/admin.php?page=about

This means that you need to make some adjustments to index.php to ensure that a page variable is passed when a user clicks the link to create a new entry.

In index.php, starting at line 100, modify the link to create a new entry as follows:

```
<p class="backlink">
    <a href="/simple_blog/admin.php?page=<?php echo $page ?>">
        Post a New Entry
    </a>
</p>
```

This entry takes the $page variable you stored at the beginning of the script and uses it to make a link for posting a new entry pass to the page. You can test this by navigating to http://localhost/simple_blog/?page=about; this URL lets you use your browser to look at the page value stored in the "Post a New Entry" link (see Figure 6-4).

■**Tip** You can view the source code in a PHP project by select View from the browser menu, then (depending on the browser being used) Source, Page Source, or View Source.

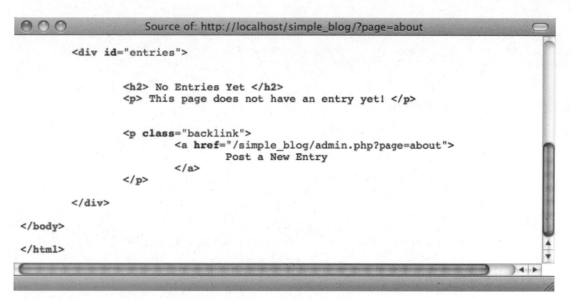

```
<div id="entries">


        <h2> No Entries Yet </h2>
        <p> This page does not have an entry yet! </p>


        <p class="backlink">
                <a href="/simple_blog/admin.php?page=about">
                        Post a New Entry
                </a>
        </p>

</div>

</body>

</html>
```

Figure 6-4. *The source code of* `http://localhost/simple_blog/?page=about`

Next, you need to make sure that you're storing the page in the hidden input properly. Click the "Post a New Entry" link on `http://localhost/simple_blog/?page=about`, which should direct you to `http://localhost/simple_blog/admin.php?page=about`. There, you can see your form as usual, but looking at the source code should reveal that the hidden input now contains the "about" value that was passed in the URL (see Figure 6-5).

```
        <title> Simple Blog </title>
</head>

<body>

        <h1> Simple Blog Application </h1>

        <form method="post" action="/simple_blog/inc/update.inc.php">
                <fieldset>
                        <legend>New Entry Submission</legend>
                        <label>Title <input type="text" name="title" maxlength="15
                        <label>Entry <textarea name="entry" cols="45" rows="10"></
                        <input type="hidden" name="page" value="about" />
                        <input type="submit" name="submit" value="Save Entry" />
                        <input type="submit" name="submit" value="Cancel" />
                </fieldset>
        </form>
</body>

</html>
```

Figure 6-5. *The source of* `http://localhost/simple_blog/admin.php?page=about`

167

Now you know that the page will be passed to the form. This means that you have access, via the $_POST superglobal, to whatever page the entry is associated with after the new entry is submitted.

However, bear in mind that the page association won't be saved until you make some adjustments to update.inc.php to handle this new information.

Saving Page Associations

Saving the page association in your database when new entries are created requires that you modify your query in update.inc.php, as well as a couple more checks to ensure that errors don't occur.

To save the entry information, you need to:

1. Make sure the page was specified before processing

2. Add the page to the query to be saved

3. Sanitize the data

4. Use the sanitized page information to send the user back to the created entry

In update.inc.php, modify the script to include the lines highlighted in bold:

```php
<?php

if($_SERVER['REQUEST_METHOD']=='POST'
    && $_POST['submit']=='Save Entry'
    && !empty($_POST['page'])
    && !empty($_POST['title'])
    && !empty($_POST['entry']))
{

    // Include database credentials and connect to the database
    include_once 'db.inc.php';
    $db = new PDO(DB_INFO, DB_USER, DB_PASS);

    // Save the entry into the database
    $sql = "INSERT INTO entries (page, title, entry)
            VALUES (?, ?, ?)";
    $stmt = $db->prepare($sql);
    $stmt->execute(
        array($_POST['page'],$_POST['title'],$_POST['entry'])
    );
    $stmt->closeCursor();

    // Sanitize the page information for use in the success URL
    $page = htmlentities(strip_tags($_POST['page']));
```

```
    // Get the ID of the entry you just saved
    $id_obj = $db->query("SELECT LAST_INSERT_ID()");
    $id = $id_obj->fetch();
    $id_obj->closeCursor();

    // Send the user to the new entry
    header('Location: /simple_blog/?page='.$page.'&id='.$id[0]);
    exit;
}

else
{
    header('Location: ../');
    exit;
}

?>
```

Making these changes, effectively ensures that a page association is passed to the update script; you can then insert the association using your prepared statement. Afterward, you sanitize the page information and store it in the $page variable. Finally, you send the user to the new entry by passing the page in the URL, along with the ID of the new entry.

Save update.inc.php and navigate to http://localhost/simple_blog/?page=about, then click the "Post a New Entry" link. Now create an "About the Author" entry and click "Save Entry"; this should take you to the entry saved with the "about" page association (see Figure 6-6).

Figure 6-6. The "About the Author" page with an entry created

Using .htaccess to Create Friendly URLs

When building applications for the web, it's important to look at some of the marketing tricks involved in getting a site noticed. There are full courses dedicated to web site marketing, but every developer should know a little bit about how sites get noticed on the web.

One of the most widely discussed areas of web site marketing is *search engine optimization*, or SEO. This is the practice of maximizing the value of a web site in the eyes of search engines like Google and Yahoo! by placing key words in important areas of the site.

One of the most important areas of any site is the URL itself. For instance, a web site selling t-shirts with rubber ducks on them would want locate its products page at an URL something like this:

```
http://rubberducktees.com/products/t-shirts
```

This is far more desirable than a URL with a bunch of confusing IDs, such as:

```
http://rubberducktees.com?page=4&category=5&product=67
```

Neither approach is wrong, but the former is far easier to read and to remember. It is also far more likely to make sense to the average user. Also, you should be aware that search engines are much more likely to *index*, or store as a search result, sites with key words in the URL.

■**Note** Some search engines won't index URLs beyond the first question mark they encounter, which means non-optimized URLs won't make it into search results at all.

Your URLs right now aren't exactly optimal because you're using variables such as ?page=blog&entry=2 to identify entries to the script. So a good next step is to figure out a way to allow your users to get to a blog using a much easier URL, such as:

```
http://localhost/simple_blog/blog/first-entry
```

Doing this requires that you use a pair of advanced coding techniques: *.htaccess* and *regular expressions.*

What .htaccess Does

One of the best parts about using Apache servers is the ability to use .htaccess files. These allow developers to control a number of things, including file-access permissions, how certain file types are handled. The files also serve as an especially useful tool for rewriting URLs.

You won't need to know too much about how .htaccess works for the examples described in this book. However, I teach you everything you need to know about rewriting a URL so it is much more user-friendly.

Using Regular Expressions

Regular expressions are, in essence, patterns that enable complex matching in strings. They are tricky, and they employ a syntax that can be very hard to understand; however, they are also one of the most powerful tools available to developers, so it behooves you to learn about them.

Once you get the basics of regular expressions (or *regex*), you can use them in your .htaccess files to match URL patterns and rewrite them so they are compatible with your scripts.

Creating Your .htaccess File

Begin by firing up Eclipse and creating a new file called .htaccess in the simple_blog project. You should place this file in the top level of the project (full path: /xampp/htdocs/simple_blog/.htaccess).

■**Note** .htaccess files start with a period, so your new file might not show up in your file list under the project in Eclipse. If you close .htaccess and need to open it, use File > Open... to access it again. Alternatively, you can set Eclipse to show resources starting with a period by selecting the upside-down triangle (third button from the right) in the "Project Explorer" panel and clicking "Customize View..." In the Filters tab, uncheck .* resources, and the .htaccess file should appear in your file list.

■**Caution** If you choose to view .* resources in project folders, be sure that you do *not* edit or delete the .project or .buildpath files. Doing so can cause Eclipse to lose its association with your projects, which means you'll have to recreate them before you can access any of your files for editing.

The file should bring up a blank file in the editor. In this file, you need to accomplish the following:

- Turn on URL rewriting
- Declare the base-level folder for rewriting
- Set up a rule to stop the rewrite if certain file types are accessed directly
- Set up a special rule for admin.php
- Set up a rule for page-only URLs
- Set up a rule for page and entry URLs

Step 1: Turn on URL Rewriting

The first line of your .htaccess file lets the server know that URL rewriting is allowed in this directory. To do this, add the following line to your currently blank .htaccess file:

```
RewriteEngine on
```

Step 2: Declare the Base-Level Folder for Rewriting

Next, you need to let the server know which folder to use as a base when rewriting. If you want the root folder to be the base folder, you could use a single forward slash (/) to set the root folder (the htdocs folder when using XAMPP) as the base folder. Your project is in the simple_blog folder in root, so you need to specify it as the base. To do so, add the following to line 2 in .htaccess:

RewriteBase /simple_blog/

Step 3: Set Up a Rule to Stop Rewriting for Certain File Types

You must be able to access some files by their real path, not a rewritten one, so you need to set up a rewrite rule that says certain file types, such as images and included scripts, will stop the rewrite engine from doing anything and exit the .htaccess file.

■**Tip** For a complete breakdown of URL rewriting, visit the mod_rewrite documentation on the Apache website at http://httpd.apache.org/docs/2.2/mod/mod_rewrite.html.

This is a slightly more complicated area of the file, and it's here you start using regex. Begin by creating the rule; I'll break down what it does and how it works afterward:

RewriteRule \.(gif|jpg|png|css|js|inc\.php)$ - [L]

In .htaccess files, rewrite rules follow this pattern:

RewriteRule pattern replacement [flags]

Adding a RewriteRule lets you signify to the server that the rest of the line contains commands for URL rewriting.

Patterns

The *pattern*, which is what you want to match, goes next. In your rule just described, the pattern section of the rule is \.(gif|jpg|png|css|js|inc\.php)$. In plain English, this means that any URL that calls a file ending with the extension .gif, .jpg, .png, .css, .js, or .inc.php will match your pattern.

The first part, a backslash followed by a period, signifies the "dot" that precedes the file extension (as in, "dot jpg"). Next, you have your file extensions wrapped in parentheses and separated with a vertical bar (|). The parentheses enclose a *group* of characters to match, and the vertical bar acts as an "or" command. Finally, the dollar sign means that the match must fall at the end of the URL, so a URL ending in image.jpg would trigger the command, but a URL ending in image.jpg?mischief would not.

■**Note** To learn more about regular expressions, check out http://regular-expressions.info.

Replacements

The *replacement* is a new format for the data matched in the rule's pattern. Each group can be accessed to create a different URL structure that scripts can use instead of the one navigated to by the user.

In the case of your rule, the replacement is a hyphen (-). This signifies that nothing is to be done. You'll near more about replacements momentarily, when I cover the next rule.

Flags

The *flags* for rewrite rules are a set of controls that allow users to determine what to do *after* a rule matches. In the preceding example, the flag for your rule is [L], which means that this is the last rule checked if this rule is matched. This means that no more rewriting will occur. Some of the other available rules include:

- nocase/NC *(no case)*: Makes the rule case-insensitive

- forbidden/F *(forbidden)*; Force a resource to return a 403 (FORBIDDEN) response

- skip/S=num *(skip the next rule)*: If current rule is matched, the next *num* rules are skipped

---

■**Note** There are many other flags that you can in .htaccess rewrite rules. For a full list, visit the RewriteRule Directive section of the mod_rewrite documentation on the Apache web site at http://httpd.apache.org/docs/2.2/mod/mod_rewrite.html#rewriterule.

Step 4: Set Up a Rule for Admin Page Access

Your admin page is a little different from the rest of your site because it relies on a different file (admin.php). This means your URL rewrites need to take this into account and behave accordingly.

You want your administrative page to be accessed with the following URL structure:

```
http://localhost/simple_blog/admin/blog
```

However, your scripts need the URL to be structured like this:

```
http://localhost/simple_blog/admin.php?page=blog
```

To do this, you need to catch any URL that begins with "admin/" and take the rest of the string and pass it as the page variable. In your .htaccess file, add the following rule:

```
RewriteRule ^admin/(\w+) admin.php?page=$1 [NC,L]
```

In this rewrite rule, you require that the URL path start with admin/ using the carat (^), then use the shorthand \w+ to store one or more word characters (a-z, 0-9, and _ [underscore]) as a *backreference*, which is functionally equivalent to a variable in PHP. When working with rewrite rules, you access backreferences using a dollar sign and the number corresponding to the group (*i.e.*, the first backreference is $1, the second is $2, and so on). You can create only nine backreferences for each rule.

The replacement URL is a link to admin.php, with the page variable set to the value of your backreference. So, if the URL path supplied to the rule is admin/blog, it is rewritten to admin.php?page=blog.

Finally, you set the flags to NC, which means the rule isn't case-sensitive (ADMIN/ is equivalent to admin/ for purposes of matching), and L, which means more rewriting will occur if this rule is matched.

You don't want the site to throw an error if the user accesses http://localhost/simple_blog/ admin, so you need to add an additional rule. This rule will go immediately above the previous rewrite rule, and handle administrative URLs that don't specify the page.

Add the following rule to .htaccess:

```
RewriteRule ^admin/?$ admin.php [NC,L]
```

This rule makes sure that the user has used either http://localhost/simple_blog/admin or http://localhost/simple_blog/admin/ to access the site. If this rule is matched, the user is directed to admin.php.

Step 5: Set Up a Rule for Page-Only URLs

You can access your publicly displayed pages in one of two ways: either page-only (*i.e.*, http:// localhost/simple_blog/blog/) or page-and-entry (*i.e.*, http://localhost/simple_blog/blog/ first-entry). Your next rewrite rule catches the page-only URLs and directs the user to the proper place.

In .htaccess, add the following rule:

```
RewriteRule ^(\w+)/?$ index.php?page=$1
```

This rule captures the beginning of the URL path, stopping at the first forward slash. The dollar sign after the forward slash means that you can't use any additional characters after the first forward slash, or the rule won't match. You can then use the captured characters as the page variable in the rewritten URL.

Also, note the use of a question mark following the slash. This makes the expression lazy, which means it doesn't need to match the last slash. This covers you if the user enters a URL without a trailing slash, like this one: http://localhost/simple_blog/blog. You don't need any flags for this rule, so you simply leave them out altogether.

Step 6: Set Up a Rule for Page-and-Entry URLs

Finally, you need a rule that passes the page and entry information to your script in a format it can understand. This is similar to the previous rule, except you're going to be using two backreferences, as well as a new concept known as *character classes*.

In .htaccess, add the following rule:

```
RewriteRule ^(\w+)/([\w-]+) index.php?page=$1&url=$2
```

The first part of the rule, ^(\w+)/, is the same as the last rule. It matches any word character that starts the URL path until the first forward slash.

The second part of the URL, ([\w-]+), creates a second backreference to a character class, which is a group of characters enclosed in square brackets that you can use for a valid match. You can match any word character in this character class, as well as the hyphen (-). The plus sign (+) means that one or more characters will be matched.

You add a hyphen in this case because you're going to use hyphens to replace spaces in your URLs (you can learn more about this in the next section, "Creating Friendly URLs Automatically").

The replacement URL generated passes the first backreference as the page variable, and it passes the second backreference as a variable called url, which you use in place of an entry ID from here on out.

Trying It Out

At this point, your blog should accept friendly URLs. You can test whether this is true by navigating to http://localhost/simple_blog/blog/ in a browser to see the results (see Figure 6-7).

Figure 6-7. *Previewing your blog entries with a friendly URL*

In the next section, you'll modify your application to use friendly entry URLs to access individual entries.

Creating Friendly URLs Automatically

Now that your site can rewrite friendly URLs for your site to process correctly, you need to modify your application to use the new format. You must implement the following steps to make your application run properly:

1. Add a url column to the entries table

2. Modify functions.inc.php to search by and return the url value

3. Modify index.php to use the url value

4. Write a function to create friendly URLs automatically

5. Modify update.inc.php to save the new URL

Step 1: Add a url Column to the entries Table

There are a few ways you can make your application use custom URLs. Perhaps the easiest method is to create a custom friendly URL and store it in the database, which is the approach you'll take in this project.

Begin by creating a new column in the entries table, which you call url. To do this, navigate to http://localhost/phpmyadmin, then select the simple_blog database, and, finally, the entries table. Click the SQL tab and enter the following command:

```
ALTER TABLE entries
ADD url VARCHAR(250)
AFTER entry
```

This creates a new column in the entries table that accepts 250 characters. This field stores your entry URLs.

You can populate this column for pre-existing entries quickly by hand. Click the Browse tab, then scroll to the bottom of the entry listings and click "Check All." To the right of the "Check All" option, click the pencil to edit all the entries at once.

The format you'll be using for entry URLs is to take the title of the entry, remove all special characters (such as apostrophes, punctuation, and so on), and replace spaces with hyphens. For example, "First Entry" would become "first-entry" after processing.

Enter a URL for each entry in the url field of each entry, then click the Go button to save.

Step 2: Modify functions.inc.php to Handle URLs

Next, open functions.inc.php in Eclipse. You need to change your queries to use the url column rather than the id column to look up entries, as well as making sure the URL is returned by your page-only query.

First, you modify the parameters of retrieveEntries() to accept the URL in place of the ID. Next, you check whether the URL was provided. If so, you retrieve the entry that matches the provided URL. If not, you retrieve entry information for all the entries that correspond to the provided page.

To accomplish this, you need to make the following modifications (shown in bold) to retrieveEntries():

```
function retrieveEntries($db, $page, $url=NULL)
{
    /*
     * If an entry URL was supplied, load the associated entry
     */
    if(isset($url))
    {
        $sql = "SELECT id, page, title, entry
                FROM entries
                WHERE url=?
                LIMIT 1";
        $stmt = $db->prepare($sql);
        $stmt->execute(array($url));
```

```php
    // Save the returned entry array
    $e = $stmt->fetch();

    // Set the fulldisp flag for a single entry
    $fulldisp = 1;
}


/*
 * If no entry URL provided, load all entry info for the page
 */
else
{
    $sql = "SELECT id, page, title, entry, url
            FROM entries
            WHERE page=?
            ORDER BY created DESC";
    $stmt = $db->prepare($sql);
    $stmt->execute(array($page));

    $e = NULL; // Declare the variable to avoid errors

    // Loop through returned results and store as an array
    while($row = $stmt->fetch()) {
        $e[] = $row;
        $fulldisp = 0;
    }

    /*
     * If no entries were returned, display a default
     * message and set the fulldisp flag to display a
     * single entry
     */
    if(!is_array($e))
    {
        $fulldisp = 1;
        $e = array(
            'title' => 'No Entries Yet',
            'entry' => 'This page does not have an entry yet!'
        );
    }
}
```

```
    // Add the $fulldisp flag to the end of the array
    array_push($e, $fulldisp);

    return $e;
}
```

Now your function can search by URL, as well as return the URL information for use in link creation.

Step 3: Modify index.php to Handle URLs

Next, you need to open index.php in Eclipse and make some changes. First, you need to swap out your check for an ID in the $_GET superglobal and check instead for a url variable. Then you need to pass the stored URL information to retrieveEntries() for processing.

In index.php, make the following modifications to the script at the top (shown in bold highlight):

```php
<?php

    /*
     * Include the necessary files
     */
    include_once 'inc/functions.inc.php';
    include_once 'inc/db.inc.php';

    // Open a database connection
    $db = new PDO(DB_INFO, DB_USER, DB_PASS);

    // Figure out what page is being requested (default is blog)
    if(isset($_GET['page']))
    {
        $page = htmlentities(strip_tags($_GET['page']));
    }
    else
    {
        $page = 'blog';
    }

    // Determine if an entry URL was passed
    $url = (isset($_GET['url'])) ? $_GET['url'] : NULL;

    // Load the entries
    $e = retrieveEntries($db, $page, $url);
```

```
    // Get the fulldisp flag and remove it from the array
    $fulldisp = array_pop($e);

    // Sanitize the entry data
    $e = sanitizeData($e);

?>
```

Your "About the Author" page is displayed as a full entry, so you need to an extra line to your full entry display to ensure that administrative links are built properly, even though the entry isn't accessed with a URL beyond this page. Add the code in bold to index.php in the code block starting on line 59:

```
<?php

// If the full display flag is set, show the entry
if($fulldisp==1)
{

    // Get the URL if one wasn't passed
    $url = (isset($url)) ? $url : $e['url'];

?>
```

You also need to change how entry previews are formatted, changing the links to reflect your new URL format. Finally, you need to switch your "Post a New Entry" link so it uses the new URL format.

Make the following code modifications in the bottom half of index.php, starting at line 78, as marked in bold:

```
// If the full display flag is 0, format linked entry titles
else
{
    // Loop through each entry
    foreach($e as $entry) {

?>

        <p>
            <a href="/simple_blog/<?php echo $entry['page'] ?>/<?php echo $entry['url'] ?>">
                <?php echo $entry['title'] ?>

            </a>
        </p>
```

```php
<?php

    } // End the foreach loop
} // End the else

?>

        <p class="backlink">
            <a href="/simple_blog/admin/<?php echo $page ?>">
                Post a New Entry
            </a>
        </p>

    </div>
```

Now navigate to http://localhost/simple_blog/blog/ in a browser to see your code in action. Click one of the entries for a full view and note that the URL is now easy to read (see Figure 6-8).

Figure 6-8. *A full entry loaded with a custom URL*

Step 4: Write a Function to Create Friendly URLs Automatically

You don't want to create a URL manually for every entry created, so you need to write a function that generates a URL following your format automatically. To do this, you need to use regular expressions again, but with the twist that this time you combine it with a PHP function called preg_replace():

mixed **preg_replace** (mixed *$pattern* , mixed *$replacement* ,
        mixed *$subject* [, int *$limit= -1* [, int *&&$count*]])

Essentially, preg_replace() works similarly to the rewrite rules you're already created. It accepts *patterns* to match ($pattern), *replacements* for those matches ($replacement), a string in which to search ($subject), and two optional parameters: the maximum number of replacements to be performed ($limit), which defaults to -1 (no limit), and the number of replacements made ($count).

One of the most convenient features of preg_replace() is its ability to accept arrays as both the $pattern and $replacement parameters, which allows you to perform multiple pattern matches and replacements with a single function call.

To create your URLs, you can accept the title of an entry as a string, which you run through preg_replace(). You want to match two patterns: first, you want to replace all spaces with a hyphen; second, you want to remove all non-word characters (excluding hyphens) by replacing them with an empty string.

You place your function, called makeUrl(), in functions.inc.php. Open the file in Eclipse and insert the following code at the bottom of the file:

```
function makeUrl($title)
{
    $patterns = array(
        '/\s+/',
        '/(?!-)\W+/'
    );
    $replacements = array('-', '');
    return preg_replace($patterns, $replacements, strtolower($title));
}
```

In this function, you begin by defining your array of patterns. The first pattern, /\s+/, matches any one or more whitespace characters, such as spaces and tabs. The special character shorthand, \s, denotes any whitespace, and the plus sign means "one or more," as explained previously.

The second pattern, /(?!-)\W+/, matches one or more non-word characters, excluding the hyphen. The first bit after the *delimiter* (see the note on using regex, which I'll introduce momentarily), (?!-), is a complicated bit of syntax called a *negative lookahead*. Essentially, it means, "if the following match can be made *without* using the character noted, consider it valid." The syntax for this is (?!*character*), where *character* is the character or characters that will render a match invalid.

The \W is shorthand for the *opposite* of word characters. This means punctuation, whitespace, and other special characters that aren't alphanumeric or the underscore character.

Next, you declare your replacement array. This follows the order of the patterns, which means that you replace the first element of the pattern array with the first element in the replacement array. Your first replacement is for whitespace characters, which you want to replace with a hyphen. You use the second replacement to get rid of other special characters, which you accomplish simply by supplying an empty string.

With your patterns and replacements stored and ready, you return the result of preg_replace() when passed your entry title (which you convert to lowercase using the function strtolower()). This return value is your custom URL.

■**Note** When using regex in PHP, or any Perl-compatible language, you need to enclose patterns in delimiters, which are forward slashes. This means that if your pattern is \w+, you must enclose it in forward slashes (/\w+/) to delimit it as a pattern.

Step 5. Modify update.inc.php to Save URLs in the Database

You now need a way to store the results of makeUrl() in the database. To do this, you need to modify your query in update.inc.php. Open this file in Eclipse and make the modifications shown in bold:

```php
<?php

// Include the functions so you can create a URL
include_once 'functions.inc.php';

if($_SERVER['REQUEST_METHOD']=='POST'
    && $_POST['submit']=='Save Entry'
    && !empty($_POST['page'])
    && !empty($_POST['title'])
    && !empty($_POST['entry']))
{
    // Create a URL to save in the database
    $url = makeUrl($_POST['title']);

    // Include database credentials and connect to the database
    include_once 'db.inc.php';
    $db = new PDO(DB_INFO, DB_USER, DB_PASS);

    // Save the entry into the database
    $sql = "INSERT INTO entries (page, title, entry, url)
            VALUES (?, ?, ?, ?)";
    $stmt = $db->prepare($sql);
    $stmt->execute(
        array($_POST['page'], $_POST['title'], $_POST['entry'], $url)
    );
    $stmt->closeCursor();

    // Sanitize the page information for use in the success URL
    $page = htmlentities(strip_tags($_POST['page']));
```

```
// Send the user to the new entry
    header('Location: /simple_blog/'.$page.'/'.$url);
    exit;
}

else
{
    header('Location: ../');
    exit;
}

?>
```

When a new entry is created now, functions.inc.php is loaded and makeUrl() is called on the new title. The result is stored in the url column of the entries table, which leaves you with a dynamically generated, custom URL for your new entry. You can then use this custom URL to direct the user to the new entry.

Navigate to http://localhost/simple_blog/admin/blog and create a new entry with the title ("Another Entry") and the text ("This is another entry."). Clicking the Save Entry button takes you to your new entry at the URL, http://localhost/simple_blog/blog/another-entry (see Figure 6-9).

Figure 6-9. *An entry with a dynamically created custom URL*

Adding a Menu

Your blog should include a menu item that enables your users to get between the "Blog" and "About the Author" pages. Accomplishing this is a simple matter of adding a snippet of HTML to index.php below the main heading.

Open index.php in Eclipse and insert the HTML code in bold into the body of the page as indicated, just below the <h1> tag:

```
<body>

    <h1> Simple Blog Application </h1>
    <ul id="menu">
        <li><a href="/simple_blog/blog/">Blog</a></li>
        <li><a href="/simple_blog/about/">About the Author</a></li>
    </ul>

    <div id="entries">
```

Next, navigate to http://localhost/simple_blog/ to see the menu (see Figure 6-10).

Figure 6-10. *Your blog application with a menu in place*

Creating Different Viewing Styles for the Pages

You're nearly finished with this stage of your blog's development. However, if you navigate to the "About the Author" page, you'll see that it shows an entry preview. This is undesirable because there should be only one entry on this page.

To fix this, you need to modify your retrieveEntries() function to force the "About the Author" entry to be a full-display entry, even without a URL being supplied.

Open functions.inc.php and modify retrieveEntries() by inserting the following code in bold into the while loop starting at line 38:

```
// Loop through returned results and store as an array
while($row = $stmt->fetch()) {
    if($page=='blog')
    {
        $e[] = $row;
        $fulldisp = 0;
    }
    else
    {
        $e = $row;
        $fulldisp = 1;
    }
}
```

You also need to remove the original line that defaults $fulldisp to 0. Remove this line from functions.inc.php:

```
// Set the fulldisp flag for multiple entries
$fulldisp = 0;
```

Now you can view the full "About the Author" entry by navigating to http://localhost/simple_blog/about/ in your browser (see Figure 6-11).

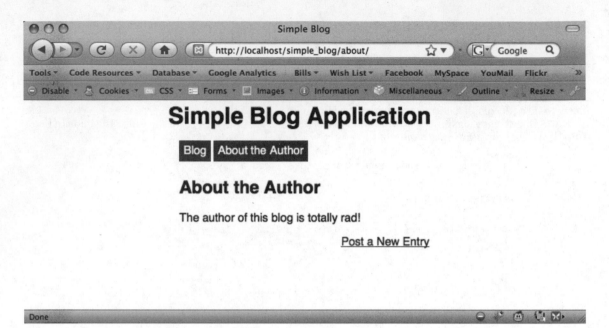

Figure 6-11. The full "About the Author" entry display

Summary

In this chapter, you've learned a ton of information. Some of it was pretty advanced, so congratulate yourself! You can now:

- Support multiple pages in your application

- Create custom URLs using regular expressions and `.htaccess`

- Differentiate between multi-entry and single-entry pages

In the next chapter, you'll learn how to update entries that have already been created, bringing you one step closer to having a fully customizable blogging application.

CHAPTER 7

■ ■ ■

Updating and Deleting Entries

In this chapter, you'll learn how to modify and delete an existing entry. To accomplish this, you need to do the following in your application:

- Create administrative links (edit and delete)
- Display the administrative links in index.php
- Populate the admin form with entry information if you're editing
- Modify .htaccess to pass a URL to admin.php
- Check whether submitted form values are edits or new entries
- Update entries in the entries table
- Check whether an entry is marked for deletion
- Remove deleted entries from the entries table

Creating Administrative Links

Your first task is to create links that will allow you to edit and delete entries. You'll eventually want this to be available to administrators only (see Chapter 11 for more information on this topic), so you're going to build these links inside a function, rather than inline in index.php.

Name your function adminLinks() and have it accept two arguments: the current page ($page) and the URL of the entry you're working with ($url).

To start, open up functions.inc.php and declare your new function just below retrieveEntries():

```
function adminLinks($page, $url)
{
    // Build admin links here
}
```

The first step in your function is to build the addresses for your links. For your editing link, this address simply appends the entry's URL to the end, which you'll use later to identify the entry being edited. The path for the link follows this format:

```
/simple_blog/admin/page/url
```

The delete link works a little differently; rather than using the page, you use the word "delete" in the address, signifying that the entry is to be deleted. The `delete` link follows this format:

```
/simple_blog/admin/delete/url
```

Now it's time to add these paths to `adminLinks()` in `functions.inc.php`. Do so by inserting the lines in bold, as shown:

```
function adminLinks($page, $url)
{
    // Format the link to be followed for each option
    $editURL = "/simple_blog/admin/$page/$url";
    $deleteURL = "/simple_blog/admin/delete/$url";

    // Finish the admin links here
}
```

Finally you need to create the hyperlinks from your URLs and return them so they can be used in `index.php`. You need to place your links in an array, so that both the edit and delete links can be returned by your function. Add the bold lines to `functions.inc.php`:

```
function adminLinks($page, $url)
{
    // Format the link to be followed for each option
    $editURL = "/simple_blog/admin/$page/$url";
    $deleteURL = "/simple_blog/admin/delete/$url";

    // Make a hyperlink and add it to an array
    $admin['edit'] = "<a href=\"$editURL\">edit</a>";
    $admin['delete'] = "<a href=\"$deleteURL\">delete</a>";

    return $admin;
}
```

Now you can generate custom `edit` and `delete` links quickly for any entry with a URL (which, in your application, is all of them). Next, you need to display those links, as well as their corresponding entries, in `index.php`.

Displaying Administrative Links

Your application can generate administrative links at this point; next you need to load those links into `index.php`. You place your administrative links only on the full display of an entry, so you must place the call to load information from `adminLinks()` within a conditional statement that fires only if `$fulldisp == 1`.

In index.php, at line 69, insert the code shown in bold:

```php
<?php

// If the full display flag is set, show the entry
if($fulldisp==1)
{

    // Get the URL if one wasn't passed
    $url = (isset($url)) ? $url : $e['url'];

    // Build the admin links
    $admin = adminLinks($page, $url);

?>
```

Now you have an array with your edit and delete links as individual array elements. This means you can insert the links in your layout by adding the code shown in bold:

```php
    // Build the admin links
    $admin = adminLinks($page, $url);

?>

        <h2> <?php echo $e['title'] ?> </h2>
        <p> <?php echo $e['entry'] ?> </p>
        <p>
            <?php echo $admin['edit'] ?>
            <?php if($page=='blog') echo $admin['delete'] ?>
        </p>
        <?php if($page=='blog'): ?>
        <p class="backlink">
            <a href="./">Back to Latest Entries</a>
        </p>
        <?php endif; ?>
```

■**Note** You're checking whether $page=='blog' before you display the delete link. This is because you don't want to delete your "About the Author" entry; doing that would leave you without any entry for that page. Instead, you want your users to edit the existing entry.

Now loading index.php in a browser and selecting an entry displays your administrative links (see Figure 7-1).

Figure 7-1. *Your administrative links for a blog entry*

Passing URL Values to admin.php with .htaccess

As your application stands right now, the URLs in your administrative links won't mean anything to admin.php. To remedy this, you need to modify .htaccess with an additional rule that handles URLs passed in a link to admin.php.

Modifying the Original Admin Rule

When you write this rule, you need to keep in mind that new entries are passed to admin.php without a URL, so you need to allow for scenarios where a URL is passed to admin.php, as well as for scenarios where it isn't. To do this, you'll modify your original admin rule to ensure that the path ends with the page name, followed by either a forward slash or nothing at all. With these modifications, your rule in .htaccess should look like this:

```
RewriteRule ^admin/(\w+)(|/)$ admin.php?page=$1 [NC,L]
```

You modify this rule in your addition of (|/)$, which tells the server to ensure that the end of the path must be encountered after one or more word characters, whether that occurs at the end of the word characters or after one occurrence of a forward slash.

The (|/) tells the server to match *either* nothing *or* a forward slash. The vertical pipe character (|) is the regular expression equivalent of "or".

Adding a dollar sign ($) to the end of the rule lets you signify the end of the string, so nothing can come after the pattern you define.

Thus, both of the following examples match your new rule:

```
http://localhost/simple_blog/admin/blog
http://localhost/simple_blog/admin/blog/
```

However, this example does not match your rule:

```
http://localhost/simple_blog/admin/blog/entry
```

The New Admin Rule

The next step is to set up a rule that catches information in the URL after the page and passes it to `admin.php` as a URL variable; this enables you to signify which entry is being edited. Accomplishing this requires that you add an additional backreference for the URL of the entry you want to edit. This backreference needs to catch the entire URL, so the word character shorthand (\w) won't be enough, since your URLs contain hyphens. To add hyphens as a matchable character, you'll have to create a character class using square brackets.

■**Note** Backreferences are named matches that you can use in the replacement. For a refresher on backreferences, see the section on `.htaccess` in Chapter 6.

You pass the first backreference in the URL query string as a page, just like your original rule. You pass the second backreference as a URL, to let `admin.php` know which entry is being edited.

To implement this rule in `.htaccess`, add the bold line to your `.htaccess` file:

```
RewriteEngine on
RewriteBase /simple_blog/

RewriteRule \.(gif|jpg|png|css|ico|swf|js|inc\.php)$ - [L]
RewriteRule ^admin/(\w+)(|/)$ admin.php?page=$1 [NC,L]
RewriteRule ^admin/(\w+)/([\w-]+) admin.php?page=$1&url=$2 [NC,L]
RewriteRule ^(\w+)(|/)$ index.php?page=$1
RewriteRule ^(\w+)/([\w-]+) index.php?page=$1&url=$2
```

Your second backreference, ([\w-]+), will match one or more word characters and/or hyphens—which is what your custom entry URLs consist of—and pass their value to `admin.php`. Now you're ready to modify `admin.php` to load entries for editing.

Populating Your Form with the Entry to Be Edited

`admin.php` is receiving entry URLs when a user clicks the edit link is clicked; next you need to write a script that identifies that URL and loads the appropriate entry. You also need to add the entry's values to the administrative form to enable editing.

Your first step is to check whether $_GET['url'] is set, which determines whether you're editing an entry or creating a new one. If an entry is being edited, you need to load the existing entry data and save each piece in a variable. Fortunately, you've already written the function to load an entry using the URL—retreiveEntries()–so you can use that to load the entry to be edited.

To use retrieveEntries() in your script, you must include the necessary files and open a database connection.

You want to avoid the possibility of having undefined variables, so you should also add an else to your conditional that will declare your entry data variables as NULL if no entry is passed.

Also, you can enhance your form's friendliness by changing the legend to indicate whether you're editing an existing entry or creating a new one. You can store this information in a variable ($legend).

To do this, open admin.php and add the lines of code in bold:

```php
<?php

    /*
     * Include the necessary files
     */
    include_once 'inc/functions.inc.php';
    include_once 'inc/db.inc.php';

    // Open a database connection
    $db = new PDO(DB_INFO, DB_USER, DB_PASS);

    $page = isset($_GET['page']) ? htmlentities(strip_tags($_GET['page'])) : 'blog';

    if(isset($_GET['url']))
    {
        // Do basic sanitization of the url variable
        $url = htmlentities(strip_tags($_GET['url']));

        // Set the legend of the form
        $legend = "Edit This Entry";

        // Load the entry to be edited
        $e = retrieveEntries($db, $page, $url);

        // Save each entry field as individual variables
        $id = $e['id'];
        $title = $e['title'];
        $entry = $e['entry'];
    }
```

```
    else
    {
        // Set the legend
        $legend = "New Entry Submission";

        // Set variables to NULL if not editing
        $id = NULL;
        $title = NULL;
        $entry = NULL;
    }
?>
```

To add these values into your form, you need to set the value attribute in your inputs and place the $entry variable between the opening and closing <textarea> tags. Also, you need to add a new hidden input named id to contain the entry ID, which will help you in your next step, when you save your changes.

You can add the values into your form by modifying admin.php with the lines of code in bold, as shown:

```
<form method="post" action="/simple_blog/inc/update.inc.php">
    <fieldset>
        <legend><?php echo $legend ?></legend>
        <label>Title
            <input type="text" name="title" maxlength="150"
                value="<?php echo htmlentities($title) ?>" />
        </label>
        <label>Entry
            <textarea name="entry" cols="45"
                rows="10"><?php echo sanitizeData($entry) ?></textarea>
        </label>
        <input type="hidden" name="id"
            value="<?php echo $id ?>" />
        <input type="hidden" name="page"
            value="<?php echo $page ?>" />
        <input type="submit" name="submit" value="Save Entry" />
        <input type="submit" name="submit" value="Cancel" />
    </fieldset>
</form>
```

Clicking the edit link on one of your entries now loads and displays the contents of that entry into the form (see Figure 7-2).

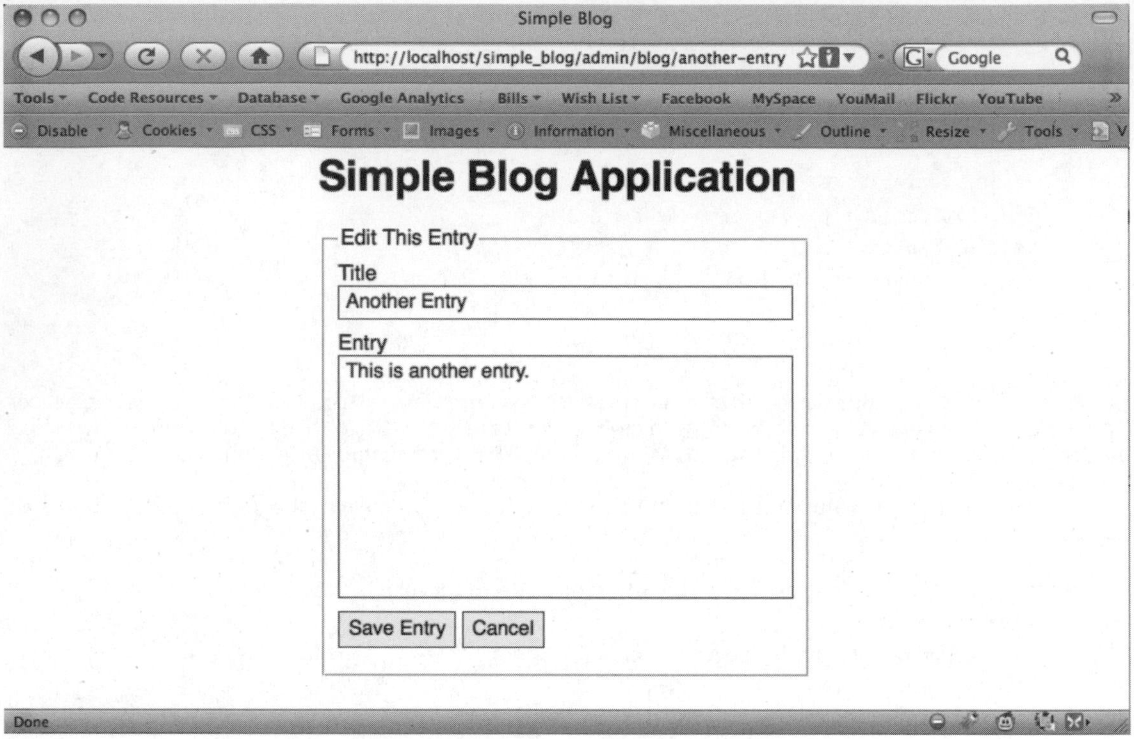

Figure 7-2. Clicking a link loads that entry into the form for editing

Next you need to modify update.inc.php so it recognizes that an entry is being edited and updates the proper entry, as opposed to creating a new entry in the database.

Updating Entries in the Database

In your form, you added a hidden input to store the entry's ID. This hidden input is what you use to determine whether a form submission is an edit or a new entry.

To make this distinction, you need to check whether $_GET['id'] is empty. If so, the entry is new, and you can proceed as usual. If $_GET['id'] has a value, however, you're editing an entry, and you must use a different query.

You update an entry in the entries table by specifying which fields are being set to which value. Your ID won't change, but the title, url, and entry fields all might, so your query needs to look like this:

```
UPDATE entries
SET title=?, entry=?, url=?
WHERE id=?
LIMIT 1
```

This query updates a maximum of one entry in the entries table by matching the supplied ID with the submitted title, entry, and url values.

You can check whether $_GET['id'] contains a value and update an entry by inserting the code highlighted in bold in update.inc.php:

```php
<?php

// Include the functions so you can create a URL
include_once 'functions.inc.php';

if($_SERVER['REQUEST_METHOD']=='POST'
    && $_POST['submit']=='Save Entry'
    && !empty($_POST['page'])
    && !empty($_POST['title'])
    && !empty($_POST['entry']))
{
    // Create a URL to save in the database
    $url = makeUrl($_POST['title']);

    // Include database credentials and connect to the database
    include_once 'db.inc.php';
    $db = new PDO(DB_INFO, DB_USER, DB_PASS);

    // Edit an existing entry
    if(!empty($_POST['id']))
    {
        $sql = "UPDATE entries
                SET title=?, entry=?, url=?
                WHERE id=?
                LIMIT 1";
        $stmt = $db->prepare($sql);
        $stmt->execute(
            array(
                $_POST['title'],
                $_POST['entry'],
                $url,
                $_POST['id']
            )
        );
        $stmt->closeCursor();
    }
```

```
    // Create a new entry
    else
    {
        // Save the entry into the database
        $sql = "INSERT INTO entries (page, title, entry, url)
                VALUES (?, ?, ?, ?)";
        $stmt = $db->prepare($sql);
        $stmt->execute(
            array(
                $_POST['page'],
                $_POST['title'],
                $_POST['entry'],
                $url
            )
        );
        $stmt->closeCursor();
    }

    // Sanitize the page information for use in the success URL
    $page = htmlentities(strip_tags($_POST['page']));

    // Send the user to the new entry
    header('Location: /simple_blog/'.$page.'/'.$url);
    exit;
}

else
{
    header('Location: ../');
    exit;
}

?>
```

■**Note** Make sure you add the closing curly brace for the else statement (just after $stmt->closeCursor();) to avoid a parsing error.

Now you can update entries in your database. To test this ability, open your application in a browser and click the edit link on one of your entries and add some new text. Click the Save Entry button to see the edited entry (see Figure 7-3).

Figure 7-3. *An edited entry*

Handling Entry Deletion

You've almost completed your administrative controls. All that's left is to add the ability to delete entries. This is fairly straightforward, due to the way that you've constructed the delete link.

The link passes delete as $_GET['page'], so it's easy to identify entries marked for deletion. In admin.php, you check whether $_GET['page'] == 'delete', then pass the entry URL to be deleted to a function called confirmDelete()—you'll write this function in the next section. This function asks the user to confirm that she does in fact wish to delete the entry.

Do this by adding the following code in bold to admin.php:

```php
<?php

    /*
     * Include the necessary files
     */
    include_once 'inc/functions.inc.php';
    include_once 'inc/db.inc.php';

    // Open a database connection
    $db = new PDO(DB_INFO, DB_USER, DB_PASS);
```

```php
$page = htmlentities(strip_tags($_GET['page']));

if(isset($_GET['url']))
{
    $url = htmlentities(strip_tags($_GET['url']));

    // Check if the entry should be deleted
    if($page == 'delete')
    {
        $confirm = confirmDelete($db, $url);
    }

    // Set the legend of the form
    $legend = "Edit This Entry";

    $e = retrieveEntries($db, $page, $url);
    $id = $e['id'];
    $title = $e['title'];
    $entry = $e['entry'];
}
else
{
    // Set the legend
    $legend = "New Entry Submission";

    // Set the variables to null if not editing
    $id = NULL;
    $title = NULL;
    $entry = NULL;
}

?>
```

confirmDelete() is called when the user clicks the delete link, and its return value is stored in the $confirm variable. This function returns an HTML form asking the user to confirm that she wishes to delete the entry in question. To display this form, you need to add a conditional statement in the body of admin.php that displays the confirmation form if the value of $page is delete.

Add the code in bold to admin.php to display your confirmation page:

```html
<!DOCTYPE html
    PUBLIC "-//W3C//DTD XHTML 1.0 Strict//EN"
    "http://www.w3.org/TR/xhtml1/DTD/xhtml1-strict.dtd">

<html xmlns="http://www.w3.org/1999/xhtml" xml:lang="en" lang="en">
```

```html
<head>
    <meta http-equiv="Content-Type" content="text/html;charset=utf-8" />
    <link rel="stylesheet" href="/simple_blog/css/default.css" type="text/css" />
    <title> Simple Blog </title>
</head>

<body>
    <h1> Simple Blog Application </h1>

<?php

    if($page == 'delete'):
    {
        echo $confirm;
    }
    else:

?>
    <form method="post"
        action="/simple_blog/inc/update.inc.php"
        enctype="multipart/form-data">
        <fieldset>
            <legend><?php echo $legend ?></legend>
            <label>Title
                <input type="text" name="title" maxlength="150"
                    value="<?php echo $title ?>" />
            </label>
            <label>Image
                <input type="file" name="image" />
            </label>
            <label>Entry
                <textarea name="entry" cols="45"
                    rows="10"><?php echo $entry ?></textarea>
            </label>
            <input type="hidden" name="id"
                value="<?php echo $id ?>" />
            <input type="hidden" name="page"
                value="<?php echo $page ?>" />
            <input type="submit" name="submit" value="Save Entry" />
            <input type="submit" name="submit" value="Cancel" />
        </fieldset>
    </form>
<?php endif; ?>
</body>

</html>
```

■**Note** Don't forget to close the else statement by inserting <?php endif; ?> just above the closing </body> tag.

Confirming Your Choice to Delete an Entry

Clicking the delete link now causes the return value of confirmDelete() to be displayed; your next step is to define confirmDelete(). This function accepts two arguments: a database object and the URL of the entry to be deleted.

The function uses the entry's URL to load the entry's information, which pops up and displays a form to the user that asks whether a given entry should be deleted. This form contains hidden inputs that store the action you want carried out by the form (delete), and the URL of the entry that will be deleted if the user confirms that he wants to delete the entry.

Add the following code to functions.inc.php to declare the function confirmDelete():

```php
function confirmDelete($db, $url)
{
    $e = retrieveEntries($db, '', $url);

    return <<<FORM
<form action="/simple_blog/admin.php" method="post">
    <fieldset>
        <legend>Are You Sure?</legend>
        <p>Are you sure you want to delete the entry "$e[title]"?</p>
        <input type="submit" name="submit" value="Yes" />
        <input type="submit" name="submit" value="No" />
        <input type="hidden" name="action" value="delete" />
        <input type="hidden" name="url" value="$url" />
    </fieldset>
</form>
FORM;
}
```

You're using the heredoc syntax to make passing formatted HTML containing PHP variables as easy as possible.

Now if you click the delete link next to an entry, you're taken to a confirmation screen to verify that you really wish to delete the entry (see Figure 7-4).

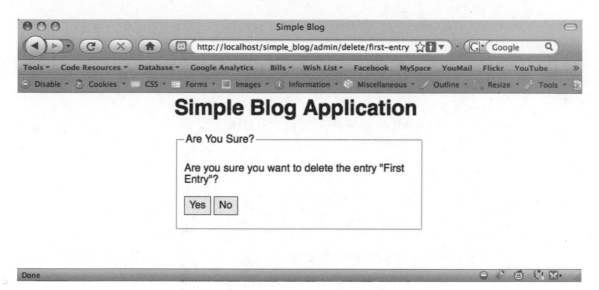

Figure 7-4. The confirmation screen displays when the delete link is clicked

Your confirmation form submits your choice, via the POST method, to admin.php. To process this, you need to add an additional block of code to the top of admin.php that determines what choices you've made and act accordingly.

Handling Your Submitted Confirmation Form

In admin.php, you need to identify whether the user reached the page from the confirmation form; you do this by checking whether the $_POST superglobal contains an *action* variable. You also need to check whether the variable value is delete. If the Yes button was clicked, you submit the entry's URL to the deleteEntry()function (which you'll write in a moment) for deletion.

If the No button was clicked, you return the user to the entry she was viewing when the delete link was clicked originally.

You can accomplish this by adding the following code in bold to the top of admin.php:

```php
<?php

    /*
     * Include the necessary files
     */
    include_once 'inc/functions.inc.php';
    include once 'inc/db.inc.php';

    // Open a database connection
    $db = new PDO(DB_INFO, DB_USER, DB_PASS);
```

```php
$page = isset($_GET['page']) ? htmlentities(strip_tags($_GET['page'])) : 'blog';

if(isset($_POST['action']) && $_POST['action'] == 'delete')
{
    if($_POST['submit'] == 'Yes')
    {
        $url = htmlentities(strip_tags($_POST['url']));
        if(deleteEntry($db, $url))
        {
            header("Location: /simple_blog/");
            exit;
        }
        else
        {
            exit("Error deleting the entry!");
        }
    }
    else
    {
        header("Location: /simple_blog/blog/$url");
        exit;          }
}

if(isset($_GET['url']))
{
    $url = htmlentities(strip_tags($_GET['url']));

    // Check if the entry should be deleted
    if($page == 'delete')
    {
        $confirm = confirmDelete($db, $url);
    }

    // Set the legend of the form
    $legend = "Edit This Entry";

    $e = retrieveEntries($db, $page, $url);
    $id = $e['id'];
    $title = $e['title'];
    $entry = $e['entry'];
}
```

```
        else
        {
            // Set the legend
            $legend = "New Entry Submission";

            // Set the variables to null if not editing
            $id = NULL;
            $title = NULL;
            $entry = NULL;
        }
    ?>
```

When a user confirms that he wishes to delete an entry, that entry's URL is passed to the yet-to-be-written deleteEntry() function, which removes the entry from the database. If the function is successful, you send the user to the main page. If it fails, you stop execution of the script and display an error, letting the user know that something went wrong.

You can complete this process by defining deleteEntry().

Removing Deleted Entries from the Database

You need to write your deleteEntry() function in functions.inc.php. This function needs to accept the entry URL as an argument, then place that URL into a DELETE query that removes a maximum of one entry from the entries table.

Your MySQL query should read like this:

```
DELETE FROM entries
WHERE url=?
LIMIT 1
```

After you prepare the statement for execution, you use your supplied URL to execute the argument. You can make sure that the function executes successfully by returning the value of $stmt->execute() as the return value of your function.

Add your deleteEntry() function below retrieveEntries() in functions.inc.php:

```
function deleteEntry($db, $url)
{
    $sql = "DELETE FROM entries
            WHERE url=?
            LIMIT 1";
    $stmt = $db->prepare($sql);
    return $stmt->execute(array($url));
}
```

You can now delete entries from the database. You can test this by creating a temporary entry (see Figure 7-5), then deleting it to see whether it is removed from the database and, therefore, from your entry list (see Figure 7-6).

Figure 7-5. *A temporary entry created using the* `Post a New Entry` *link*

Figure 7-6. *The temporary entry has been deleted, so it is no longer available in the title summary*

Summary

This chapter was short, but it covered a lot of ground. In it, you learned how to create administrative links, as well as how to use those links to edit and delete entries from the database.

In the next chapter, you'll dive into new territory and learn how to upload and manipulate images using PHP's *GD library*. This section will be much longer and will present you with a great deal of new material, so get ready!

CHAPTER 8

■ ■ ■

Adding the Ability to Upload Images

Up to this point, you've been dealing exclusively with text on your blog. However, you can make your blog much more interesting by incorporating images.

I'll cover a lot of information in this chapter. For example, I'll explain how to use PHP's GD library (in the section on resizing images), as well as functions that manipulate the file system. I'll even begin to cover the relatively advanced topic of your object-oriented programming.

By the end of this chapter, your blog should be able to:

- Accept image uploads

- Save uploaded images in a folder of your choosing

- Save the uploaded image's path in the database

- Display images to your blog's users

- Resize images to fit into your layout

- Delete images when necessary

Adding a File Input to the Admin Form

Before you can start processing images with PHP, you must first add the ability to upload images to your administrative form on `admin.php`. To do this, you' need to add a file upload input to your administrative form.

When using file inputs, you also have to change the *enctype*, or content type, of the form. By default, HTML forms are set to `application/x-www-form-urlencoded`. However, this won't work when you're uploading files; instead, you need to set the `enctype` of the form to multipart/form-data, which can accept files *and* standard form values.

Modify the form in `admin.php` to include the code in bold:

```
<form method="post"
    action="/simple_blog/inc/update.inc.php"
    enctype="multipart/form-data">
    <fieldset>
        <legend><?php echo $legend ?></legend>
        <label>Title
            <input type="text" name="title" maxlength="150"
                value="<?php echo $title ?>" />
        </label>
        <label>Image
            <input type="file" name="image" />
        </label>
        <label>Entry
            <textarea name="entry" cols="45"
                rows="10"><?php echo $entry ?></textarea>
        </label>
        <input type="hidden" name="id"
            value="<?php echo $id ?>" />
        <input type="hidden" name="page"
            value="<?php echo $page ?>" />
        <input type="submit" name="submit" value="Save Entry" />
        <input type="submit" name="submit" value="Cancel" />
    </fieldset>
</form>
```

Load `admin.php` in a browser to see the added file input.

Accessing the Uploaded File

File uploads work differently than standard inputs, which means you must handle them a little differently. In this case, you must modify `update.inc.php` to deal with uploaded images.

You don't want to force your users to upload an image to post a new entry, so you need to check whether a file was uploaded *after* you verify that the rest of the entry form was filled out. To check whether a file was uploaded, you look in the `$_FILES` superglobal array.

A Quick Refresher on the $_FILES Superglobal Array

You learned about the `$_FILES` superglobal in Chapter 3, but it might be helpful to review what it does before moving on.

Whenever a file is uploaded via an HTML form, that file is stored in temporary memory and information about the file is passed in the $_FILES superglobal. You can see this in action by taking a look at what's being passed to your update.inc.php script. To do this, add the code in bold to the top of the file:

```php
<?php

// Include the functions so you can create a URL
include_once 'functions.inc.php';

if($_SERVER['REQUEST_METHOD']=='POST'
    && $_POST['submit']=='Save Entry'
    && !empty($_POST['page'])
    && !empty($_POST['title'])
    && !empty($_POST['entry']))
{
    // Create a URL to save in the database
    $url = makeUrl($_POST['title']);

    // Output the contents of $_FILES
    echo "<pre>"; // <pre> tags make the output easy to read
    print_r($_FILES);
    echo "</pre>";

    /*
     * You don't want to save this test, so you exit the script to
     * prevent further execution.
     */
    exit;
```

After you save this file, you can navigate to create a new entry and try uploading an image by pointing your browser to http://localhost/simple_blog/admin/blog.

Click the Browse... button on the file input and select any image off your computer. You can fill in the Title and Entry fields with any information you want because this information won't be saved (see Figure 8-1).

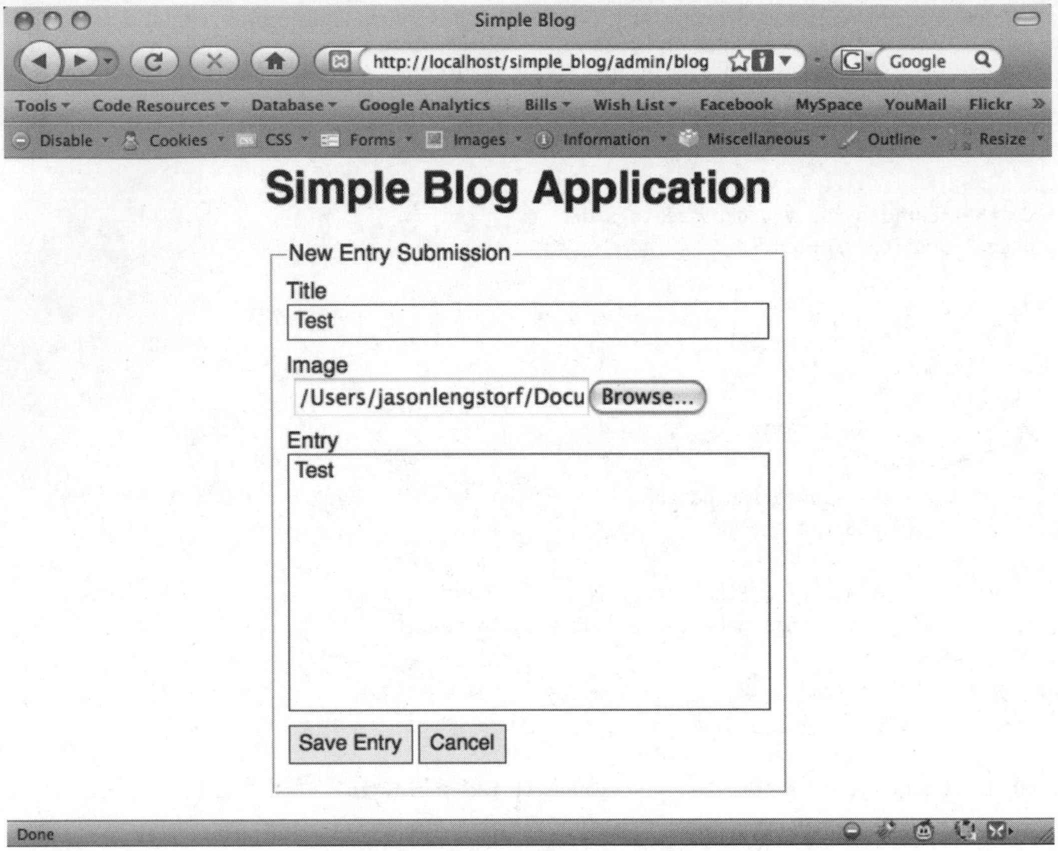

Figure 8-1. An image selected in the new file input in **admin.php**

Click the Save Entry buttonto send this information to update.inc.php, which will display the contents of $_FILES and stop execution. The output will look similar to this:

```
Array
(
    [image] => Array
        (
            [name] => IMG001.jpg
            [type] => image/jpeg
            [tmp_name] => /Applications/XAMPP/xamppfiles/temp/phpHQLHjt
            [error] => 0
            [size] => 226452
        )

)
```

Examining this output enables you to determine that your image is stored in the array located at `$_FILES['image']` (named for the name attribute of the file input) and that five pieces of information were stored:

- `$_FILES['image']['name']` : The name of the uploaded file

- `$_FILES['image']['type']` : The MIME type of the uploaded file

- `$_FILES['image']['tmp_name']` : The temporary location of the uploaded file

- `$_FILES['image']['error']` : An error code for the upload (0 means no error)

- `$_FILES['image']['size']` : The size of the uploaded file in bytes

You're ready to start processing the uploaded image now that you know what information is being sent from your form to `update.inc.php`.

Object-Oriented Programming

To handle your uploaded images, you need to leverage *object-oriented programming* (OOP) to write a class that handles your image processing. Classes and objects are extremely useful in programming; both have been well supported in PHP scripts since the release of PHP 5.

Drill Down on Objects

An object is a collection of information in a program. An object behaves similarly to an array, except that the information in an object provides a little more flexibility in how the information can be accessed and processed. To use objects in PHP, you must define a *class* to provide a structure for the object.

Classes vs. Objects

It's not uncommon to hear the terms "class" and "object" used interchangeably when talking about programming, but it's important to recognize that classes and objects are *not* the same thing, albeit they are bound tightly together.

A class is a blueprint for information. It provides a map of properties and methods that give a collection of information meaning. However, a class by itself doesn't really mean anything.

Objects contain a mass of information that conforms to the blueprint laid out by the class: an object is to a class as a house is to a blueprint. Each object is an instantiation of a class—just as each house built from a blueprint is an instantiation of the blueprint.

Here's another example that might help you understand the difference between a class and an object. Imagine that you have a toy robot that stores one *property*, or class-specific variable (its name) and one *method*, or class-specific function (the ability to write its name). The methods and properties that describe and define your robot are the class. However, before your toy robot can actually perform any of its abilities, you must first supply it with its required information—its name, in this case. The robot's name represents an object.

Why Objects Are Useful

One neat feature about objects: they enable you to have multiple instances of a given class that run simultaneously, but use different information.

Let's continue with the toy robot example. If you have two toy robots that are exactly the same, you can store the name "Tom" in the first robot, and the name "Jim" in the second, and they will both perform their duties in the same way, but with different information. If you set them loose at the same time, they will both start writing their names—Tom and Jim, respectively.

The advantage of using classes and objects in programming over procedural code is that an object can save its state. This means that you can set a property in an object once, then reference it for as long as the object exists.

In procedural code, you would need to pass that same property to every function to take advantage of it. This makes function calls cumbersome, and this process can prove confusing if the same functions must handle two or more sets of data.

Imagining Your Robot as a PHP Class

Let's explore the benefits of OOP by building your toy robots with PHP.

Begin by defining the class, which you should call ToyRobot. Do this using the reserved class keyword, followed by the class name, and then a pair of curly braces to enclose the class's properties and methods.

Next, create a new test file called ToyRobot.php in your simple_blog project, then define the class by adding the following code:

```php
<?php

class ToyRobot
{

}

?>
```

Class Properties

A property in a PHP class behaves similarly to a regular variable. The difference is that a class property is specific to the instance of your class and available to the methods without being passed as an argument.

In your ToyRobot class, you have only one property: the robot's name. You want to control how the robot's name is accessed and manipulated, so set this property as *private*, which ensures that only the ToyRobot class's methods can access the property's value.

MEMBER VISIBILITY IN OOP

Depending on how you use your classes, you need to assign the appropriate visibility declarations to their methods and properties. The available visibility declarations include:

- public: Public properties and methods can be accessed anywhere in a script after the object has been instantiated
- protected: Protected properties and methods can be accessed only within the class that defines them, parent classes, or inherited classes (you can learn more about inheritance in the PHP manual at http://us.php.net/manual/en/language.oop5.basic.php#language.oop5.basic.extends)
- private: Private properties and methods can only be accessed by the class that defines them

You must assign all properties with a visibility declaration. Methods declared without a declaration default to public visibility. In PHP4, developers used the var keyword to define object properties because visibility declarations weren't supported yet. For the sake of backward compatibility, PHP5 recognizes var as an alias for public, although it does raise an E_STRICT warning. For more information on visibility declarations, read the entry on it in the PHP manual, which you can find at http://us.php.net/manual/en/language.oop5.visibility.php.

To declare a private property in your ToyRobot class, you need to add the lines in bold to test.php:

```php
<?php

class ToyRobot
{
    // Stores the name of this instance of the robot
    private $_name;
}

?>
```

■**Note** Using an underscore before a private property name ($_name) is a widely accepted way of denoting private properties.

Each instance of the ToyRobot class will likely have a different name, so you don't specify a value for the $_name property; instead, you accomplish this using the object's *constructor*.

Class Constructors

PHP5 introduced *magic methods*, which are essentially methods that execute when a certain action occurs in a script. There are several available, but this book won't delve into them because they don't apply to your blogging application. You can learn more about magic methods in its PHP manual entry at http://us.php.net/manual/en/language.oop5.magic.php.

Constructors are one of the most commonly used magic methods available in PHP5. A constructor is called when an object is *instantiated*, or first created. This allows you to initialize certain parameters or other settings for an object when you create the object. You can leverage a constructor in your ToyRobot class by declaring it in the __construct() magic method. You use this constructor to define the $_name property.

Test this by adding the following code in bold to test.php:

```php
<?php

class ToyRobot
{
    // Stores the name of this instance of the robot
    private $_name;

    // Sets the name property upon class instantiation
    public function __construct($name)
    {
        $this->_name = $name;
    }
}

?>
```

Note the use of $this in your class. In object-oriented PHP, $this is a reserved variable that refers to the current object.

$this enables an object to refer to itself without needing to know what it's called. This enables multiple instances of a class to exist without conflict.

Next, consider the use of an arrow (->) after the $this keyword. This arrow indicates that you're accessing a property or method contained within the object. Again, this enables you to have multiple instances of a class without conflict.

Finally, the preceding script lets you add the name of the property or method you want to access (the $_name property, in this case). When accessing properties, you leave off the dollar sign because you already use it with $this.

Your declared constructor will now allow you to define the name of each ToyRobot instance right as you create it. The next step is to create the method that enables your ToyRobot class to write its name.

Class Methods

You define a method in your ToyRobot class much as you declare a function in a procedural script. The only difference is the visibility declaration and the ability to access class properties without needing to accept them as function arguments.

You en able your ToyRobot to write its name by defining a public method called writeName(). Add the code in bold to test.php:

```php
<?php

class ToyRobot
{
    // Stores the name of this instance of the robot
    private $_name;

    // Sets the name property upon class instantiation
    public function __construct($name)
    {
        $this->_name = $name;
    }

    // Writes the robot's name
    public function writeName()
    {
        echo 'My name is ', $this->_name, '.<br />';
    }
}

?>
```

This method is straightforward: when called, it causes the robot to introduce itself. All that's left is to learn how to use objects in your scripts.

Using Classes in Your Scripts

The toy robot example initially discussed two robots: Tom and Jim. You're now ready to use your new PHP skills to build this pair of robots.

You use the new keyword to create a new instance of an object, followed by the name of the class. You use the name of the class like a function call, which allows you to pass arguments (assuming any are necessary) to your constructor.

Begin building Tom by adding the lines in bold to test.php:

```php
<?php

// Create an instance of ToyRobot with the name "Tom"
$tom = new ToyRobot("Tom");

class ToyRobot
{
    // Stores the name of this instance of the robot
    private $_name;
```

215

```php
    // Sets the name property upon class instantiation
    public function __construct($name)
    {
        $this->_name = $name;
    }

    // Writes the robot's name
    public function writeName()
    {
        echo 'My name is ', $this->_name, '.<br />';
    }
}

?>
```

At this point, you have created and instantiated your first PHP class. Passing Tom as an argument to the object enables you to set the private $_name property to Tom, effectively giving your robot its name.

Now you can have Tom write his name by calling his writeName() method. Add the lines in bold to test.php:

```php
<?php

// Create an instance of ToyRobot with the name "Tom"
$tom = new ToyRobot("Tom");

// Have Tom introduce himself
$tom->writeName();

class ToyRobot
{
    // Stores the name of this instance of the robot
    private $_name;

    // Sets the name property upon class instantiation
    public function __construct($name)
    {
        $this->_name = $name;
    }

    // Writes the robot's name
    public function writeName()
    {
        echo 'My name is ', $this->_name, '.<br />';
    }
}

?>
```

Now you have some actual output to look at. Load `test.php` in your browser to see what Tom had to say:

```
My name is Tom.
```

You're now ready to build Jim and have him introduce himself; add the bold to `test.php`:

```php
<?php

// Create an instance of ToyRobot with the name "Tom"
$tom = new ToyRobot("Tom");

// Have Tom introduce himself
$tom->writeName();

// Build Jim and have him introduce himself
$jim = new ToyRobot("Jim");
$jim->writeName();

class ToyRobot
{
    // Stores the name of this instance of the robot
    private $_name;

    // Sets the name property upon class instantiation
    public function __construct($name)
    {
        $this->_name = $name;
    }

    // Writes the robot's name
    public function writeName()
    {
        echo 'My name is ', $this->_name, '.<br />';
    }
}

?>
```

You should see the following when you load `test.php` in a browser:

```
My name is Tom.
My name is Jim.
```

Your ToyRobot class is admittedly simple, but it exemplifies the power of using objects with PHP. You can have two instances in use at the same time without any conflicts and without needing to keep track of a bunch of variables.

Even if your objects are mixed in together, you still get the proper result. For instance, you can replace the class instantiations in test.php with the following:

```php
<?php

$tom = new ToyRobot("Tom");
$jim = new ToyRobot("Jim");

$tom->writeName();
$jim->writeName();

?>
```

This still outputs the following:

```
My name is Tom.
My name is Jim.
```

Armed with your new understanding of OOP, you're ready to take on a new task: writing a class to handle images.

Writing the Image Handling Class

Your first step, of course, is to define the ImageHandler class. You want this class to be portable, so you should create a separate file for it called images.inc.php. You save this file in the inc folder (full path: /xampp/htdocs/simple_blog/inc/images.inc.php). After you create images.inc.php, insert the following code to define the class:

```php
<?php

class ImageHandler
{

}

?>
```

Saving the Image

So far you've defined your class is defined; next, you need to determine what methods and properties you need to define.

You need a public method that saves the uploaded image in a folder and returns its path. You also need a public property that stores the folder you want your images saved in. This property is vital, so set it in your constructor.

To be as descriptive as possible, call your method for uploading an image processUploadedImage.. Call the property that holds the folder's location $save_dir.

In images.inc.php, define your properties and constructor first by adding the lines in bold:

```php
<?php

class ImageHandler
{
    // The folder in which to save images
    public $save_dir;

    // Sets the $save_dir on instantiation
    public function __construct($save_dir)
    {
        $this->save_dir = $save_dir;
    }
}

?>
```

At this point, instantiating the ImageHandler class gives you an object that sets a folder where you can save your images. At last you're ready to save an image. Do this by creating your public processUploadedImage() method.

Next, define the method by adding the lines in bold to images.inc.php:

```php
<?php

class ImageHandler
{
    // The folder in which to save images
    public $save_dir;

    // Sets the $save_dir on instantiation
    public function __construct($save_dir)
    {
        $this->save_dir = $save_dir;
    }
```

```
    /**
     * Resizes/resamples an image uploaded via a web form
     *
     * @param array $upload the array contained in $_FILES
     * @return string the path to the resized uploaded file
     */
    public function processUploadedImage($file)
    {
        // Process the image
    }
}

?>
```

■**Note** The block comment immediately before `processUploadedImage()` is a special comment known as a PHP DocBlock. This is a special comment that provides information about a class, property, or method. DocBlocks are indicated by opening a comment using `/**`, then providing a short description of the class, method, or property. This process also lists a method's list of parameters and its return value. All classes you write from now on will take advantage of DocBlocks to help you keep track of the code you're writing. An additional point of interest: Some IDEs and SDKs (including Eclipse) use DocBlocks to provide descriptions of methods as they're used, including a list of parameters (defined using `@param [datatype] [var_name] [description]`) and the return value (defined using `@return [datatype] [description]`).

You accept the file as an argument, which is the array you find in `$_FILES`. To process this file, you need to break the array apart into individual values. You do this using the `list()` function, which allows you to create named variables for each array index as a comma-separated list.

What that means becomes clear if you look at how you previously defined an array:

```
$array = array(
    'First value',
    'Second value'
);
```

The array values are separated by `list()` as follows:

```
list($first, $second) = $array;
echo $first, "<br />", $second;
```

This produces the following output:

```
First value
Second value
```

In processUploadedImage(), you need to pull out the five pieces of information supplied about your uploaded file. You can accomplish this by adding the following code in bold to images.inc.php:

```php
<?php

class ImageHandler
{
    // The folder in which to save images
    public $save_dir;

    // Sets the $save_dir on instantiation
    public function __construct($save_dir)
    {
        $this->save_dir = $save_dir;
    }

    /**
     * Resizes/resamples an image uploaded via a web form
     *
     * @param array $upload the array contained in $_FILES
     * @return string the path to the resized uploaded file
     */
    public function processUploadedImage($file)
    {
        // Separate the uploaded file array
        list($name, $type, $tmp, $err, $size) = array_values($file);

        // Finish processing
    }
}

?>
```

Checking for Errors Using Exceptions

Next, you need to check whether there an error occurred during the upload. When you're dealing with files uploaded through an HTML form, you have access to a special constant called UPLOAD_ERR_OK that tells you whether a file uploaded successfully.

Before you try to process the file, you need to make sure that your $err value is equivalent to UPLOAD_ERR_OK. Add the following code in bold to images.inc.php:

```php
<?php

class ImageHandler
{
    // The folder in which to save images
    public $save_dir;

    // Sets the $save_dir on instantiation
    public function __construct($save_dir)
    {
        $this->save_dir = $save_dir;
    }

    /**
     * Resizes/resamples an image uploaded via a web form
     *
     * @param array $upload the array contained in $_FILES
     * @return string the path to the resized uploaded file
     */
    public function processUploadedImage($file)
    {
        // Separate the uploaded file array
        list($name, $type, $tmp, $err, $size) = array_values($file);

        // If an error occurred, throw an exception
        if($err != UPLOAD_ERR_OK) {
            throw new Exception('An error occurred with the upload!');
            return;
        }

        // Finish processing
    }
}

?>
```

Note the use of the throw new Exception() line. This is a special form of error handling available in object-oriented scripts. Exceptions give you the ability to catch errors in your scripts without displaying ugly error messages to your end user.

In its simplest form, an exception can return a custom error message to your user in the event of an error. The preceding script takes this approach. Passing a string as an argument to the exception lets you define a custom error message; I'll cover how you handle Exceptions in a moment.

Saving the File

So far you can determine whether your file was uploaded without error; the next step is to save an uploaded file to your file system. Begin by assigning a path and filename to save. For now, you can use the original name of the file, which you can grab from $save_dir of the instantiated object. This is the path that displays the image.

However, you still don't have enough information to save your file. Specifically, your site isn't stored at the web root, so you need to get the root path of your site to generate an absolute path, which you can use to save the file. Fortunately, the $_SERVER superglobal stores the document root path for you, so all you need to do is include its value to save the image.

You can establish your paths by adding the code in bold to images.inc.php:

```php
<?php

class ImageHandler
{
    // The folder in which to save images
    public $save_dir;

    // Sets the $save_dir on instantiation
    public function __construct($save_dir)
    {
        $this->save_dir = $save_dir;
    }

    /**
     * Resizes/resamples an image uploaded via a web form
     *
     * @param array $upload the array contained in $_FILES
     * @return string the path to the resized uploaded file
     */
    public function processUploadedImage($file)
    {
        // Separate the uploaded file array
        list($name, $type, $tmp, $err, $size) = array_values($file);

        // If an error occurred, throw an exception
        if($err != UPLOAD_ERR_OK) {
            throw new Exception('An error occurred with the upload!');
            exit;
        }

        // Create the full path to the image for saving
        $filepath = $this->save_dir . $name;
```

```php
        // Store the absolute path to move the image
        $absolute = $_SERVER['DOCUMENT_ROOT'] . $filepath;

        // Finish processing
    }
}

?>
```

For example, if your $filepath is simple_blog/images/IMG001.jpg, your $absolute value might be /Applications/XAMPP/xamppfiles/htdocs/simple_blog/images/IMG001.jpg.

Now that you have your paths on hand, you can save your image to the file system. Do this using the move_uploaded file() function, which accepts two arguments: the temporary location of an uploaded file and the location where that file should be saved permanently.

You can save your image by adding the following code in bold to images.inc.php:

```php
<?php

class ImageHandler
{
    // The folder in which to save images
    public $save_dir;

    // Sets the $save_dir on instantiation
    public function __construct($save_dir)
    {
        $this->save_dir = $save_dir;
    }

    /**
     * Resizes/resamples an image uploaded via a web form
     *
     * @param array $upload the array contained in $_FILES
     * @return string the path to the resized uploaded file
     */
    public function processUploadedImage($file)
    {
        // Separate the uploaded file array
        list($name, $type, $tmp, $err, $size) = array_values($file);

        // If an error occurred, throw an exception
        if($err != UPLOAD_ERR_OK) {
            throw new Exception('An error occurred with the upload!');
            exit;
        }
```

```php
        // Create the full path to the image for saving
        $filepath = $this->save_dir . '/' . $name;

        // Store the absolute path to move the image
        $absolute = $_SERVER['DOCUMENT_ROOT'] . $filepath;

        // Save the image
        if(!move_uploaded_file($tmp, $absolute))
        {
            throw new Exception("Couldn't save the uploaded file!");
        }

        return $filepath;
    }
}

?>
```

At this point, you're ready to try out your class!

Modifying update.inc.php to Save Images

You've put your class together; next, you need to instantiate it in update.inc.php and feed it your uploaded image.

You can do this by opening update.inc.php and modifying it so it contains the lines in bold:

```php
<?php

// Include the functions so you can create a URL
include_once 'functions.inc.php';

// Include the image handling class
include_once 'images.inc.php';

if($_SERVER['REQUEST_METHOD']=='POST'
    && $_POST['submit']=='Save Entry'
    && !empty($_POST['page'])
    && !empty($_POST['title'])
    && !empty($_POST['entry']))
{
    // Create a URL to save in the database
    $url = makeUrl($_POST['title']);
```

```php
if(isset($_FILES['image']['tmp_name']))
{
    try
    {
        // Instantiate the class and set a save path
        $img = new ImageHandler("/simple_blog");

        // Process the file and store the returned path
        $img_path = $img->processUploadedImage($_FILES['image']);

        // Output the uploaded image as it was saved
        echo '<img src="', $img_path, '" /><br />';
    }
    catch(Exception $e)
    {
        // If an error occurred, output your custom error message
        die($e->getMessage());
    }
}
else
{
    // Avoids a notice if no image was uploaded
    $img_path = NULL;
}

// Outputs the saved image path
echo "Image Path: ", $img_path, "<br />";
exit; // Stops execution before saving the entry

// Include database credentials and connect to the database
include_once 'db.inc.php';
$db = new PDO(DB_INFO, DB_USER, DB_PASS);
```

The most important task this code accomplishes is to make your ImageHandler class available by including images.inc.php. Next, you need to check whether an image was uploaded, which you accomplish by making sure the temporary file exists.

Using try...catch with Exceptions

Your next task introduces a new construct: the try...catch statement. You use this construct with exceptions to handle errors gracefully. Essentially it says: "Run this snippet of code. If an exception is thrown, catch it and perform the following snippet."

In your image handling snippet, you place your object instantiation and processing within a `try` block. Doing so ensures that you can output the custom error message by grabbing the message within the catch block if any of the custom errors you define within the class are thrown.

Inside your `try` block, you instantiate the ImageHandler object and pass "/simple_blog" as its argument, which sets the `$save_dir` property. Next, you call `processUploadedImage()` and pass the uploaded file as its argument. `processUploadedImage()` returns the file's path, so you store that in a variable called `$img_path`, which you use (for now) to output the image for viewing via an `<img>` HTML tag.

Finally, you output the image path as plain text and exit the script to prevent your test entries from being saved to the database.

You can test your class by uploading an image. Navigate to your admin form in a browser and fill out the form with test data (you don't save this), then select a file to upload. When you press the Save Entry button, you should see your image displayed, along with its path (see Figure 8-2).

*Figure 8-2. An image uploaded by your **ImageHandler** class*

If you look at your `simple_blog` folder in the file system, you'll see that the image has been saved (see Figure 8-3).

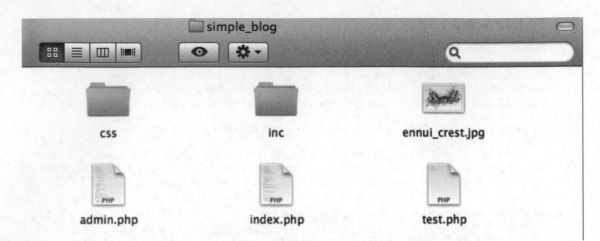

Figure 8-3. *The uploaded image saved in the* **simple_blog** *folder*

This isn't necessarily bad, but it does cause clutter in your folder. You can clear this up by creating a new folder to store images in.

Creating a New Folder

You could simply create the folder manually, but it's better to use PHP to check whether a folder exists, then create it if it doesn't. This way, you have to change only the path if the folder you wish to save images in changes in the future; the alternative is to go in and manipulate the file system directly.

You can make a new folder by creating a new method in your ImageHandler class called checkSaveDir() that creates a directory if it doesn't exist already.

Begin by declaring your method in ImageHandler. This method is private, so you want to make sure you control its use. In images.inc.php, after processUploadedImage(), define your new method by adding the code in bold:

```php
<?php

class ImageHandler
{
    public $save_dir;

    public function __construct($save_dir)
    {
        $this->save_dir = $save_dir;
    }
```

```php
/**
 * Resizes/resamples an image uploaded via a web form
 *
 * @param array $upload the array contained in $_FILES
 * @return string the path to the resized uploaded file
 */
public function processUploadedImage($file, $rename=TRUE)
{
    // Separate the uploaded file array
    list($name, $type, $tmp, $err, $size) = array_values($file);

    // If an error occurred, throw an exception
    if($err != UPLOAD_ERR_OK) {
        throw new Exception('An error occurred with the upload!');
        exit;
    }

    // Create the full path to the image for saving
    $filepath = $this->save_dir . $name;

    // Store the absolute path to move the image
    $absolute = $_SERVER['DOCUMENT_ROOT'] . $filepath;

    // Save the image
    if(!move_uploaded_file($tmp, $absolute))
    {
        throw new Exception("Couldn't save the uploaded file!");
    }

    return $filepath;
}

/**
 * Ensures that the save directory exists
 *
 * Checks for the existence of the supplied save directory,
 * and creates the directory if it doesn't exist. Creation is
 * recursive.
 *
 * @param void
 * @return void
 */
```

```
    private function checkSaveDir()
    {
        // Check for the dir
    }

}

?>
```

You've declared your method. Next you need to figure out which path to check. As with processUploadedImage(), you use the $_SERVER superglobal and your $save_dir property to create your path to check. The only difference is that you don't attach a file name this time.

Add the lines in bold to checkSaveDir() to store your path to check:

```
/**
 * Ensures that the save directory exists
 *
 * Checks for the existence of the supplied save directory,
 * and creates the directory if it doesn't exist. Creation is
 * recursive.
 *
 * @param void
 * @return void
 */
private function checkSaveDir()
{
    // Determines the path to check
    $path = $_SERVER['DOCUMENT_ROOT'] . $this->save_dir;

    // Check for the dir
}
```

Next, you need to see whether the $path you've stored exists. PHP provides a function to do exactly this in is_dir(). If the path exists, is_dir() returns TRUE; otherwise, it returns FALSE. You want to continue processing only if the directory doesn't exist, so add a check to see whether is_dir() returns FALSE before continuing. Insert the lines in bold into checkSaveDir():

```
/**
 * Ensures that the save directory exists
 *
 * Checks for the existence of the supplied save directory,
 * and creates the directory if it doesn't exist. Creation is
 * recursive.
 *
 * @param void
 * @return void
 */
private function checkSaveDir()
{
    // Determines the path to check
    $path = $_SERVER['DOCUMENT_ROOT'] . $this->save_dir;

    // Checks if the directory exists
    if(!is_dir($path))
    {
        // Create the directory
    }
}
```

If the directory doesn't exist, you need to create it. You accomplished in PHP with the mkdir() function, which translates in plain English to *make directory*. You need to pass three arguments to mkdir() for it to work properly: the path, the mode, and a value that indicates whether directories should be created recursively.

The first argument, the path, is what you just created and stored in the $path variable.

The second argument, the mode, describes how to set the folder permissions. The default mode is 0777, which provides the widest possible access. Your image files are not sensitive, so you display them to any user viewing your page.

■**Note** For more information on file permissions, check the PHP manual entry on chmod()at http://php.net/chmod. Basically, you set folder permissions using an octal number, where each number represents who can access the file (owner, owner's group, and everyone else). Each number represents a level of permission, with 7 being the highest (read, write, and execute).

Your third argument is a boolean value that tells the function whether directories should be created recursively. Only one directory at a time can be created when set to FALSE (the default). This means you need to call mkdir() twice if you want to add two subdirectories to the simple_blog folder with the path, simple_blog/images/uploads/. If you set the third argument to TRUE, however, you can create both directories with a single function call.

You need to control access to this method, so you allow the function to create directories recursively.

231

You can create the directory in the simple_blog folder by adding the lines in bold to checkSaveDir():

```
/**
 * Ensures that the save directory exists
 *
 * Checks for the existence of the supplied save directory,
 * and creates the directory if it doesn't exist. Creation is
 * recursive.
 *
 * @param void
 * @return void
 */
private function checkSaveDir()
{
    // Determines the path to check
    $path = $_SERVER['DOCUMENT_ROOT'] . $this->save_dir;

    // Checks if the directory exists
    if(!is_dir($path))
    {
        // Creates the directory
        if(!mkdir($path, 0777, TRUE))
        {
            // On failure, throws an error
            throw new Exception("Can't create the directory!");
        }
    }
}
```

This code includes a provision to throw an exception if mkdir() returns FALSE, which means it failed. Your method is finally ready. You want to call it from the processUploadedImage() method before you attempt to move the uploaded file. Implement this by adding the lines in bold lines to processUploadedImage():

```
/**
 * Resizes/resamples an image uploaded via a web form
 *
 * @param array $upload the array contained in $_FILES
 * @return string the path to the resized uploaded file
 */
public function processUploadedImage($file)
{
    // Separate the uploaded file array
    list($name, $type, $tmp, $err, $size) = array_values($file);
```

```
        // If an error occurred, throw an exception
        if($err != UPLOAD_ERR_OK) {
            throw new Exception('An error occurred with the upload!');
            exit;
        }

        // Check that the directory exists
        $this->checkSaveDir();

        // Create the full path to the image for saving
        $filepath = $this->save_dir . $name;

        // Store the absolute path to move the image
        $absolute = $_SERVER['DOCUMENT_ROOT'] . $filepath;

        // Save the image
        if(!move_uploaded_file($tmp, $absolute))
        {
            throw new Exception("Couldn't save the uploaded file!");
        }

        return $filepath;
    }
```

It's time to test your new function. In update.inc.php, modify your object instantiation to use this path as the $save_dir: /simple_blog/images/.

Your code should look like this:

```php
<?php

// Include the functions so you can create a URL
include_once 'functions.inc.php';

// Include the image handling class
include_once 'images.inc.php';

if($_SERVER['REQUEST_METHOD']=='POST'
    && $_POST['submit']=='Save Entry'
    && !empty($_POST['page'])
    && !empty($_POST['title'])
    && !empty($_POST['entry']))
{
    // Create a URL to save in the database
    $url = makeUrl($_POST['title']);
```

```php
if(isset($_FILES['image']['tmp_name']))
{
    try
    {
        // Instantiate the class and set a save path
        $img = new ImageHandler("/simple_blog/images/");

        // Process the file and store the returned path
        $img_path = $img->processUploadedImage($_FILES['image']);

        // Output the uploaded image as it was saved
        echo '<img src="', $img_path, '" /><br />';
    }
    catch(Exception $e)
    {
        // If an error occurred, output your custom error message
        die($e->getMessage());
    }
}
else
{
    // Avoids a notice if no image was uploaded
    $img_path = NULL;
}

// Outputs the saved image path
echo "Image Path: ", $img_path, "<br />";
exit; // Stops execution before saving the entry

// Include database credentials and connect to the database
include_once 'db.inc.php';
$db = new PDO(DB_INFO, DB_USER, DB_PASS);
```

Save update.inc.php and navigate to your admin form in a browser, then fill out the form and submit an image. After you click the Save Entry button, you should see the image you uploaded previously, as well as its path; your script places the image in the newly created images folder (see Figure 8-4).

Figure 8-4. *The image uploaded shows that it's been stored in the new images folder.*

You can check the file system manually to see your new folder and the saved, uploaded image (see Figure 8-5).

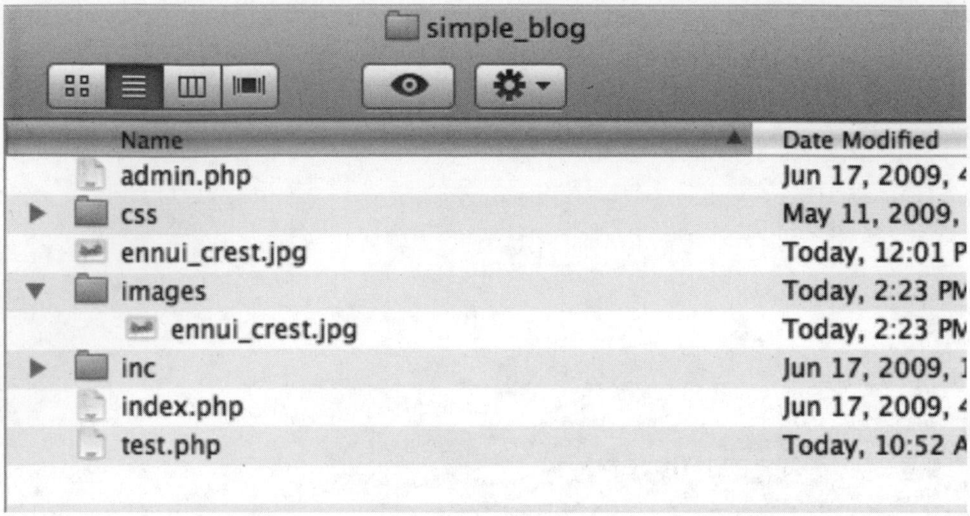

Figure 8-5. The images folder has been created, and the image has been saved in it.

You're almost ready to start working with the database. First, however, you need to make sure that your images have unique names, so you don't accidentally overwrite older uploads with new ones.

Renaming the Image

You can't trust that every file uploaded to your blog will be uniquely named, so you need to rename any image that is uploaded to your blog. Otherwise, it's possible for a user who uploads an image named to overwrite that image later if he submits a future image with the same name. In this case, the new image would suddenly appear for the older entry, as well as the new one, and you would lose the old image.

You can avoid this by creating a new private method in ImageHandler that generates a new, unique name for any uploaded image. You can make sure this name is unique by using the current timestamp and a random four-digit number between 1000 and 9999. This way, even images uploaded during the same second will receive unique names.

■**Note** This method is not 100% effective, but the likelihood of two images being uploaded at the exact same second and generating the exact same random number is so slim that it will most likely never be a problem.

This method is a one-liner that accepts one argument: the file extension you want to use (we'll get to how you know what file extension to send in just a moment). The method returns the current timestamp, an underscore, a random number, and a file extension.

It's time to add your method to `ImageHandler` by inserting the code in boldafter `processUploadedImage()` in `images.inc.php`:

```
/**
 * Generates a unique name for a file
 *
 * Uses the current timestamp and a randomly generated number
 * to create a unique name to be used for an uploaded file.
 * This helps prevent a new file upload from overwriting an
 * existing file with the same name.
 *
 * @param string $ext the file extension for the upload
 * @return string the new filename
 */
private function renameFile($ext)
{
    /*
     * Returns the current timestamp and a random number
     * to avoid duplicate filenames
     */
    return time() . '_' . mt_rand(1000,9999) . $ext;
}
```

Determining the File Extension

Before `renameFile()` can work, you need to figure out the uploaded image's extension. Do this by accessing the image's type with the value stored in `$type` in `processUploadedImage()`.

All uploaded files have a content type, which you can use to determine the proper file extension to use. You need to make sure you're processing only images, so you use a switch and match the known content types you want to accept, then set a default action to throw an error if an unexpected content type is passed.

The content types you want to accept are:

- `image/gif`: A GIF image (`.gif`)

- `image/jpeg`: A JPEG image (`.jpg`)

- `image/pjpeg`: A JPEG image as it is recognized by certain browsers, which uses the same file extension as a "normal" JPEG (`.jpg`)

- `image/png`: A PNG image (`.png`)

To check for content types, you create a new private method called `getImageExtension()`. This method contains the switch just discussed and returns the proper file extension. Add the following code in bold to `images.inc.php` just after `renameFile()`:

237

```
/**
 * Determines the filetype and extension of an image
 *
 * @param string $type the MIME type of the image
 * @return string the extension to be used with the file
 */
private function getImageExtension($type)
{
    switch($type) {
        case 'image/gif':
            return '.gif';

        case 'image/jpeg':
        case 'image/pjpeg':
            return '.jpg';

        case 'image/png':
            return '.png';

        default:
            throw new Exception('File type is not recognized!');
    }
}
```

Now you can retrieve the file extension to pass to renameFile(), which means you're ready to implement the methods in processUploadedImage().

There might be a point at which you no longer wish to rename files, so you should add an argument to processUploadedImage() that holds a boolean value. If set to TRUE (the default), the image is renamed; if set to FALSE, the original filename is used.

You can add file renaming to your method by adding the following code in bold to processUploadedImage():

```
/**
 * Resizes/resamples an image uploaded via a web form
 *
 * @param array $upload the array contained in $_FILES
 * @param bool $rename whether or not the image should be renamed
 * @return string the path to the resized uploaded file
 */
public function processUploadedImage($file, $rename=TRUE)
{
    // Separate the uploaded file array
    list($name, $type, $tmp, $err, $size) = array_values($file);
```

```php
        // If an error occurred, throw an exception
        if($err != UPLOAD_ERR_OK) {
            throw new Exception('An error occurred with the upload!');
            exit;
        }

        // Check that the directory exists
        $this->checkSaveDir();

        // Rename the file if the flag is set to TRUE
        if($rename===TRUE) {
            // Retrieve information about the image
            $img_ext = $this->getImageExtension($type);

            $name = $this->renameFile($img_ext);
        }

        // Create the full path to the image for saving
        $filepath = $this->save_dir . $name;

        // Store the absolute path to move the image
        $absolute = $_SERVER['DOCUMENT_ROOT'] . $filepath;

        // Save the image
        if(!move_uploaded_file($tmp, $absolute))
        {
            throw new Exception("Couldn't save the uploaded file!");
        }

        return $filepath;
    }
```

Save images.inc.php and try uploading another image through the admin form. You should see a renamed file stored in the file system, as well as on your screen (see Figure 8-6).

Figure 8-6. *An image renamed by your script*

Your ImageHandler class now accepts, renames, and stores images in your file system, which means you're ready to start working with the database.

Storing and Retrieving Images from the Database

If you need to, you can store the image itself in the database as a BLOB column. However, it's much more efficient to save the path to the image in the database instead. This means you need to do three things to save an image:

- Add an image column to the entries table
- Modify update.inc.php to save the image path along with the rest of the entry
- Modify retrieveEntries() to select the new image column

Modifying the entries Table

Your next step is to add the image column to your entries table. You do this the same way that you added all the other columns to your table.

Navigate to http://localhost/phpmyadmin, open the simple_blog database, select the entries table, and open the SQL tab. Insert the following command to add the image column:

```
ALTER TABLE entries
ADD image VARCHAR(150) DEFAULT NULL
AFTER title
```

This creates an image column after the title column, which stores a 150-character string and defaults to NULL if no value is supplied.

Modifying update.inc.php to Save Images

Now that your entries table can store the image path, it's time to modify update.inc.php to save the image path.

You've already done everything necessary to make the image path available. All you need to do is remove the sections of code that output the image and exit the script.

After the code no longer outputs image data, you need to modify your queries to include the image path. You do this for both new entries and updated entries.

You can save the image path in the database by modifying update.inc.php to reflect the changes shown in bold:

```php
<?php

// Include the functions so you can create a URL
include_once 'functions.inc.php';

// Include the image handling class
include_once 'images.inc.php';

if($_SERVER['REQUEST_METHOD']=='POST'
    && $_POST['submit']=='Save Entry'
    && !empty($_POST['page'])
    && !empty($_POST['title'])
    && !empty($_POST['entry']))
```

```php
{
    // Create a URL to save in the database
    $url = makeUrl($_POST['title']);

    if(isset($_FILES['image']['tmp_name']))
    {
        try
        {
            // Instantiate the class and set a save dir
            $img = new ImageHandler("/simple_blog/images/");

            // Process the uploaded image and save the returned path
            $img_path = $img->processUploadedImage($_FILES['image']);
        }
        catch(Exception $e)
        {
            // If an error occurred, output your custom error message
            die($e->getMessage());
        }
    }
    else
    {
        // Avoids a notice if no image was uploaded
        $img_path = NULL;
    }

    // Include database credentials and connect to the database
    include_once 'db.inc.php';
    $db = new PDO(DB_INFO, DB_USER, DB_PASS);

    // Edit an existing entry
    if(!empty($_POST['id']))
    {
        $sql = "UPDATE entries
                SET title=?, image=?, entry=?, url=?
                WHERE id=?
                LIMIT 1";
```

```php
    $stmt = $db->prepare($sql);
    $stmt->execute(
        array(
            $_POST['title'],
            $img_path,
            $_POST['entry'],
            $url,
            $_POST['id']
        )
    );
    $stmt->closeCursor();
}

// Create a new entry
else
{
    // Save the entry into the database
    $sql = "INSERT INTO entries (page, title, image, entry, url)
            VALUES (?, ?, ?, ?, ?)";
    $stmt = $db->prepare($sql);
    $stmt->execute(
        array(
            $_POST['page'],
            $_POST['title'],
            $img_path,
            $_POST['entry'],
            $url
        )
    );
    $stmt->closeCursor();
}

// Sanitize the page information for use in the success URL
$page = htmlentities(strip_tags($_POST['page']));

// Send the user to the new entry
header('Location: /simple_blog/'.$page.'/'.$url);
exit;
}
```

```
else
{
    header('Location: ../');
    exit;
}

?>
```

At this point, you're ready to create a new entry with an image. Navigate to your admin form in a browser and create an entry with the following information:

- *Title*: Entry with an image

- *Body*: This entry is created with an accompanying image

Add an image, then click Save Entry. If you look in the database, you should see that an image path has been saved in the image column.

Now you need to retrieve the path from the database to display uploaded images with the entry.

Modifying retrieveEntries() to Retrieve Images

Your first step in displaying saved images is to add the image column to the array returned from retrieveEntries(). This is easy to do; it requires only that you add the column name to the SQL query.

Modify retrieveEntries() in functions.inc.php to reflect the changes shown in bold:

```
function retrieveEntries($db, $page, $url=NULL)
{
    /*
     * If an entry URL was supplied, load the associated entry
     */
    if(isset($url))
    {
        $sql = "SELECT id, page, title, image, entry
                FROM entries
                WHERE url=?
                LIMIT 1";
        $stmt = $db->prepare($sql);
        $stmt->execute(array($url));

        // Save the returned entry array
        $e = $stmt->fetch();

        // Set the fulldisp flag for a single entry
        $fulldisp = 1;
    }
```

```
/*
 * If no entry ID was supplied, load all entry titles for the page
 */
else
{
    $sql = "SELECT id, page, title, image, entry, url
            FROM entries
            WHERE page=?
            ORDER BY created DESC";
    $stmt = $db->prepare($sql);
    $stmt->execute(array($page));

    $e = NULL; // Declare the variable to avoid errors

    // Loop through returned results and store as an array
    while($row = $stmt->fetch()) {
        if($page=='blog')
        {
            $e[] = $row;
            $fulldisp = 0;
        }
        else
        {
            $e = $row;
            $fulldisp = 1;
        }
    }

    /*
     * If no entries were returned, display a default
     * message and set the fulldisp flag to display a
     * single entry
     */
    if(!is_array($e))
    {
        $fulldisp = 1;
        $e = array(
            'title' => 'No Entries Yet',
            'entry' => 'This page does not have an entry yet!'
        );
    }
}
```

```
    // Add the $fulldisp flag to the end of the array
    array_push($e, $fulldisp);

    return $e;
}
```

Now you can access the value stored in the image column, just as you access all the other information in an entry. Next, you need to use this information to display the image for the world to see.

Modifying index.php to Display Images

Unlike text entries, images require a little bit of special treatment when you retrieve them from the database. You can't simply check whether the value is set, then output it; instead, you need to create some extra HTML markup to display images properly.

For the sake of keeping your code clean, you need to write a function that checks whether an image exists and return the appropriate HTML markup if it does.

Adding a Function to Format Images for Output

You add this function to functions.inc.php. The function accepts two arguments: the path to the image and the title of the entry (you use this as an alt attribute).

Its functionality is simple: if an image path is supplied, return valid HTML markup; if not, return NULL.

Open functions.inc.php and add the new function after the existing functions:

```
function formatImage($img=NULL, $alt=NULL)
    {
    if(isset($img))
    {
        return '<img src="'.$img.'" alt="'.$alt.'" />';
    }
    else
        {
        return NULL;
    }
}
```

With your new function in place, you can add your image to the displayed entry. For the sake of organization, you display images only with a fully displayed entry.

246

Your image handling is taken care of in an external function, so you can add your image to the display with just two lines of code. In index.php, where the block of code that handles full display is located, modify the script to contain the lines in bold:

```php
<?php

// If the full display flag is set, show the entry
if($fulldisp==1)
{

    // Get the URL if one wasn't passed
    $url = (isset($url)) ? $url : $e['url'];

    // Build the admin links
    $admin = adminLinks($page, $url);

    // Format the image if one exists
    $img = formatImage($e['image'], $e['title']);

?>

        <h2> <?php echo $e['title'] ?> </h2>
        <p> <?php echo $img, $e['entry'] ?> </p>
        <p>
            <?php echo $admin['edit'] ?>
            <?php if($page=='blog') echo $admin['delete'] ?>
        </p>
        <?php if($page=='blog'): ?>
        <p class="backlink">
            <a href="./">Back to Latest Entries</a>
        </p>
        <?php endif; ?>
```

If you navigate to http://localhost/simple_blog/ and select your new entry, "Entry with an Image"; you should see the image displayed with your text (see Figure 8-7).

Unfortunately, the layout doesn't look very good if a large image is displayed (as shown in Figure 8-7). You don't want to resize every image uploaded manually, so you need to add new functionality to your ImageHandler class that resizes large images automatically.

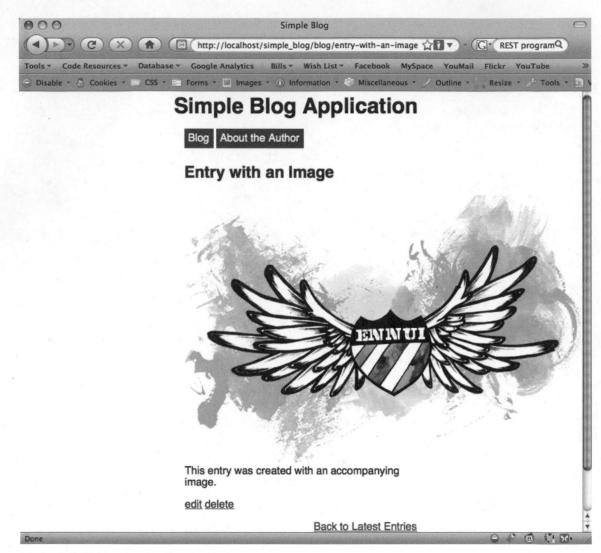

Figure 8-7. Your image displayed with the accompanying text

Resizing Images

Resizing images is a little tricky, but you can break the process down into small sections. Resizing an image requires several steps:

- Determine new dimensions based on the defined maximum dimensions
- Determine which image handling functions are necessary for resampling
- Resample the image at the proper size

Determining the New Image Dimensions

Begin the process of resizing an image by determining what size the image should actually be. Unfortunately, you can't simply tell your script that all images should be 350 pixels by 240 pixels because forcing an image to match dimensions that aren't proportional to an image's original dimensions causes distortion, which doesn't look good.

Instead, you need to determine the proportional size of the image that will fit *within* the maximum dimensions you set. You can accomplish this following several math steps:

- Determine which side of the image is the longer
- Divide the maximum dimension that corresponds to the long side by the long side's size
- Use the resulting decimal point to multiply both sides of the image
- Round the product to keep an integer value
- Use the product of this multiplication as the new width and height of the image

Adding a Property for Maximum Dimensions

Before you can start performing any resizing, you need to define maximum dimensions for uploaded images. This might need to change at some future point, so you define a new property in the ImageHandler class, called $max_dims. This property stores an array of the maximum width and height allowed for uploaded images.

You set this property in the constructor, but be aware that you need to use a default value so that it doesn't *need* to be set for the class to work.

At the top of the ImageHandler class, modify the property declarations and constructor as shown by the code in bold:

```
class ImageHandler
{
    public $save_dir;
    public $max_dims;

    public function __construct($save_dir, $max_dims=array(350, 240))
    {
        $this->save_dir = $save_dir;
        $this->max_dims = $max_dims;
    }
```

The maximum dimensions of 350 pixels by 240 pixels are acceptable for the layout of your current site. These are the default values, so don't worry about adding maximum dimensions to the class instantiation. However, if you needed to change the size of your images, you can change the dimensions using the following instantiation of ImageHandler:

```
$obj = new ImageHandler('/images/', array(400, 300));
```

This snippet sets the maximum dimensions allowed to 400 pixels wide by 300 pixels high.

Creating the Method to Determine New Width and Height

You have your maximum dimensions prepared; next, you need to define a new private method in the ImageHandler class. Place this method at the bottom of the class and accept one argument: the image for which you need new dimensions.

In images.inc.php, add the following method declaration:

```
/**
 * Determines new dimensions for an image
 *
 * @param string $img the path to the upload
 * @return array the new and original image dimensions
 */
private function getNewDims($img)
{
    // Get new image dimensions
}
```

You can determine the original dimensions of your image with a function called getimagesize().This function returns the width and height of the image supplied as an argument (as well as other information I'll address in a moment).

You use the list() function to define the first two array elements as the $src_w (source width) and $src_h (source height) variables.

Next, you use the maximum dimensions that you just added to the class. Again, use the list() function to separate their values into $max_w (maximum width) and $max_h (maximum height), then add the following code in bold to getNewDims():

```
/**
 * Determines new dimensions for an image
 *
 * @param string $img the path to the upload
 * @return array the new and original image dimensions
 */
private function getNewDims($img)
{
    // Assemble the necessary variables for processing
    list($src_w, $src_h) = getimagesize($img);
    list($max_w, $max_h) = $this->max_dims;

    // Finish processing
}
```

Before you start resizing your image, you need to check that it is, in fact, larger than your maximum dimensions. Otherwise, small images will be blown up, which can make them look bad. You accomplish this by checking whether either the original image's width or height is greater than the maximum corresponding dimension.

If so, you need to determine the scale to which you should resize the image. You can determine this by dividing the maximum length of both sides by the original length and returning the smaller of the two values using the min() function, which compares two or more expressions and returns the lowest value.

After you know what side is longer, you use the corresponding maximum dimension to determine the scale. You determine the scale by dividing the smaller maximum dimension by the original dimension, which gives you a decimal value (for instance, if your maximum size is 60 pixels, and the original size is 100 pixels, the scale is .6).

In the event that your image is smaller than the maximum allowed dimensions, you want to keep it the same size. Do this by setting the scale to 1.

Add the code in bold to getNewDims() to determine the scale:

```
/**
 * Determines new dimensions for an image
 *
 * @param string $img the path to the upload
 * @return array the new and original image dimensions
 */
private function getNewDims($img)
{
    // Assemble the necessary variables for processing
    list($src_w, $src_h) = getimagesize($img);
    list($max_w, $max_h) = $this->max_dims;

    // Check that the image is bigger than the maximum dimensions
    if($src_w > $max_w || $src_h > $max_h)
    {
        // Determine the scale to which the image will be resized
        $s = min($max_w/$src_w,$max_h/$src_h);
    }
    else
    {
        /*
         * If the image is smaller than the max dimensions, keep
         * its dimensions by multiplying by 1
         */
        $s = 1;
    }

    // Finish processing
}
```

Finally, you need to multiply the original dimensions by the scale you've just determined, then return the new dimensions (as well as the old dimensions for reasons I'll cover momentarily) as an array.

To accomplish this, insert the lines bold into getNewDims():

```
/**
 * Determines new dimensions for an image
 *
 * @param string $img the path to the upload
 * @return array the new and original image dimensions
 */
private function getNewDims($img)
{
    // Assemble the necessary variables for processing
    list($src_w, $src_h) = getimagesize($img);
    list($max_w, $max_h) = $this->max_dims;

    // Check that the image is bigger than the maximum dimensions
    if($src_w > $max_w || $src_h > $src_h)
    {
        // Determine the scale to which the image will be resized
        $s = min($max_w/$src_w,$max_h/$src_h);
    }
    else
    {
        /*
         * If the image is smaller than the max dimensions, keep
         * its dimensions by multiplying by 1
         */
        $s = 1;
    }

    // Get the new dimensions
    $new_w = round($src_w * $s);
    $new_h = round($src_h * $s);

    // Return the new dimensions
    return array($new_w, $new_h, $src_w, $src_h);
}
```

Determining Which Image Functions to Use

You use two functions when resampling your images: one to create an image resource and one to save your resampled image in a format of your choosing.

Your blog accepts three types of image files (JPEG, GIF, and PNG),, and each of these image types requires an individual set of functions to create and save images. Specifically, you use imagecreatefromjpeg(), imagecreatefromgif(), or imagecreatefrompng() to create the images, depending on the named file type.

Similarly, you save the images using imagejpeg(), imagegif(), or imagepng()—again, depending on the appropriate file type.

You want to eliminate redundant code, so you need to write a method that checks what type of image you're using and returns the names of the functions you should use with the uploaded image.

Call this private method getImageFunctions(); you will use it to return an array containing the names of the functions for creating and saving your images, which you determine with a switch statement.

Your original $type variable is out of the scope for this method, so use the getimagesize() function again. However, this time you need to access the array element that holds the image's MIME type, which you access using the mime array key.

In images.inc.php, declare the getImageFunctions() method and store the output of getimagesize(). Next, pass the MIME type to a switch statement that returns the proper array of function names. You accomplish all of this by adding the following method at the bottom of the ImageHandler class:

```
/**
 * Determines how to process images
 *
 * Uses the MIME type of the provided image to determine
 * what image handling functions should be used. This
 * increases the perfomance of the script versus using
 * imagecreatefromstring().
 *
 * @param string $img the path to the upload
 * @return array the image type-specific functions
 */
private function getImageFunctions($img)
{
    $info = getimagesize($img);

    switch($info['mime'])
    {
        case 'image/jpeg':
        case 'image/pjpeg':
            return array('imagecreatefromjpeg', 'imagejpeg');
            break;
        case 'image/gif':
            return array('imagecreatefromgif', 'imagegif');
            break;
        case 'image/png':
            return array('imagecreatefrompng', 'imagepng');
            break;
        default:
            return FALSE;
            break;
    }
}
```

Now you're able to get functions specific to the image type quickly; I'll cover how you use these in a moment.

Resampling the Image at the Proper Size

Finally, you're ready to resample the image. You do this inside a new private method called doImageResize(), which accepts one argument: the image to be resampled.

This method performs its magic in five steps:

- It determines the new dimensions for the image

- It determines the functions needed to resample the image

- It creates image resources to use in the resampling

- It resamples the image at the proper size

- It saves the resampled image

The first two steps are already done; you simply need to call the getNewDims() and getImageFunctions() methods you defined previously.

Begin by defining your method in ImageHandler and calling your methods. Add the following to images.inc.php in the ImageHandler class:

```
/**
 * Generates a resampled and resized image
 *
 * Creates and saves a new image based on the new dimensions
 * and image type-specific functions determined by other
 * class methods.
 *
 * @param array $img the path to the upload
 * @return void
 */
private function doImageResize($img)
{
    // Determine the new dimensions
    $d = $this->getNewDims($img);

    // Determine what functions to use
    $funcs = $this->getImageFunctions($img);

    // Finish resampling
}
```

Next you need to create the image resources that PHP uses to deal with images. For your resampling, you need to create two resources. The first is the original image, which you save as a resource using the first of your two functions specific to the image type. The second is a new, blank image resource, which you copy the resampled image into. You create the second image resource with a different function called imagecreatetruecolor(); this function accepts two arguments: the width and height of the new image resource you want to create.

To create your image resources, add the lines in bold to doImageResize():

```
/**
 * Generates a resampled and resized image
 *
 * Creates and saves a new image based on the new dimensions
 * and image type-specific functions determined by other
 * class methods.
 *
 * @param array $img the path to the upload
 * @return void
 */
private function doImageResize($img)
{
    // Determine the new dimensions
    $d = $this->getNewDims($tmp);

    // Determine what functions to use
    $funcs = $this->getImageFunctions($img);

    // Create the image resources for resampling
    $src_img = $funcs[0]($img);
    $new_img = imagecreatetruecolor($d[0], $d[1]);

    // Finish resampling
}
```

Note that you're calling your image type-specific function with the snippet, $funcs[0]($img). This is a trick available to developers for instances just like this one, where the function you want to call varies based on the current data being handled.

So far you have your image resources; next, you can copy the original image into the new image resource using the complicated-looking imagecopyresampled() function, which accepts a whopping *ten* arguments:

- $dst_image: This is the destination image that serves as your new image resource ($new_img).

- $src_image: This is the source image that you copy your new image from ($src_img).

- $dst_x: This is the offset from the new image's left-hand side; you use this to start inserting the source image. This value is usually 0, but if you overlay something like a watermark, you might need to insert the source image in the bottom-right corner, which would require a different value.

- $dst_y: The is the offset from the new image's top; you use this to start inserting the source image.

- $src_x: This is the offset from the source image's left-hand side; you use this to start copying image data. This value is usually 0, but this value can vary if you're cropping an image.

- $src_y: This is the offset from the top of the source image; you use this to start copying the source image.

- $dst_w: This argument specifies thewidth at which you should insert the copied image. You use the new width value stored at $d[0].

- $dst_h: This argument specifies the height at which you insert the copied image. You use the new height value stored at $d[1].

- $src_w: This argument describes the distance from the starting point to copy horizontally. Usually, this value matches the original size of the image, but this value can shorter than the original width if your image is cropped. You use the original width value stored at $d[2].

- $src_h: This argument describes the distance from the starting point to copy vertically. You use the original height value stored at $d[3].

You need to check whether the imagecopyresampled() call is successful, then destroy the source image ($src_img) to free system resources because you won't need it again. If the function fails for some reason, you throw a new exception to create a custom error message. To do this, add the following code in bold to doImageResize():

```
/**
 * Generates a resampled and resized image
 *
 * Creates and saves a new image based on the new dimensions
 * and image type-specific functions determined by other
 * class methods.
 *
 * @param array $img the path to the upload
 * @return void
 */
private function doImageResize($img)
{

    // Determine the new dimensions
    $d = $this->getNewDims($tmp);

    // Determine what functions to use
    $funcs = $this->getImageFunctions($img);

    // Create the image resources for resampling
    $src_img = $funcs[0]($img);
    $new_img = imagecreatetruecolor($d[0], $d[1]);
```

```
        if(imagecopyresampled(
            $new_img, $src_img, 0, 0, 0, 0, $d[0], $d[1], $d[2], $d[3]
        ))
        {
            imagedestroy($src_img);

            // Finish resampling

        }
        else
        {
            throw new Exception('Could not resample the image!');
        }
    }
```

Now $new_img contains the resized and resampled image. All that's left to do at this point is to save the image. You can accomplish this by using the second image type-specific function that saves the image resource to a location of your choosing. You can save it over the top of the original image because you no longer need it at its original size in your blog application.

You need to make sure that the image type-specific function fires successfully, then destroy the new image resource ($new_img) to free the memory it consumes. If the function fails, you throw an error. Add the following code in bold to doImageResize() to complete your function:

```
/**
 * Generates a resampled and resized image
 *
 * Creates and saves a new image based on the new dimensions
 * and image type-specific functions determined by other
 * class methods.
 *
 * @param array $img the path to the upload
 * @return void
 */
private function doImageResize($img)
{

    // Determine the new dimensions
    $d = $this->getNewDims($tmp);

    // Determine what functions to use
    $funcs = $this->getImageFunctions($img);

    // Create the image resources for resampling
    $src_img = $funcs[0]($img);
    $new_img = imagecreatetruecolor($d[0], $d[1]);
```

```php
        if(imagecopyresampled(
            $new_img, $src_img, 0, 0, 0, 0, $d[0], $d[1], $d[2], $d[3]
        ))
        {
            imagedestroy($src_img);
            if($new_img && $funcs[1]($new_img, $img))
            {
                imagedestroy($new_img);
            }
            else
            {
                throw new Exception('Failed to save the new image!');
            }
        }
        else
        {
            throw new Exception('Could not resample the image!');
        }
    }
```

You can now resize any JPEG, GIF, or PNG image to fit within your maximum dimensions. Next, add a call to your new method to processUploadedImage() and try it out!

Adding Your New Method to processUploadedImage()

You need to add only one line of code to the function to resample images processed with processUploadedImage(). In images.inc.php, add the lines in bold to processUploadedImage():

```php
/**
 * Resizes/resamples an image uploaded via a web form
 *
 * @param array $upload the array contained in $_FILES
 * @param bool $rename whether or not the image should be renamed
 * @return string the path to the resized uploaded file
 */
public function processUploadedImage($file, $rename=TRUE)
{
    // Separate the uploaded file array
    list($name, $type, $tmp, $err, $size) = array_values($file);

    // If an error occurred, throw an exception
    if($err != UPLOAD_ERR_OK) {
        throw new Exception('An error occurred with the upload!');
        exit;
    }
```

```php
    // Generate a resized image
    $this->doImageResize($tmp);

    // Rename the file if the flag is set to TRUE
    if($rename===TRUE) {
        // Retrieve information about the image
        $img_ext = $this->getImageExtension($type);

        $name = $this->renameFile($img_ext);
    }

    // Check that the directory exists
    $this->checkSaveDir();

    // Create the full path to the image for saving
    $filepath = $this->save_dir . $name;

    // Store the absolute path to move the image
    $absolute = $_SERVER['DOCUMENT_ROOT'] . $filepath;

    // Save the image
    if(!move_uploaded_file($tmp, $absolute))
    {
        throw new Exception("Couldn't save the uploaded file!");
    }

    return $filepath;
}
```

You can test this by re-uploading your original image to the "Entry with an Image" entry. Navigate to the entry in a browser at http://localhost/simple_blog/entry-with-an-image and click the edit link to bring up the admin form. Select the image you uploaded previously and click the Save Entry button. You should now see that the resampled, properly-sized image (see Figure 8-8).

259

Figure 8-8. *A resized image that is displayed with an entry*

Summary

This chapter has been intense. You've covered several advanced topics, including object-oriented programming and image handling. The next chapter is a little less complex, but the still important: you'll learn how to create an RSS feed for your blog, which is a great feature to add to your blog's functionality.

PART 3

Reaching Out to Site Visitors

Now that you have a functional blog, you need to consider how you can interact with your users. In this section, you'll learn some of the different methods available to you to make your site more interactive.

CHAPTER 9

Syndicating the Blog

One of the easiest ways to reach out to your users is to create an RSS feed for your blog. This is fairly simple to do, and it allows your readers to subscribe to your posts, which means they'll receive notifications whenever you post a new entry.

This is a mutually beneficial system because you, as a content provider, have the comfort of knowing that people who subscribe will likely come back to your site when you publish new content, and your readers are saved the trouble of coming to your site to find that nothing has changed.

In the course of this chapter, you'll learn several skills that will enable you to create an RSS feed for your blog:

- What RSS is, and how it works

- What XML is, and how RSS uses it

- How to create a new file to generate an RSS feed for your blog

- How to repurpose your existing functions to minimize effort

- How to use some of the methods available to publish your feed

What Is RSS?

RSS is a format used by content providers to publish content. Originally, RSS stood for *Rich Site Summary*, but with the release of the RSS 2.0 spec in 2002, the name was changed to *Really Simple Syndication*.

RSS simplifies publishing by providing a standardized, no-frills approach to releasing content. No formatting is included with an RSS entry; only the content is sent. This allows for RSS aggregators, commonly referred to as *feed readers*, to accept and display RSS feeds from any number of sites in a uniform, easy-to-read manner.

The RSS format is built in XML, which learn more about in the next section.

■**Note** For a history of RSS, visit this article: `http://en.wikipedia.org/wiki/RSS`.

What Is XML?

XML stands for *Extensible Markup Language*. In the context of programming, extensible means that the developer can define the markup elements. This might sound odd, but it's actually incredibly useful.

XML is, on a basic level, extremely simple. In a parallel with HTML, XML information is enclosed in tags; however, you can name the tags anything you want, and these tags are basically labels for the enclosed information.

For example, assume you want to send personal information about someone via XML. The markup might read as follows:

```
<person>
    <name>Jason</name>
    <age>24</age>
    <gender>male</gender>
</person>
```

The benefit of XML is that it's easy to read. Take another look at the information in the preceding example—you don't need to be an XML expert to understand what the markup means. In the next section, you'll learn how RSS uses XML to syndicate content.

Creating an RSS Feed

RSS feeds follow a general format that allows for large-scale, easy compatibility with any feed reader in use right now. The basic format for an RSS consists of a channel that includes a title, description, link, and language setting.

Within the channel, you declare each entry as an item. Each item contains a title, description, link, the date it was published, and a unique identifier.

To create your feed, you need to create a new folder and file in the simple_blog project. Next, add a new folder called feeds, and then create a new file called rss.php and in that folder (the full path: http://localhost/simple_blog/feeds/rss.php).

Before you can run your file, you need to modify .htaccess. This is as simple as adding an additional file extension to the first RewriteRule that prevents any rewrite from occurring if a file ending in .php is accessed. To accomplish this, add the following line in bold to your .htaccess file:

```
RewriteEngine on
RewriteBase /simple_blog/

RewriteRule \.(gif|jpg|png|css|ico|swf|js|inc\.php|php)$ - [L]
RewriteRule ^admin/?$ admin.php [NC,L]
RewriteRule ^admin/(\w+)/?$ admin.php?page=$1 [NC,L]
RewriteRule ^admin/(\w+)/([\w-]+) admin.php?page=$1&url=$2 [NC,L]
RewriteRule ^(\w+)/?$ index.php?page=$1
RewriteRule ^(\w+)/([\w-]+) index.php?page=$1&url=$2
```

Describing Your Feed

Now that your file is created and being handled properly, you can start to mark up your feed.

Begin by adding a Content-Type header to the document (using the aptly named header() function). This header tells the browser to serve the file as XML.

Next, you need to output an XML declaration. However, this causes issues because XML declarations conflict with PHP short tags. You can get around this by using the echo command to output the declaration in double quotes, which eliminates the conflict.

Now you need to state what you are doing, which you accomplish by adding an <rss> tag with a version attribute. This tells any feed reader what it's receiving and ensures the information received is handled properly.

Next, you add the channel declaration and your feed's basic information. As mentioned previously, the basic information consists of the title, description, link, and language of your feed.

Add the following code to rss.php to create your feed:

```php
<?php

// Add a content type header to ensure proper execution
header('Content-Type: application/rss+xml');

// Output the XML declaration
echo "<?xml version=\"1.0\" encoding=\"UTF-8\"?>\n";

?>
<rss version="2.0">
<channel>

    <title>My Simple Blog</title>
    <link>http://localhost/simple_blog/</link>
    <description>This blog is awesome.</description>
    <language>en-us</language>

</channel>
</rss>
```

At this point, you can load your RSS feed in a browser to see what it looks like without any items; you can load the information at http://localhost/simple_blog/feeds/rss.php (see Figure 9-1).

■**Note** You don't want to do anything further with the feed as it appears in your browser. The blog is not available publicly, so subscribing to the feed won't work in a feed reader at this time.

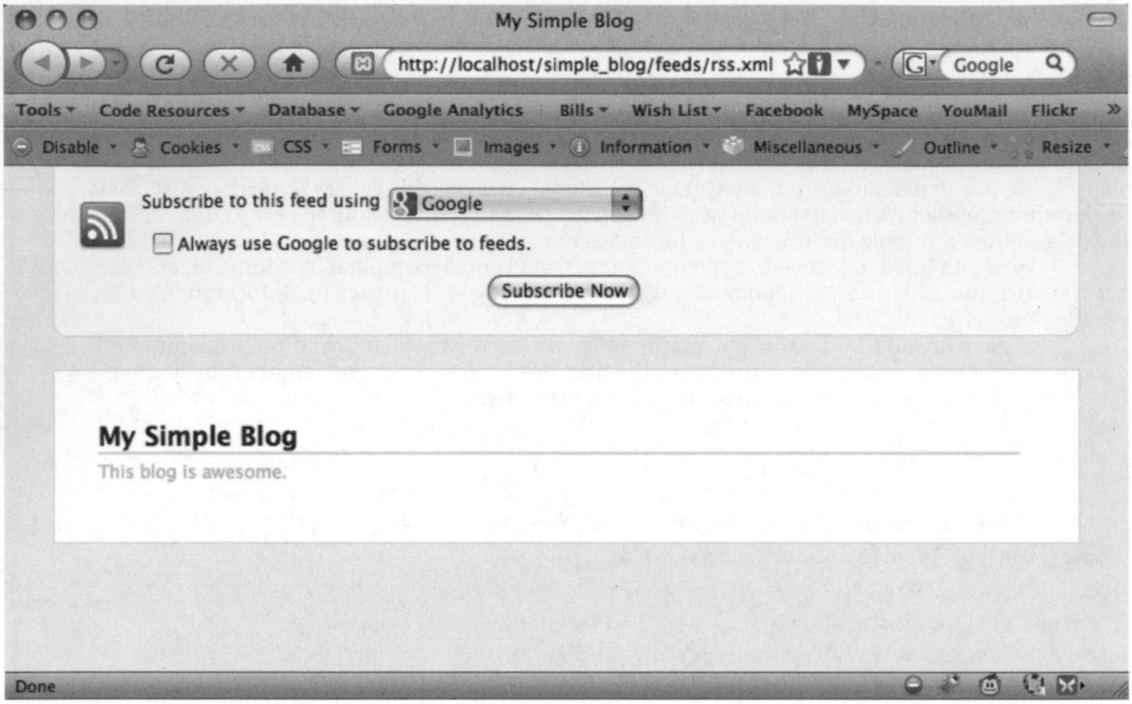

Figure 9-1. *Your feed as it appears in Firefox 3 on a Mac*

Creating Feed Items

Now that your feed is working properly, you need to add your blog entries as feed items. This process is similar to the way you display your entries in index.php, except that you simplify the process by displaying only the latest blog entries (your feed will send data to the browser in only one way, unlike index.php, which has view options for multiple pages, entry previews, and full entries).

Using Existing Functions to Minimize Effort

You've already written a function to retrieve your entries from the database, so you don't need to write a new one. Including functions.inc.php in rss.php enables you to access retrieveEntries(), which you use to return all of your blog entries as an array. Next, you can loop through the entries to generate your feed items.

For retrieveEntries() to work, you also need a database connection to exist. For this, you include db.inc.php in rss.php as well. After you include the necessary files in rss.php, you open a database connection by inserting the code in bold at the very top of the file:

```php
<?php

// Include necessary files
include_once '../inc/functions.inc.php';
include_once '../inc/db.inc.php';

// Open a database connection
$db = new PDO(DB_INFO, DB_USER, DB_PASS);

// Add a content type header to ensure proper execution
header('Content-Type: application/rss+xml');

// Output the XML declaration
echo "<?xml version=\"1.0\" encoding=\"UTF-8\"?>\n";

?>
<rss version="2.0">
<channel>

    <title>My Simple Blog</title>
    <link>http://localhost/simple_blog/</link>
    <description>This blog is awesome.</description>
    <language>en-us</language>

</channel>
</rss>
```

Next, you need to load the entries from the database. You do this by storing the return value of retrieveEntries() in a variable called $e. Also, retrieveEntries() attaches a $fulldisp flag to the end of the returned array, so you want to pop the last element off $e to remove the flag. You can accomplish this using array_pop(). Finally, you need to do some basic data sanitization before you try to output anything, just to be on the safe side.

Do this by adding the code in bold to rss.php:

```php
<?php

// Include necessary files
include_once '../inc/functions.inc.php';
include_once '../inc/db.inc.php';

// Open a database connection
$db = new PDO(DB_INFO, DB_USER, DB_PASS);

// Load all blog entries
$e = retrieveEntries($db, 'blog');
```

267

```php
// Remove the fulldisp flag
array_pop($e);

// Perform basic data sanitization
$e = sanitizeData($e);

// Add a content type header to ensure proper execution
header('Content-Type: application/rss+xml');

// Output the XML declaration
echo "<?xml version=\"1.0\" encoding=\"UTF-8\"?>\n";

?>
<rss version="2.0">
<channel>

    <title>My Simple Blog</title>
    <link>http://localhost/simple_blog/</link>
    <description>This blog is awesome.</description>
    <language>en-us</language>

</channel>
</rss>
```

At this point, you have an array that contains your entries ready for output. You use a foreach loop to display each entry.

Begin by generating an item with a title, a description, and a link. The only extra step is to escape all HTML entities in your description—you need to convert special characters to their HTML entity equivalents, such as < to <. This is necessary because unescaped HTML will cause an error for RSS readers. You accomplish this by calling htmlentities() on the contents of the entry column.

Add the following code in bold to rss.php:

```php
<?php

// Include necessary files
include_once '../inc/functions.inc.php';
include_once '../inc/db.inc.php';

// Open a database connection
$db = new PDO(DB_INFO, DB_USER, DB_PASS);

// Load all blog entries
$e = retrieveEntries($db, 'blog');
```

```php
// Remove the fulldisp flag
array_pop($e);

// Perform basic data sanitization
$e = sanitizeData($e);

// Add a content type header to ensure proper execution
header('Content-Type: application/rss+xml');

// Output the XML declaration
echo "<?xml version=\"1.0\" encoding=\"UTF-8\"?>\n";

?>
<rss version="2.0">
<channel>

    <title>My Simple Blog</title>
    <link>http://localhost/simple_blog/</link>
    <description>This blog is awesome.</description>
    <language>en-us</language>

<?php

// Loop through the entries and generate RSS items
foreach($e as $e):
    // Escape HTML to avoid errors
    $entry = htmlentities($e['entry']);

    // Build the full URL to the entry
    $url = 'http://localhost/simple_blog/blog/' . $e['url'];

?>
    <item>
        <title><?php echo $e['title']; ?></title>
        <description><?php echo $entry; ?></description>
        <link><?php echo $url; ?></link>
    </item>

<?php endforeach; ?>

</channel>
</rss>
```

To keep your script as legible as possible, you need to use the alternative syntax for your `foreach` loop, using a colon to start the loop and `endforeach` to close the loop.

You can see your feed items displayed if you load `http://localhost/simple_blog/feeds/rss.php` into your browser at this point (see Figure 9-2).

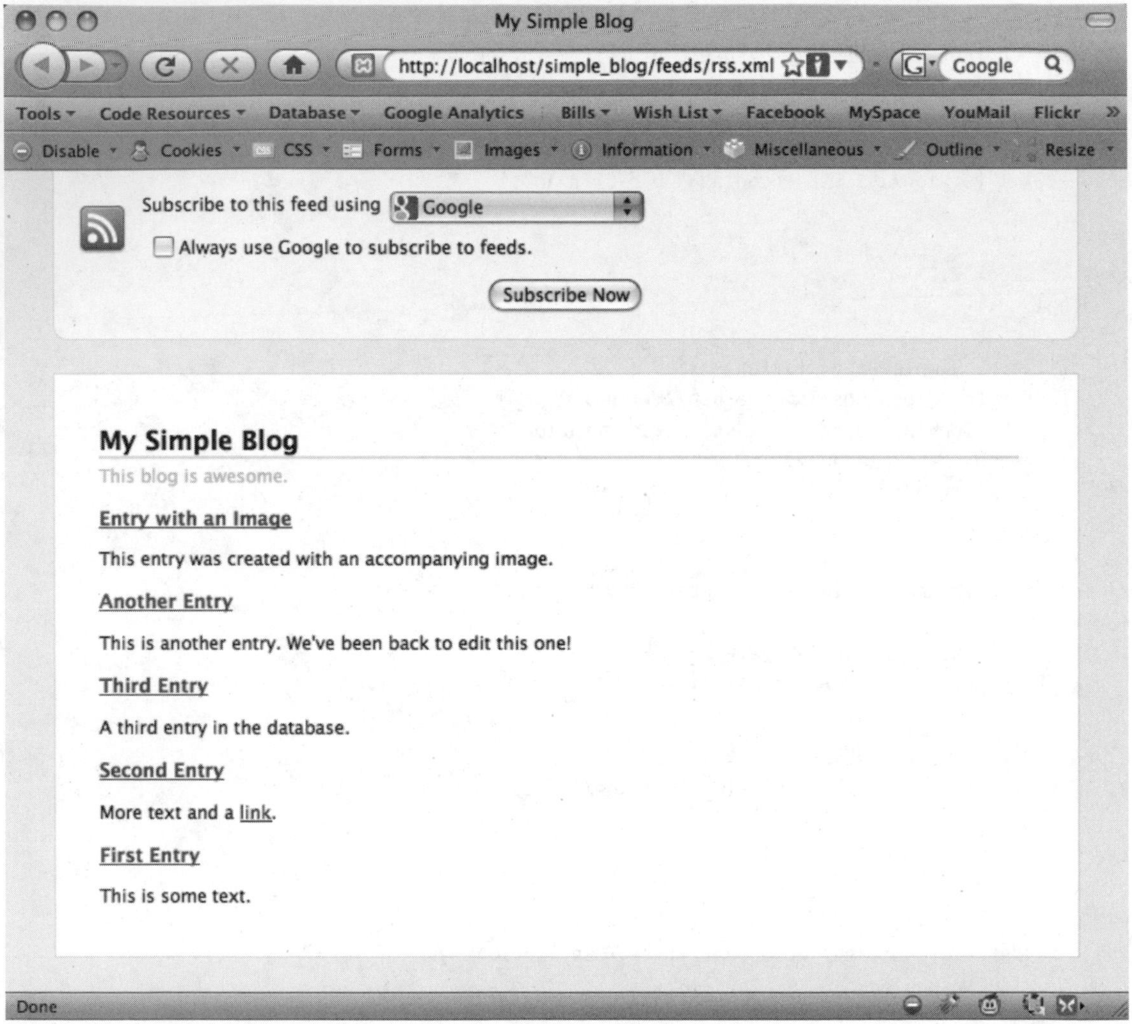

Figure 9-2. *Your feed with items, as displayed in Firefox 3*

On the most basic level, your RSS feed is now running. However, you still need to add a couple things to feed items to ensure widespread compatibility with feed readers: a GUID and a publishing date.

What Is a GUID?

In RSS, publishers are encouraged to include a *Globally Unique Identifier* (GUID) . There is no hard-and-fast rule for what to use as an item's GUID, but the most common GUID tends to be the permanent URL of the item because this is generally a unique path that won't be duplicated.

In your feed, you use each item's URL as a GUID, which means that adding it is as simple as including a second element that displays the link value. It's not uncommon for RSS feed items to have identical link and GUID values.

You can insert a GUID by adding the code in bold to rss.php:

```php
<?php

// Include necessary files
include_once '../inc/functions.inc.php';
include_once '../inc/db.inc.php';

// Open a database connection
$db = new PDO(DB_INFO, DB_USER, DB_PASS);

// Load all blog entries
$e = retrieveEntries($db, 'blog');

// Remove the fulldisp flag
array_pop($e);

// Perform basic data sanitization
$e = sanitizeData($e);

// Add a content type header to ensure proper execution
header('Content-Type: application/rss+xml');

// Output the XML declaration
echo "<?xml version=\"1.0\" encoding=\"UTF-8\"?>\n";

?>
<rss version="2.0">
<channel>

    <title>My Simple Blog</title>
    <link>http://localhost/simple_blog/</link>
    <description>This blog is awesome.</description>
    <language>en-us</language>
```

```php
<?php

// Loop through the entries and generate RSS items
foreach($e as $e):
    // Escape HTML to avoid errors
    $entry = htmlentities($e['entry']);

    // Build the full URL to the entry
    $url = 'http://localhost/simple_blog/blog/' . $e['url'];

?>
    <item>
        <title><?php echo $e['title']; ?></title>
        <description><?php echo $entry; ?></description>
        <link><?php echo $url; ?></link>
        <guid><?php echo $url; ?></guid>
    </item>

<?php endforeach; ?>

</channel>
</rss>
```

What Is a Publishing Date?

The publishing date of a feed item is the date it was created on. RSS requires that this date conform to the RFC-822 guidelines, which means the date must be formatted as follows:

```
Sat, 23 May 2009 18:54:16 -0600
```

You might remember that, when you created your entries table, you included a column called created that stores the date automatically when an entry is created. However, as things stand now, the created column isn't returned from retrieveEntries(). Before you can generate a publishing date for your feed items, you need to add the created column to the array of values returned from retrieveEntries().

Modifying retrieveEntries() to Return the created Column

Your first task is to add the created column to the array returned from retrieveEntries(). To do this, you simply need to add the created column to your SQL query. Do this by opening functions.inc.php and modifying the lines in bold in retrieveEntries():

```
function retrieveEntries($db, $page, $url=NULL)
{
    /*
     * If an entry URL was supplied, load the associated entry
     */
    if(isset($url))
    {
        $sql = "SELECT id, page, title, image, entry, created
                FROM entries
                WHERE url=?
                LIMIT 1";
        $stmt = $db->prepare($sql);
        $stmt->execute(array($url));

        // Save the returned entry array
        $e = $stmt->fetch();

        // Set the fulldisp flag for a single entry
        $fulldisp = 1;
    }

    /*
     * If no entry ID was supplied, load all entry titles for the page
     */
    else
    {
        $sql = "SELECT id, page, title, image, entry, url, created
                FROM entries
                WHERE page=?
                ORDER BY created DESC";
        $stmt = $db->prepare($sql);
        $stmt->execute(array($page));

        $e = NULL; // Declare the variable to avoid errors

        // Loop through returned results and store as an array
        while($row = $stmt->fetch()) {
            if($page=='blog')
            {
                $e[] = $row;
                $fulldisp = 0;
            }
```

```
        else
        {
            $e = $row;
            $fulldisp = 1;
        }
    }

    /*
     * If no entries were returned, display a default
     * message and set the fulldisp flag to display a
     * single entry
     */
    if(!is_array($e))
    {
        $fulldisp = 1;
        $e = array(
            'title' => 'No Entries Yet',
            'entry' => 'This page does not have an entry yet!'
        );
    }
}

// Add the $fulldisp flag to the end of the array
array_push($e, $fulldisp);

return $e;
}
```

Creating a pubDate from the MySQL Timestamp

Now your entry array contains the MySQL timestamp that was generated when each entry was created. However, the MySQL timestamp is formatted like this:

```
2009-05-23 18:54:16
```

Using the MySQL timestamp renders your RSS feed invalid, so you need to somehow convert it to the proper RFC-822 format. Fortunately, PHP provides two functions that allow you to do exactly that: strtotime() and date().

This means that string to timestamp—strtotime()—can convert a variety of date strings, including your MySQL timestamp, to a UNIX timestamp. You can then use the UNIX timestamp in the date() function, which accepts a format and a timestamp and outputs a formatted date string.

RSS is widely used, so PHP provides a constant for use with date() that returns a properly formatted RFC-822 date string, called DATE_RSS.

The next step is to add the code in bold to `rss.php` to reformat your date and add a publishing date to each item:

```php
<?php

// Include necessary files
include_once '../inc/functions.inc.php';
include_once '../inc/db.inc.php';

// Open a database connection
$db = new PDO(DB_INFO, DB_USER, DB_PASS);

// Load all blog entries
$e = retrieveEntries($db, 'blog');

// Remove the fulldisp flag
array_pop($e);

// Perform basic data sanitization
$e = sanitizeData($e);

// Add a content type header to ensure proper execution
header('Content-Type: application/rss+xml');

// Output the XML declaration
echo "<?xml version=\"1.0\" encoding=\"UTF-8\"?>\n";

?>
<rss version="2.0">
<channel>

    <title>My Simple Blog</title>
    <link>http://localhost/simple_blog/</link>
    <description>This blog is awesome.</description>
    <language>en-us</language>
```

```php
<?php

// Loop through the entries and generate RSS items
foreach($e as $e):
    // Escape HTML to avoid errors
    $entry = htmlentities($e['entry']);

    // Build the full URL to the entry
    $url = 'http://localhost/simple_blog/blog/' . $e['url'];

    // Format the date correctly for RSS pubDate
    $date = date(DATE_RSS, strtotime($e['created']));

?>
    <item>
        <title><?php echo $e['title']; ?></title>
        <description><?php echo $entry; ?></description>
        <link><?php echo $url; ?></link>
        <guid><?php echo $url; ?></guid>
        <pubDate><?php echo $date; ?></pubDate>
    </item>

<?php endforeach; ?>

</channel>
</rss>
```

Your feed now contains all the elements it needs to be compatible with nearly all feed readers. When you load http://localhost/simple_blog/feeds/rss.php in a browser, you see your items displayed with the date they were published (see Figure 9-3).

Figure 9-3. *Your feed as it appears in Firefox 3, complete with the publishing date*

Publishing Your Feed

Now that you have a functional RSS feed for your blog, you need to make it available to your users, so they can take advantage of your syndicated content.

Adding the Feed to the Blog

To make your feed available to users, add it to your blog by including it within `index.php`. You can do this in either of two ways (I'll show you how to use both approaches). First, you can add a `<link>` tag in the head of your HTML. Alternatively, you can place a direct link to the feed within the body of your document.

Using the <link> Tag to Signify an RSS Feed

Most modern browsers have RSS readers built in, so they recognize when a site has an available RSS feed. To make your feed recognizable, you need to add a `<link>` tag to the head section of `index.php`.

You've already used the `<link>` tag in this project to include an external CSS style sheet. To include the RSS feed, you use a similar process to you provide attributes that describe the document's title, location, type, and relationship of the feed. The relationship you provide is called `alternate` because the feed is an alternative method to view your content.

To mark this link as a feed, you set its type to `application/rss+xml`, which is the accepted content type for RSS feeds. The `title` and `href` attributes identify your feed.

To insert your feed, add the code in bold to the head section of `index.php`:

```
<!DOCTYPE html
    PUBLIC "-//W3C//DTD XHTML 1.0 Strict//EN"
    "http://www.w3.org/TR/xhtml1/DTD/xhtml1-strict.dtd">

<html xmlns="http://www.w3.org/1999/xhtml" xml:lang="en" lang="en">

<head>
    <meta http-equiv="Content-Type"
        content="text/html;charset=utf-8" />
    <link rel="stylesheet"
        href="/simple_blog/css/default.css" type="text/css" />
    <link rel="alternate" type="application/rss+xml"
        title="My Simple Blog - RSS 2.0"
        href="/simple_blog/feeds/rss.php" />
    <title> Simple Blog </title>
</head>
```

Once you add your feed, you can load `http://localhost/simple_blog/` and see a new RSS icon in the address bar of some browsers (see Figure 9-4).

Figure 9-4. *An RSS icon (circled in red) appears in the address bar after you include a link to your feed*

Adding an RSS Link

Next, you need to provide a direct link to the feed for users who have a feed reader other than a browser. This is as simple as adding an anchor element to the bottom of the page, just before the closing `</div>` and `</body>` tags.

Add the lines in bold to the bottom of `index.php` to link to your feed:

```
<p class="backlink">
<?php if($page=='blog'): ?>
    <a href="/simple_blog/admin/<?php echo $page ?>">
        Post a New Entry
    </a>
<?php endif; ?>
</p>
```

```
    <p>
        <a href="/simple_blog/feeds/rss.php">
            Subscribe via RSS!
        </a>
    </p>

    </div>

</body>

</html>
```

This link enables users to point their feed readers at your feed. When you reload `http://localhost/simple_blog/` in your browser, you see the new link at the bottom of the blog entry previews (see Figure 9-5).

Figure 9-5. *A link to your feed is added to the bottom of the page*

Summary

In this chapter, you learned how to add an RSS feed to your blog. Syndicating content is one of the easiest and best ways to extend your blog to as many eyes as possible.

In the next chapter, you dive into some more complex programming as you add a commenting system to your blog in an effort to connect with your users further.

CHAPTER 10

Adding a Commenting System to Your Blog

One of the most important features of modern web applications is the ability to allow users to interact via a commenting system. Nearly every blog in existence allows its readers to comment on entries. This adds to the experience of the users and the blog author by enabling everyone to continue the conversations the author initiates with his posts.

In this chapter, I'll show you now to add a commenting system to the blog. To get the system up and running, you need to do the following:

- Create a comments table in the database to store comment entries
- Build a Comments class to perform all comment-related actions
- Build a method for displaying a form to enter new comments
- Modify index.php to display the comment form
- Build a method to store comments in the comments table
- Modify update.inc.php to handle new comments
- Build a method to retrieve comments for an entry
- Modify index.php to display entry comments
- Build a method to delete unwanted comments
- Modify update.inc.php to handle comment deletion

We'll be using object-oriented programming in this chapter again, so if you need to, refer to Chapter 8 for a quick refresher on the basics.

Creating a comments Table in the Database

Before you can begin working with comments, you need to have a place to store them. Create a table called comments in the simple_blog database; you'll use this to store all of your comment information.

You need to store several different kinds of information in this table:

- Id: A unique identifier for the comment. This is the table's primary key. You can use the AUTO_INCREMENT property to simplify adding new comments.

- blog_id: The identifier of the blog entry to which the comment corresponds. This column is an INT value. To speed up your queries, you can also create an index on this column.

- name: The name of the commenter. This column accepts a maximum of 75 characters and is of the VARCHAR type.

- email: The email address of the commenter. This column accepts a maximum of 150 characters and is of the VARCHAR type.

- comment: The actual comment. This column is of the TEXT type.

- date: The date the comment was posted. You set this column to store the CURRENT_TIMESTAMP when a user adds a comment i to the table, which means it is of the TIMESTAMP type.

To create this table, navigate to http://localhost/phpmyadmin in a browser and open the SQL tab. Executing the following command creates the comments table and prepares it for use:

```
CREATE TABLE simple_blog.comments
(
id INT PRIMARY KEY AUTO_INCREMENT,
blog_id INT,
name VARCHAR(75),
email VARCHAR(150),
comment TEXT,
date TIMESTAMP DEFAULT CURRENT_TIMESTAMP,
INDEX(blog_id)
)
```

Once you click the Go button, you can click the comments table in the simple_blog database to see the structure of your table (see Figure 10-1).

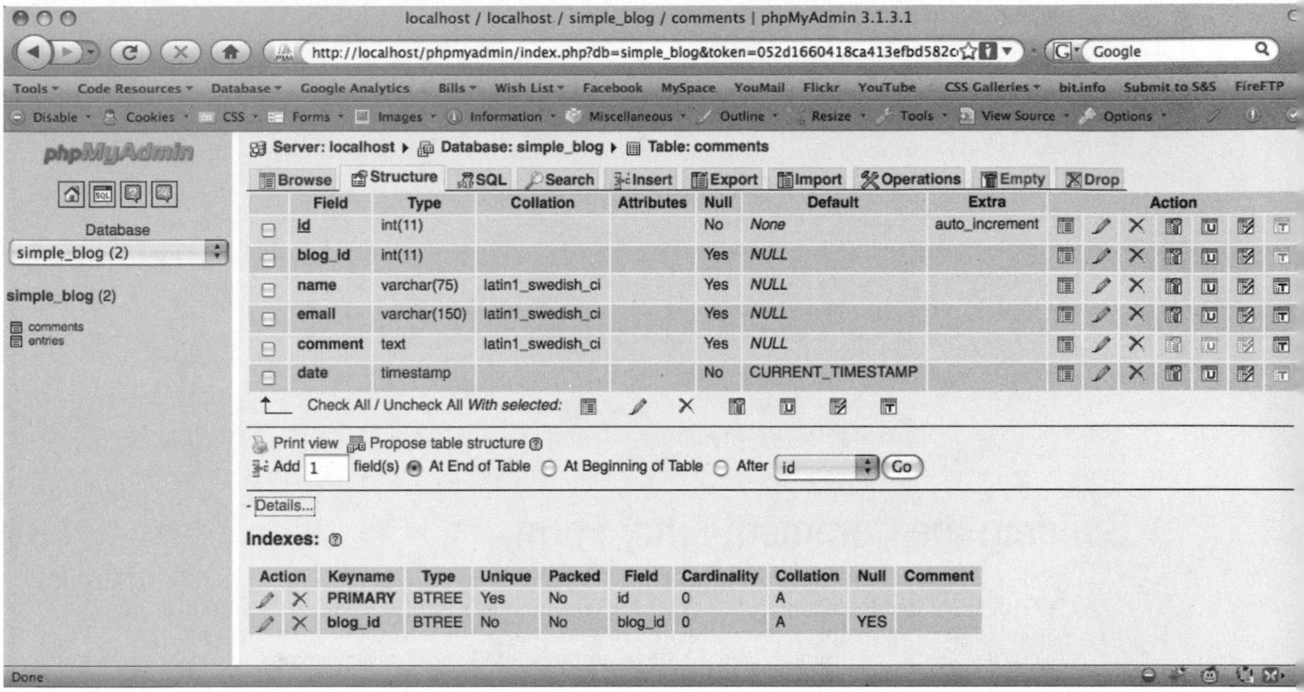

Figure 10-1. *The comments table as viewed in phpMyAdmin*

Building a Comments Class

Separating your commenting system separate from the rest of your blog makes it easier to maintain and extend in the future; you'll leverage the object-oriented approach you learned about in Chapter 8 to implement this feature.

Begin by creating a new file that will contain the class. Call this file comments.inc.php, and store it in the inc folder in the simple_blog project (full path: /xampp/htdocs/simple_blog/inc/comments.inc.php).

Once you create the file, you need to declare the class and a constructor for it. This class must be able to read and write from the database, so you need to include the database information stored in db.inc.php.

Your class needs a property to hold the database variable. Your class also needs to open a database connection in the constructor that you store in the aforementioned property, which you will call $db.

Next, include the database info, create the class, and define a property and constructor for Comments by adding the code in bold to your newly created comments.inc.php:

```php
<?php


include_once 'db.inc.php';
```

```php
class Comments
{
    // Our database connection
    public $db;

    // Upon class instantiation, open a database connection
    public function __construct()
    {
        // Open a database connection and store it
        $this->db = new PDO(DB_INFO, DB_USER, DB_PASS);
    }
}

?>
```

Building the Comment Entry Form

You enable users to add new comments to your blog entries by providing them with a form to fill out.
This form needs to contain fields for the commenter's name, email address, and comment.
Also, you need to store the blog entry's identifier to associate the comment with the blog.
To display this form, you create a new method called showCommentForm(), which accepts one argument, $blog_id, and outputs a form in HTML.
You can create this method by adding the code in bold to your Comments class in comments.inc.php:

```php
<?php

include_once 'db.inc.php';

class Comments
{
    // Our database connection
    public $db;

    // Upon class instantiation, open a database connection
    public function __construct()
    {
        // Open a database connection and store it
        $this->db = new PDO(DB_INFO, DB_USER, DB_PASS);
    }
```

```php
     // Display a form for users to enter new comments with
     public function showCommentForm($blog_id)
     {
          return <<<FORM
<form action="/simple_blog/inc/update.inc.php"
     method="post" id="comment-form">
     <fieldset>
          <legend>Post a Comment</legend>
          <label>Name
               <input type="text" name="name" maxlength="75" />
          </label>
          <label>Email
               <input type="text" name="email" maxlength="150" />
          </label>
          <label>Comment
               <textarea rows="10" cols="45" name="comment"></textarea>
          </label>
          <input type="hidden" name="blog_id" value="$blog_id" />
          <input type="submit" name="submit" value="Post Comment" />
          <input type="submit" name="submit" value="Cancel" />
     </fieldset>
</form>
FORM;
     }
}

?>
```

Note that you're using the heredoc syntax; this allows you to return HTML and PHP values easily, without requiring that you use escape quotes.

Modifying index.php to Display the Comment Form

You have a method to display a comment form; your next step is to show it to your users.

You want this form to be visible only on blog entries that are being fully displayed, so you want to work inside the conditional statement that checks whether $fulldisp is set to 1. Then you need to set up a second conditional to make sure you're on the blog and not any other page.

After you're sure the user is in the right place to see the form, you need to include your comment class, instantiate it, and load the form into a variable, which you can call $comment_form.

Finally, you add the comment form to the output, just after the Back to Latest Entries link.

To do this, add the code in bold to index.php, starting at line 78:

```php
// If the full display flag is set, show the entry
if($fulldisp==1)
{

    // Get the URL if one wasn't passed
    $url = (isset($url)) ? $url : $e['url'];

    // Build the admin links
    $admin = adminLinks($page, $url);

    // Format the image if one exists
    $img = formatImage($e['image'], $e['title']);

    if($page=='blog')
    {
        // Load the comment object
        include_once 'inc/comments.inc.php';
        $comments = new Comments();
        $comment_form = $comments->showCommentForm($e['id']);
    }
    else
    {
        $comment_form = NULL;
    }

?>

        <h2> <?php echo $e['title'] ?> </h2>
        <p> <?php echo $img, $e['entry'] ?> </p>
        <p>
            <?php echo $admin['edit'] ?>
            <?php if($page=='blog') echo $admin['delete'] ?>
        </p>
        <?php if($page=='blog'): ?>
        <p class="backlink">
            <a href="./">Back to Latest Entries</a>
        </p>
        <?php echo $comment_form; endif; ?>

<?php

} // End the if statement
```

Viewing a full entry in a browser reveals your new comment form beneath the entry (see Figure 10-2).

Figure 10-2. Your comment form

Storing New Comments in the Database

When the user fills out your form and clicks the Post Comment box, the data from the form is submitted to update.inc.php. But before you do anything with update.inc.php, you need to determine how you be handle information from the form by creating a new method, called saveComment(), that cleans posted data and stores it in the database.

This method accepts the posted data as an argument, then cleans the data using strip_tags() and htmlentities(). You store the clean data in variables, which you pass to a prepared SQL statement and save in the comments table.

If nothing goes wrong, the method returns TRUE. Otherwise, it returns FALSE.

You can build this method by adding the code in bold to comments.inc.php:

```php
<?php

include_once 'db.inc.php';

class Comments
{
    // Our database connection
    public $db;

    // Upon class instantiation, open a database connection
    public function __construct()
    {
        // Open a database connection and store it
        $this->db = new PDO(DB_INFO, DB_USER, DB_PASS);
    }

    // Display a form for users to enter new comments with
    public function showCommentForm($blog_id)
    {
        return <<<FORM
<form action="/simple_blog/inc/update.inc.php"
    method="post" id="comment-form">
    <fieldset>
        <legend>Post a Comment</legend>
        <label>Name
            <input type="text" name="name" maxlength="75" />
        </label>
        <label>Email
            <input type="text" name="email" maxlength="150" />
        </label>
        <label>Comment
            <textarea rows="10" cols="45" name="comment"></textarea>
        </label>
        <input type="hidden" name="blog_id" value="$blog_id" />
        <input type="submit" name="submit" value="Post Comment" />
        <input type="submit" name="submit" value="Cancel" />
    </fieldset>
</form>
FORM;
    }
```

```php
// Save comments to the database
public function saveComment($p)
{
    // Sanitize the data and store in variables
    $blog_id = htmlentities(strip_tags($p['blog_id']),ENT_QUOTES);
    $name = htmlentities(strip_tags($p['name']),ENT_QUOTES);
    $email = htmlentities(strip_tags($p['email']),ENT_QUOTES);
    $comment = htmlentities(strip_tags($p['comment']),ENT_QUOTES);
    // Keep formatting of comments and remove extra whitespace
    $comment = nl2br(trim($comments));

    // Generate and prepare the SQL command
    $sql = "INSERT INTO comments (blog_id, name, email, comment)
            VALUES (?, ?, ?, ?)";
    if($stmt = $this->db->prepare($sql))
    {
        // Execute the command, free used memory, and return true
        $stmt->execute(array($blog_id, $name, $email, $comment));
        $stmt->closeCursor();
        return TRUE;
    }
    else
    {
        // If something went wrong, return false
        return FALSE;
    }
}
}

?>
```

■ **Note** You'll learn how to add email validation in the next chapter, as well as implement some basic spam-prevention measures.

Modifying update.inc.php to Handle New Comments

Your script knows how to handle data from the comment form, so you're ready to modify update.inc.php to call saveComment() when the comment form is submitted.

You can do this by adding a check to see whether the user clicked the Post Comment button. You add this check after your check for the admin form in update.inc.php. If the comment form was submitted, you need to include and instantiate the Comments class, then call your new saveComment() method and pass the $_POST superglobal array as an argument.

If the call to saveComment() returns TRUE, you try to use the value of $_SERVER['HTTP_REFERER'] to send the user back to the entry where she posted the comment. If that value isn't available, you send user back to the default entry listings.

You should also add a check that outputs an error message if the saveComment() call returns FALSE. To accomplish this, add the code in bold to the bottom of update.inc.php, just before the last else block:

```php
// If a comment is being posted, handle it here
else if($_SERVER['REQUEST_METHOD'] == 'POST'
    && $_POST['submit'] == 'Post Comment')
{
    // Include and instantiate the Comments class
    include_once 'comments.inc.php';
    $comments = new Comments();

    // Save the comment
    if($comments->saveComment($_POST))
    {
        // If available, store the entry the user came from
        if(isset($_SERVER['HTTP_REFERER']))
        {
            $loc = $_SERVER['HTTP_REFERER'];
        }
        else
        {
            $loc = '../';
        }

        // Send the user back to the entry
        header('Location: '.$loc);
        exit;
    }

    // If saving fails, output an error message
    else
    {
        exit('Something went wrong while saving the comment.');
    }
}
```

```
else
{
    header('Location: ../');
    exit;
}


?>
```

You're now ready to test your system. Navigate to an entry in a browser and fill out the form with test information. Press the Post Comment button, and you should be redirected to the entry.

If you navigate to `http://localhost/phpmyadmin` and open the `comments` table in the `simple_blog` database, you can see your entry in the database (see Figure 10-3).

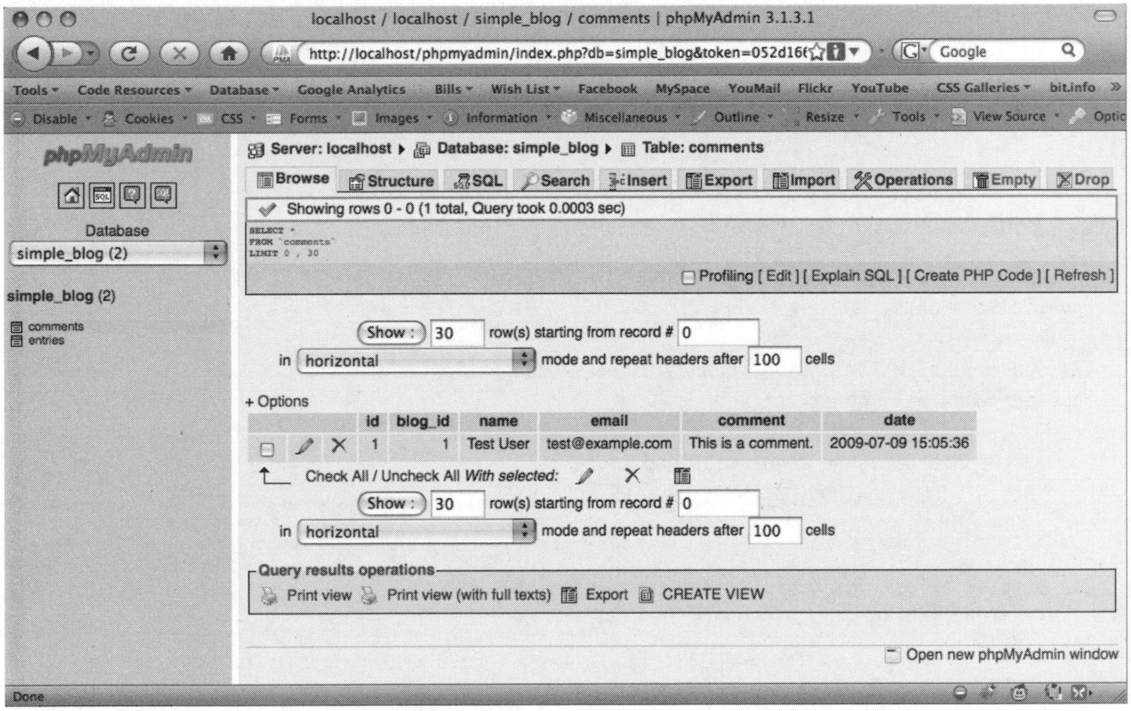

Figure 10-3: *A comment stored in the* `comments` *table*

Retrieving All Comments for a Given Entry

You can now that store comments in the database; your next task is to write a method that retrieves them.

This method, called `retrieveComments()`, accepts one argument: the ID of the blog that you need to retrieve comments for (`$blog_id`).

This new method works similarly to your retrieveEntries() function, except that you store the entries as an array in a property of the Comments class itself, for use with other methods.

Begin by declaring a new $comments property in the class; you use this property to store the loaded comments in memory.

Next, you need to write a SQL query that pulls all the entries from the comments table that match the given blog ID. Be sure to retrieve every column from the table with your query.

The next step is to prepare your SQL statement and execute it using the value of $blog_id that was passed as an argument to your method.

Now loop through the returned entries and store each row in the $comments property as an array element.

Finally, check to see whether any comments exist for the given blog entry. If not, place some default text in the array to let users know that no comments have been posted yet.

You can create this method by adding the code in bold to comments.inc.php:

```php
<?php

include_once 'db.inc.php';

class Comments
{
    // Our database connection
    public $db;

    // An array for containing the entries
    public $comments;

    // Upon class instantiation, open a database connection
    public function __construct()
    {
        // Open a database connection and store it
        $this->db = new PDO(DB_INFO, DB_USER, DB_PASS);
    }

    // Display a form for users to enter new comments with
    public function showCommentForm($blog_id)
    {
        return <<<FORM
<form action="/simple_blog/inc/update.inc.php"
    method="post" id="comment-form">
    <fieldset>
        <legend>Post a Comment</legend>
        <label>Name
            <input type="text" name="name" maxlength="75" />
        </label>
```

```
            <label>Email
                <input type="text" name="email" maxlength="150" />
            </label>
            <label>Comment
                <textarea rows="10" cols="45" name="comment"></textarea>
            </label>
            <input type="hidden" name="blog_id" value="$blog_id" />
            <input type="submit" name="submit" value="Post Comment" />
            <input type="submit" name="submit" value="Cancel" />
        </fieldset>
</form>
FORM;
    }


    // Save comments to the database
    public function saveComment($p)
    {
        // Sanitize the data and store in variables
        $blog_id = htmlentities(strip_tags($p['blog_id']),ENT_QUOTES);
        $name = htmlentities(strip_tags($p['name']),ENT_QUOTES);
        $email = htmlentities(strip_tags($p['email']),ENT_QUOTES);
        $comment = htmlentities(strip_tags($p['comment']),ENT_QUOTES);

        // Generate and prepare the SQL command
        $sql = "INSERT INTO comments (blog_id, name, email, comment)
                VALUES (?, ?, ?, ?)";
        if($stmt = $this->db->prepare($sql))
        {
            // Execute the command, free used memory, and return true
            $stmt->execute(array($blog_id, $name, $email, $comment));
            $stmt->closeCursor();
            return TRUE;
        }
        else
        {
            // If something went wrong, return false
            return FALSE;
        }
    }
```

```php
// Load all comments for a blog entry into memory
public function retrieveComments($blog_id)
{
    // Get all the comments for the entry
    $sql = "SELECT id, name, email, comment, date
            FROM comments
            WHERE blog_id=?
            ORDER BY date DESC";
    $stmt = $this->db->prepare($sql);
    $stmt->execute(array($blog_id));

    // Loop through returned rows
    while($comment = $stmt->fetch())
    {
        // Store in memory for later use
        $this->comments[] = $comment;
    }

    // Set up a default response if no comments exist
    if(empty($this->comments))
    {
        $this->comments[] = array(
            'id' => NULL,
            'name' => NULL,
            'email' => NULL,
            'comment' => "There are no comments on this entry.",
            'date' => NULL
        );
    }
}
}

?>
```

Displaying Comments for a Given Entry

With retrieveComments() functional, you can now display the entries loaded when a user views an entry on the blog.

You can do this by creating a new showComments() method that accepts the blog ID as an argument ($blog_id). This method begins by initializing an empty variable ($display) to contain the formatted comments, then calls the retrieveComments() method to get the entry's comments loaded into memory.

With the comments loaded into $display, you can loop through each comment and create HTML markup to display them. Inside the loop, you want to check whether retrieveComments() has returned the default value, which means no comments exist for the entry. To do this, you set up a conditional statement that verifies that both the date and name values aren't empty before you create a byline.

Begin by setting up the method, loading the entry comments, and starting the loop. Next, add the showComments() method to comments.inc.php by adding the code in bold to the Comments class:

```
// Generates HTML markup for displaying comments
public function showComments($blog_id)
{
    // Initialize the variable in case no comments exist
    $display = NULL;

    // Load the comments for the entry
    $this->retrieveComments($blog_id);

    // Loop through the stored comments
    foreach($this->comments as $c)
    {
        // Prevent empty fields if no comments exist
        if(!empty($c['date']) && !empty($c['name']))
        {
            // Generate a byline and delete link for each comment
        }
        else
        {
            // If we get here, no comments exist
        }

        // Assemble the pieces into a formatted comment
    }

    // Return all the formatted comments as a string
}
```

Your next step is to create a byline for each comment, as well as an administrative link that lets you delete unwanted comments. You accomplish this with an if-else statement.

You need to format a byline if the date and name values aren't empty. You want this byline to display the name of the commenter, as well as the date and time the comment was posted. The format looks like this:

```
John Doe    [Posted on July 10, 2009 at 6:54PM]
```

Think back to how you handled dates in previous chapter. You take a similar approach here, changing the format of the MySQL timestamp stored in the database to fit your needs. You use the `strtotime()` and `date()` methods again, but this time you need to create a custom date formatting string.

FORMATTING DATES IN PHP USING THE DATE() FUNCTION

PHP provides you with many options for formatting dates when you use the `date()` function. You can format each part of a date (day, month, year, and so on) using one of several available formatting characters, which you can combine as necessary to create custom dates.

For example, you would use the formatting string "`M d, Y`" to create the date format, "Jan 01, 2009". Any character used that is not a formatting character—like the comman in the previous example—is output as-is.

If you wish to output text that features a formatting character, you must escape it using a backslash (\\). For example, this format "`m/d/y \a\\t g:IA`" outputs a date similar to "01/01/09 at 4:10PM".

Commonly Used Formatting Characters Recognized by the `Date()` Function

Format Character	Description	Example Return Value
Day		
d	Day of the month, two digits with leading zeros	01 to 31
D	A textual representation of a day, three letters	Mon through Sun
j	Day of the month without leading zeros	1 to 31
l	Full textual representation of the day of the week	Sunday through Saturday
S	English ordinal suffix for the day of the month	st, nd, rd or th; this works well with j
Month		
F	A full textual representation of a month	January through December
m	Numeric representation with leading zeros	01 through 12
M	A short textual representation of a month	Jan through Dec
n	Numeric representation without leading zeros	1 through 12
t	Number of days in the given month	28 through 31

Year		
Y	A full numeric representation of a year, four digits	Examples: 1999 or 2003
y	A two digit representation of a year	Examples: 99 or 03

Time		
a	Lowercase *ante meridiem* and *post meridiem*	am or pm
A	Uppercase *ante meridiem* and *post meridiem*	AM or PM
g	12-hour format of an hour without leading zeros	1 through 12
G	24-hour format of an hour without leading zeros	0 through 23
h	12-hour format of an hour with leading zeros	01 through 12
H	24-hour format of an hour with leading zeros	00 through 23
I	Minutes with leading zeros	00 to 59
s	Seconds, with leading zeros	00 through 59

Time zone		
T	Time zone abbreviation	Examples: EST, MDT, and so on

Note that this table doesn't list all of the available formatting characters. For a full reference of such characters, look up the date() entry in the PHP manual at http://php.net/date.

You store your formatting string in a variable called $format, which makes it easy to identify and change in the future, if necessary. Use this formatting string for your comment byline: F j, Y \a\\t g:iA.

■**Note** In the "F j, Y \a\\t g:iA" formatting string, the "t" is escaped twice. You need to do it this way because \t is a whitespace character in PHP, which means that it would result in unexpected output if you don't double-escape it. The same goes for other whitespace characters, including \n and \r.

With our format stored, you're ready to convert the MySQL timestamp to a Unix timestamp using strtotime(), then use date() to produce the desired date format, which you store in a variable called $date.

Next, place the commenter's name and the formatted date into HTML tags to create the desired output; store this output in a variable called $byline.

Finally, you create the markup for a link to delete the comment, which you store in a variable called $admin.

In the else block, which you get to only if no comments exist for the blog entry, you set $byline and $admin to NULL because they are unnecessary if no comments exist.

Add the code in bold to showComments() in comments.inc.php:

```php
// Generates HTML markup for displaying comments
public function showComments($blog_id)
{
    // Initialize the variable in case no comments exist
    $display = NULL;

    // Load the comments for the entry
    $this->retrieveComments($blog_id);

    // Loop through the stored comments
    foreach($this->comments as $c)
    {
        // Prevent empty fields if no comments exist
        if(!empty($c['date']) && !empty($c['name']))
        {
            // Outputs similar to: July 8, 2009 at 4:39PM
            $format = "F j, Y \a\\t g:iA";

            // Convert $c['date'] to a timestamp, then format
            $date = date($format, strtotime($c['date']));

            // Generate a byline for the comment
            $byline = "<span><strong>$c[name]</strong>
                        [Posted on $date]</span>";

            // Generate delete link for the comment display
            $admin = "<a href=\"/simple_blog/inc/update.inc.php"
                . "?action=comment_delete&id=$c[id]\""
                . "class=\"admin\">delete</a>";
        }
```

```
        else
        {
            // If no comments exist, set $byline & $admin to NULL
            $byline = NULL;
            $admin = NULL;
        }

        // Assemble the pieces into a formatted comment
    }

    // Return all the formatted comments as a string
}
```

■ **Note** You'll learn about the `delete` link and how it works in the "Deleting Comments" section.

You've stored your byline and administrative links; now place them into HTML markup with the comment itself. You append each comment to the $display variable, which is returned from the function after the loop is finished.

To finish the showComments()method, add the code in bold to your method in comments.inc.php:

```
// Generates HTML markup for displaying comments
public function showComments($blog_id)
{
    // Initialize the variable in case no comments exist
    $display = NULL;

    // Load the comments for the entry
    $this->retrieveComments($blog_id);

    // Loop through the stored comments
    foreach($this->comments as $c)
    {
        // Prevent empty fields if no comments exist
        if(!empty($c['date']) && !empty($c['name']))
        {
            // Outputs similar to: July 8, 2009 at 4:39PM
            $format = "F j, Y \a\\t g:iA";

            // Convert $c['date'] to a timestamp, then format
            $date = date($format, strtotime($c['date']));
```

```
                // Generate a byline for the comment
                $byline = "<span><strong>$c[name]</strong>
                          [Posted on $date]</span>";

                // Generate delete link for the comment display
                $admin = "<a href=\"/simple_blog/inc/update.inc.php
?action=comment_delete&id=$c[id]\" class=\"admin\">delete</a>";
            }
            else
            {
                // If no comments exist, set $byline & $admin to NULL
                $byline = NULL;
                $admin = NULL;
            }

            // Assemble the pieces into a formatted comment
            $display .= "
<p class=\"comment\">$byline$c[comment]$admin</p>";
        }

        // Return all the formatted comments as a string
        return $display;
    }
```

Modifying index.php to Display Entry Comments

You have your methods for loading and formatting comments in place. Now you're ready to open index.php and insert the comment display into your blog entries.

You've already done most of the work necessary by adding the comment form. All that remains is to create new variable called $comment_disp and store the output of showComments(). Place this new variable (in bold) just before the value of $comment_form in the index.php file, starting at line 83:

```
// If the full display flag is set, show the entry
if($fulldisp==1)
{

    // Get the URL if one wasn't passed
    $url = (isset($url)) ? $url : $e['url'];

    // Build the admin links
    $admin = adminLinks($page, $url);

    // Format the image if one exists
    $img = formatImage($e['image'], $e['title']);
```

```php
    if($page=='blog')
    {
        // Load the comment object
        include_once 'inc/comments.inc.php';
        $comments = new Comments();
        $comment_disp = $comments->showComments($e['id']);
        $comment_form = $comments->showCommentForm($e['id']);
    }
    else
    {
        $comment_form = NULL;
    }

?>

        <h2> <?php echo $e['title'] ?> </h2>
        <p> <?php echo $img, $e['entry'] ?> </p>
        <p>
            <?php echo $admin['edit'] ?>
            <?php if($page=='blog') echo $admin['delete'] ?>
        </p>
        <?php if($page=='blog'): ?>
        <p class="backlink">
            <a href="./">Back to Latest Entries</a>
        </p>
        <h3> Comments for This Entry </h3>
        <?php echo $comment_disp, $comment_form; endif; ?>

<?php

} // End the if statement
```

Once you save the file, you can navigate to the blog entry you've created a test comment for, and you should see the comment displayed with a byline and an administrative link in place (see Figure 10-4).

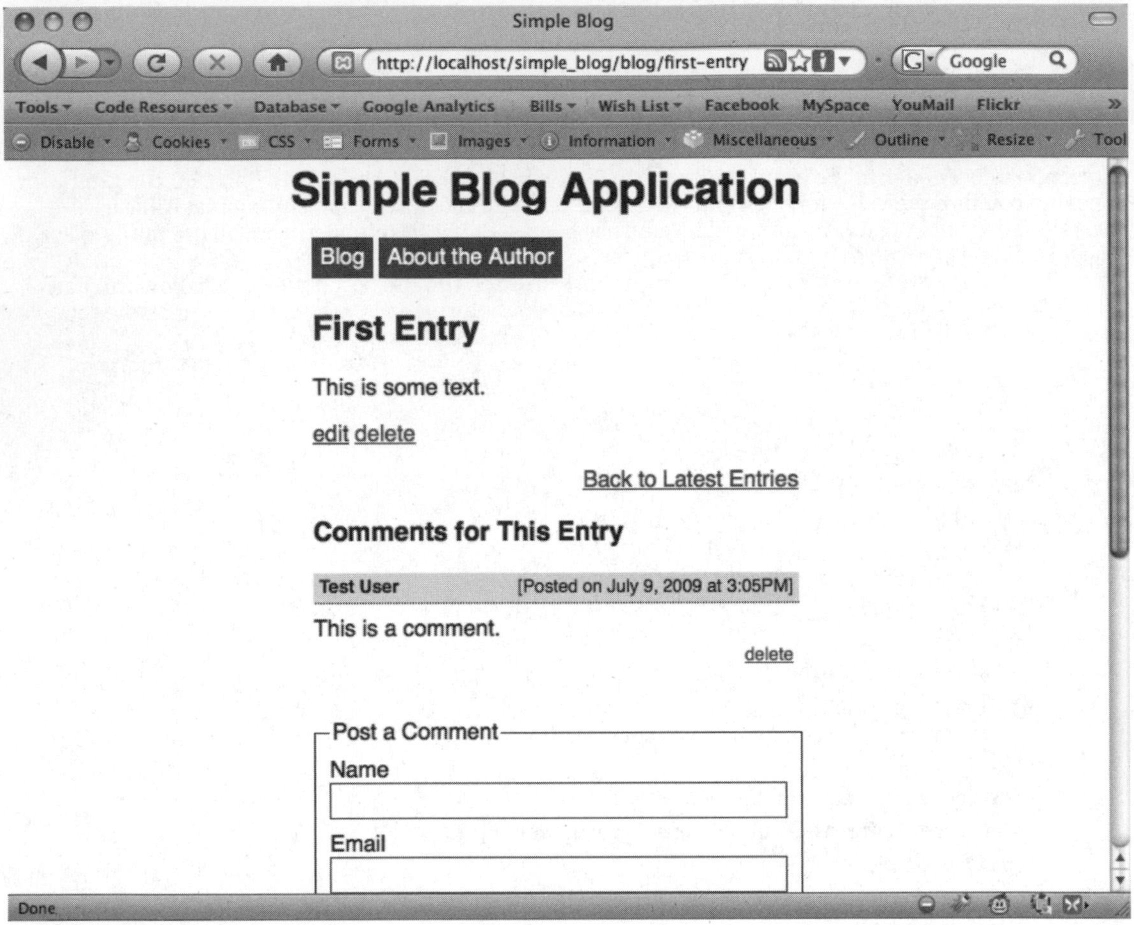

Figure 10-4. *Comments displayed for an entry*

Deleting Comments

Your last step is to provide site administrators with the ability to remove comments from entries. You've already created the link to delete comments; now you need to tell your application what to do when the link is clicked.

The link you've built directs you to `update.inc.php`. It also passes two values using the GET method: an `action`, set to `comment_delete`; and an `id`, set to the value of the comment you created the link for.

To avoid accidental comment deletion, you can use a two-step process to delete comments. After clicking the link, the user receives a confirmation form generated by the `confirmDelete()` method (which you'll write in a moment). The form asks the user to confirm his decision to delete the comment. If he clicks "Yes,", you call the yet-to-be-written `deleteComment()` method, which removes the comment from the database.

Creating a Confirmation Form

When building the confirmation form, begin by writing a method in the Comments class that displays a confirmation form to a user when a delete link is clicked. This method, named confirmDelete(), accepts one argument: the ID of the comment the user wants to delete ($id). When this method is called:, your first step is to attempt to retrieve the URL of the user's entry form. You want to have this available so you can send the user back to the entry she was viewing when she clicked the delete link. You can do this by checking whether the value of $_SERVER['HTTP_REFERER'] has been set, then storing that value in a variable called $url (again, assuming the value has been set). If it hasn't been set, you use the "../" value to send the user to the default entry preview page.

After you store the URL of the previous entry in $url, use the heredoc syntax to construct an HTML form using the $id and $url variables; this form asks the user if she really wants to delete the comment. You provide the user with "Yes" and "No" buttons to answer.

Do this by adding the confirmDelete() method to the Comments class in comments.inc.php:

```
    // Ensure the user really wants to delete the comment
    public function confirmDelete($id)
    {
        // Store the entry url if available
        if(isset($_SERVER['HTTP_REFERER']))
        {
            $url = $_SERVER['HTTP_REFERER'];
        }

        // Otherwise use the default view
        else
        {
            $url = '../';
        }


        return <<<FORM
<html>
<head>
<title>Please Confirm Your Decision</title>
<link rel="stylesheet" type="text/css"
    href="/simple_blog/css/default.css" />
</head>
<body>
<form action="/simple_blog/inc/update.inc.php" method="post">
    <fieldset>
        <legend>Are You Sure?</legend>
        <p>
            Are you sure you want to delete this comment?
        </p>
```

```
        <input type="hidden" name="id" value="$id" />
        <input type="hidden" name="action" value="comment_delete" />
        <input type="hidden" name="url" value="$url" />
        <input type="submit" name="confirm" value="Yes" />
        <input type="submit" name="confirm" value="No" />
    </fieldset>
</form>
</body>
</html>
FORM;
    }
```

■**Note** You build this form with a page title and a link to your stylesheet because update.inc.php outputs this form directly, which means that no output is generated before or after the markup returned by this function. For this reason, you need to create a full HTML page with this method; this enables you to keep your form consistent with the styling of your blog.

Removing the Comment from the Database

Your next step is to create the method that removes a comment from the database. This method, which you call deleteComment(), accepts one argument: the ID of the comment you want to delete ($id).

This method is simple: you construct a SQL query, prepare it, and execute it using the value of $id. If no errors occur, you return TRUE; otherwise, you return FALSE.

Add this code to the Comments class in comments.inc.php to create the deleteComment() method:

```
// Removes the comment corresponding to $id from the database
public function deleteComment($id)
{
    $sql = "DELETE FROM comments
            WHERE id=?
            LIMIT 1";
    if($stmt = $this->db->prepare($sql))
    {
        // Execute the command, free used memory, and return true
        $stmt->execute(array($id));
        $stmt->closeCursor();
        return TRUE;
    }
```

```
        else
        {
            // If something went wrong, return false
            return FALSE;
        }
    }
```

Modifying update.inc.php to Handle Comment Deletion

You now have methods in place to confirm that a comment is to be deleted and to remove that comment from the database. This means you're ready to modify update.inc.php to handle the comment's deletion.

Begin by adding an else if block to update.inc.php. This block of code checks whether the $_GET superglobal contains an index called "action" that you set to comment_delete. If so, you load and instantiate the Comments class and output the return value of confirmDelete().

Add the code in bold to the bottom of update.inc.php, just before the last else block:

```
// If the delete link is clicked on a comment, confirm it here
else if($_GET['action'] == 'comment_delete')
{
    // Include and instantiate the Comments class
    include_once 'comments.inc.php';
    $comments = new Comments();
    echo $comments->confirmDelete($_GET['id']);
    exit;
}

else
{
    header('Location: ../');
    exit;
}

?>
```

To see the confirmation form, navigate to the blog entry with your test comment and click the delete link just below the test comment. This takes you to your confirmation form (see Figure 10-5).

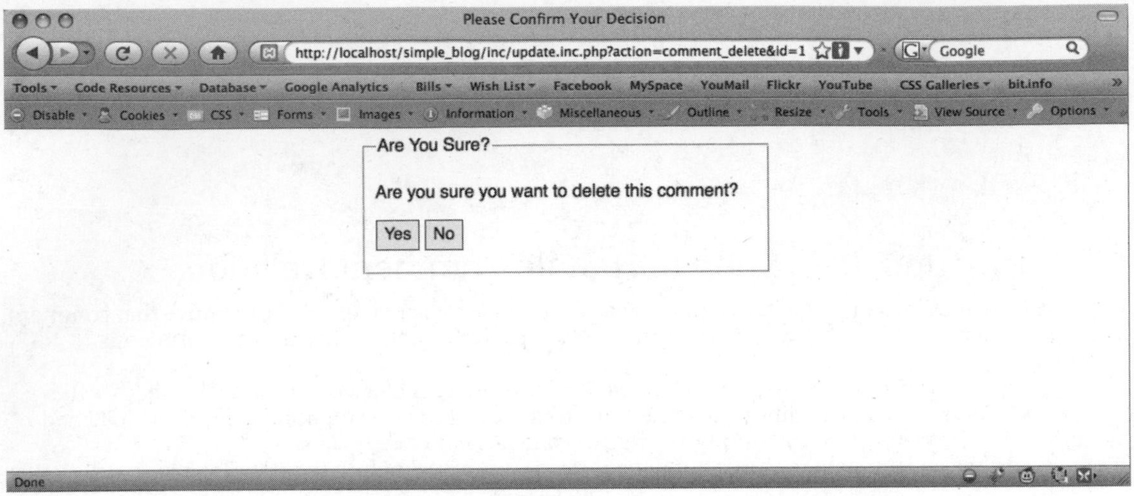

Figure 10-5. *Your form that confirms comment deletion*

Next, you need to add another elseif block to update.inc.php that checks whether the comment deletion form was submitted via the POST method. You can make sure the confirmation form was submitted by checking whether the $_POST superglobal contains an index called action with a value of comment_delete,.

You need to store the URL you passed via your form in the $_POST['url'] variable. Just to be safe, you check whether the variable was set and provide a default value it wasn't, which you store in the variable $url.

Next, you check whether the "Yes" button was clicked. If so, you include and instantiate the Comments class, then pass the comment ID stored in $_POST['id'] to the deleteComment() method. If the method returns TRUE, you send the user to the URL stored in $url.

If the user clicked No, you send her to the URL stored in $url, doing nothing with the comment.

To implement this, you add the code in bold to the bottom of update.inc.php, just above the last else block:

```
// If the delete link is clicked on a comment, confirm it here
else if($_GET['action'] == 'comment_delete')
{
    // Include and instantiate the Comments class
    include_once 'comments.inc.php';
    $comments = new Comments();
    echo $comments->confirmDelete($_GET['id']);
    exit;
}

// If the confirmDelete() form was submitted, handle it here
else if($_SERVER['REQUEST_METHOD'] == 'POST'
    && $_POST['action'] == 'comment_delete')
```

```php
{
    // If set, store the entry from which we came
    $loc = isset($_POST['url']) ? $_POST['url'] : '../';

    // If the user clicked "Yes", continue with deletion
    if($_POST['confirm'] == "Yes")
    {
        // Include and instantiate the Comments class
        include_once 'comments.inc.php';
        $comments = new Comments();

        // Delete the comment and return to the entry
        if($comments->deleteComment($_POST['id']))
        {
            header('Location: '.$loc);
            exit;
        }

        // If deleting fails, output an error message
        else
        {
            exit('Could not delete the comment.');
        }
    }

    // If the user clicked "No", do nothing and return to the entry
    else
    {
        header('Location: '.$loc);
        exit;
    }
}

else
{
    header('Location: ../');
    exit;
}

?>
```

At this point, you can delete comments from the database, thus removing them from your entry display. You can test this out by deleting your test comment. Navigate to the entry that you we entered for the comment in a browser, then click the delete link. Next, click Yes to confirm that you want to delete the comment. This takes you back to the entry, but the comment is no longer there. Instead, you see the default message: "There are no comments for this entry" (see Figure 10-6).

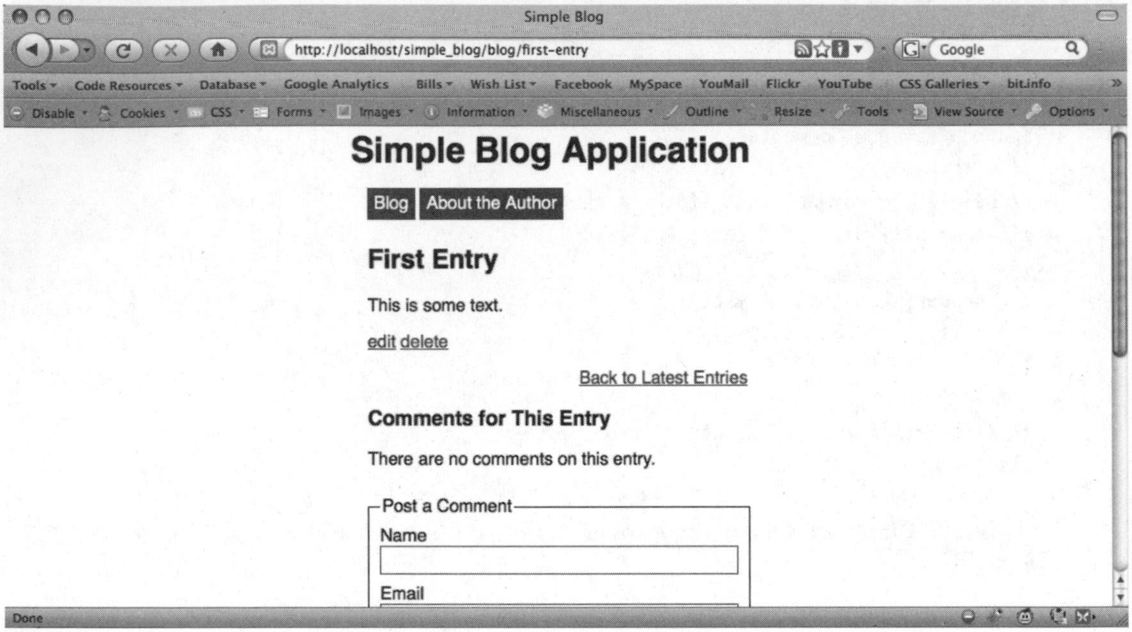

Figure 10-6. *After deleting your test comment, you see this default message*

Summary

In this chapter, you learned how to add an interactive element to your blog by allowing users to comment on your blog entries. In doing so, you also learned a little more about object-oriented programming.

In the next chapter, you'll learn how to build a login system that lets you hide administrative controls from users who aren't logged in, giving you better control over your blog.

■ ■ ■

CHAPTER 11

Adding Password Protection to Administrative Links

One of the last things you need to add before you can call your blog "web-ready" is to hide the administrative links from users who aren't authorized to view them. In this chapter, you'll learn how to build a system that lets you create administrators and require them to log in with a password before they can create, edit, and delete entries on the blog.

Creating this system requires that you master the following tasks:

- Adding an admin table to the simple_blog database

- Building a function to place administrators in the admin table

- Using sessions to hide controls from unauthorized users

- Creating a login form that allows administrators to log in to the blog

- Writing code to check submitted form data and display its controls if valid

Adding an admin Table to the Database

Enabling administrators for your site requires that you create a table to store their information. This simple table, admin, stores the following information:

- username: The administrator's login name

- password: The administrator's password

Your username needs to be unique, so make it the table's primary key. Specify both fields as of the VARCHAR type, limit the username to 75 characters, and limit the password to 40 characters.

To create the admin table, navigate to http://localhost/phpmyadmin in a browser and open the SQL tab. Enter the following command to create your table:

```
CREATE TABLE simple_blog.admin
(
username VARCHAR(75) PRIMARY KEY,
password VARCHAR(40)
)
```

Adding Administrators in the Database

You have a place to store administrators; now you're ready to start creating them. Your first step is to create a form that allows you to enter a username and password in an HTML form. Once you accomplish this, you need to store the information in the database for later use.

Building an HTML Form

To build your HTML form, you need to write a new function, named createUserForm(). When called, this function returns a string of HTML that displays a form that asks for a username and password for the new admin.

You can add the code in bold to functions.inc.php to make the createUserForm() function:

```
function createUserForm()
{
    return <<<FORM
<form action="/simple_blog/inc/update.inc.php" method="post">
    <fieldset>
        <legend>Create a New Administrator</legend>
        <label>Username
            <input type="text" name="username" maxlength="75" />
        </label>
        <label>Password
            <input type="password" name="password" />
        </label>
        <input type="submit" name="submit" value="Create" />
        <input type="submit" name="submit" value="Cancel" />
        <input type="hidden" name="action" value="createuser" />
    </fieldset>
</form>
FORM;
}
```

Next, you need to add code to call this function if the user chooses to create a new admin. Use the http://localhost/simple_blog/admin/createuser URL as your call to create a new admin for your blog.

To make this URL call the createUserForm() function, you need to add an if block to admin.php that triggers when the $page variable you use to determine what page is being edited is set to createuser.

Next, modify admin.php with the code in bold to incorporate the new form into your blog:

```
<?php

    /*
     * Include the necessary files
     */
```

```php
include_once 'inc/functions.inc.php';
include_once 'inc/db.inc.php';

// Open a database connection
$db = new PDO(DB_INFO, DB_USER, DB_PASS);

if(isset($_GET['page']))
{
    $page = htmlentities(strip_tags($_GET['page']));
}
else
{
    $page = 'blog';
}

if(isset($_POST['action']) && $_POST['action'] == 'delete')
{
    if($_POST['submit'] == 'Yes')
    {
        $url = htmlentities(strip_tags($_POST['url']));
        if(deleteEntry($db, $url))
        {
            header("Location: /simple_blog/");
            exit;
        }
        else
        {
            exit("Error deleting the entry!");
        }
    }
    else
    {
        header("Location: /simple_blog/blog/$_POST[url]");
    }
}

if(isset($_GET['url']))
{
    $url = htmlentities(strip_tags($_GET['url']));

    // Check if the entry should be deleted
    if($page == 'delete')
    {
        $confirm = confirmDelete($db, $url);
    }
```

```php
        // Set the legend of the form
        $legend = "Edit This Entry";

        $e = retrieveEntries($db, $page, $url);
        $id = $e['id'];
        $title = $e['title'];
        $img = $e['image'];
        $entry = $e['entry'];
    }
    else
    {

        // Check if we're creating a new user
        if($page == 'createuser')
        {
            $create = createUserForm();
        }

         // Set the legend
        $legend = "New Entry Submission";

        // Set the variables to null if not editing
        $id = NULL;
        $title = NULL;
        $img = NULL;
        $entry = NULL;
    }
?>
<!DOCTYPE html
    PUBLIC "-//W3C//DTD XHTML 1.0 Strict//EN"
    "http://www.w3.org/TR/xhtml1/DTD/xhtml1-strict.dtd">

<html xmlns="http://www.w3.org/1999/xhtml" xml:lang="en" lang="en">

<head>
    <meta http-equiv="Content-Type" content="text/html;charset=utf-8" />
    <link rel="stylesheet" href="/simple_blog/css/default.css" type="text/css" />
    <title> Simple Blog </title>
</head>

<body>
    <h1> Simple Blog Application </h1>
```

```php
<?php

    if($page == 'delete'):
    {
        echo $confirm;
    }
    elseif($page == 'createuser'):
    {
        echo $create;
    }
    else:

?>
```

You are now able to navigate to `http://localhost/simple_blog/admin/createuser` and see your form (see Figure 11-1).

Figure 11-1. *The form you use to create site administrators*

Saving New Administrators in the Database

You submit your form to update.inc.php with a hidden input named action that sends the value, createuser. To store administrators created through your createUserForm() HTML form, you need to modify update.inc.php to catch form information with an action of createuser.

You need to prepare an SQL statement that places the username and password into the admin table. Do this after you ensure that the form was sent using the POST method, that the action is set to createuser, and that the username and password inputs were not submitted with empty values.

Dealing with Passwords

You need to take extra precautions now that you're dealing with passwords. Passwords are sensitive information, and you do not want to store a password as plain text in the database. Fortunately, both PHP and MySQL provide means for encrypting strings.

For the blog, you can use SHA1(), which is a basic encryption algorithm. Calling SHA1() on a string returns a 40-character string that is difficult to decode.

■**Note** For more information on encrypting passwords, look up the PHP manual entries on md5() and sha1().

Saving the Admin

To save the admin information, you need to include the database credentials and open a new connection to your database.

The SQL statement you use for this is a standard insert, except that you need to use MySQL's built-in support for creating SHA1 hashes. After you insert the new entry into the table, you send the user back to the default blog home page.

In update.inc.php, insert the following code in bold just before the last else block:

```
// If an admin is being created, save it here
else if($_SERVER['REQUEST_METHOD'] == 'POST'
    && $_POST['action'] == 'createuser'
    && !empty($_POST['username'])
    && !empty($_POST['password']))
{
    // Include database credentials and connect to the database
    include_once 'db.inc.php';
    $db = new PDO(DB_INFO, DB_USER, DB_PASS);
    $sql = "INSERT INTO admin (username, password)
            VALUES(?, SHA1(?))";
    $stmt = $db->prepare($sql);
    $stmt->execute(array($_POST['username'], $_POST['password']));
    header('Location: /simple_blog/');
    exit;
}
```

```
else
{
    header('Location: ../');
    exit;
}


?>
```

You can now save new administrators to your admin table. Navigate to http://localhost/simple_blog/admin/createuser in a browser and create a new user with the username of admin and the password of admin. Now click the Create button, navigate to http://localhost/phpmyadmin in a browser, select the simple_blog database and the admin table, then click the Browse tab. Your administrator is now saved in the table, and the password is saved as an encrypted hash (see Figure 11-2).

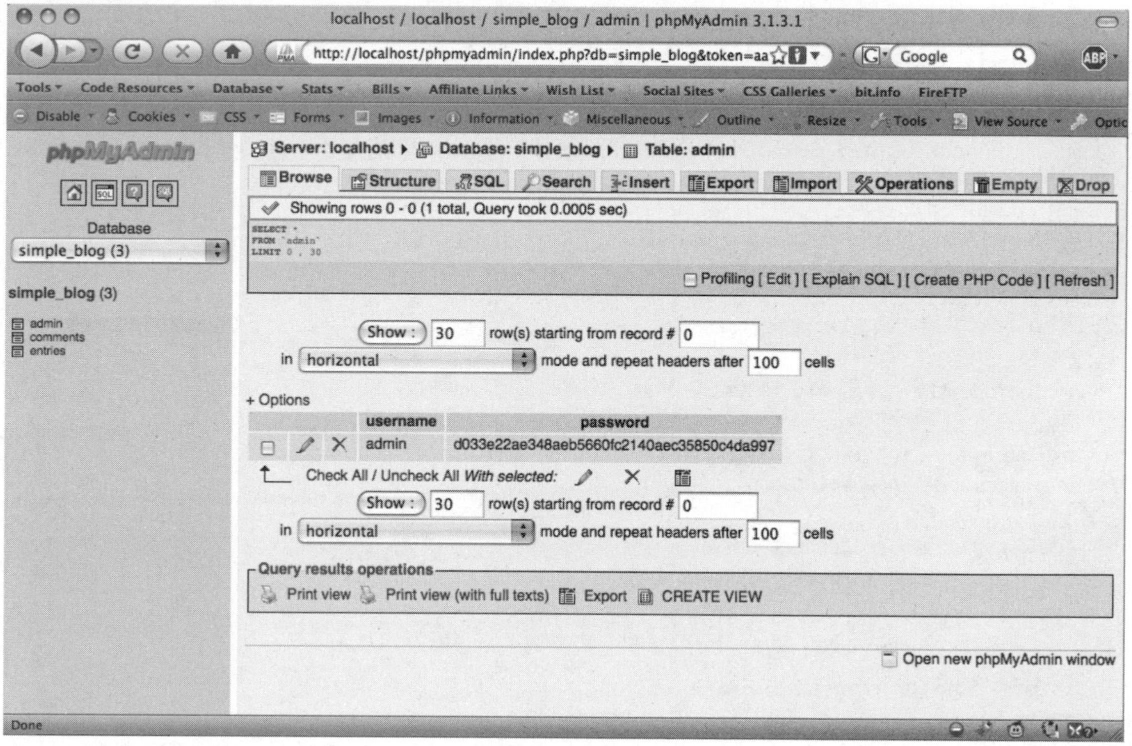

Figure 11-2. Your first administrator

Hiding Controls from Unauthorized Users

You can use *sessions* to keep track of which users are authorized to view administrative links on your blog. A session allows the user to log in once, then navigate anywhere on the site without losing his administrative privileges.

■**Note** For a refresher on how sessions work, refer to the section on sessions in Chapter 3.

Your first task is to wrap all administrative links in an if block; this ensures that a session variable is set for the current user. Call your session variable loggedin and store it in the $_SESSION['loggedin'] string.

Modifying index.php

Your next task is to hide all the admin links in index.php from unauthorized users. You need to enable sessions, which you can accomplish in a couple steps: call session_start(), then wrap all the admin links in your check for the $_SESSION['loggedin'] variable. Now modify index.php with the code in bold to make your changes:

```php
<?php

    session_start();

    /*
     * Include the necessary files
     */
    include_once 'inc/functions.inc.php';
    include_once 'inc/db.inc.php';

    // Open a database connection
    $db = new PDO(DB_INFO, DB_USER, DB_PASS);

    // Figure out what page is being requested (default is blog)
    if(isset($_GET['page']))
    {
        $page = htmlentities(strip_tags($_GET['page']));
    }
    else
    {
        $page = 'blog';
    }
```

```php
        // Determine if an entry URL was passed
        $url = (isset($_GET['url'])) ? $_GET['url'] : NULL;

        // Load the entries
        $e = retrieveEntries($db, $page, $url);

        // Get the fulldisp flag and remove it from the array
        $fulldisp = array_pop($e);

        // Sanitize the entry data
        $e = sanitizeData($e);

?>
<!DOCTYPE html
    PUBLIC "-//W3C//DTD XHTML 1.0 Strict//EN"
    "http://www.w3.org/TR/xhtml1/DTD/xhtml1-strict.dtd">

<html xmlns="http://www.w3.org/1999/xhtml" xml:lang="en" lang="en">

<head>
    <meta http-equiv="Content-Type"
        content="text/html;charset=utf-8" />
    <link rel="stylesheet" href="/simple_blog/css/default.css"
        type="text/css" />
    <link rel="alternate" type="application/rss+xml"
        title="My Simple Blog - RSS 2.0"
        href="http://localhost/simple_blog/feeds/rss.xml" />
    <title> Simple Blog </title>
</head>

<body>

    <h1> Simple Blog Application </h1>
    <ul id="menu">
        <li><a href="/simple_blog/blog/">Blog</a></li>
        <li><a href="/simple_blog/about/">About the Author</a></li>
    </ul>

    <div id="entries">

<?php
```

```php
// If the full display flag is set, show the entry
if($fulldisp==1)
{

    // Get the URL if one wasn't passed
    $url = (isset($url)) ? $url : $e['url'];

    if(isset($_SESSION['loggedin']) && $_SESSION['loggedin'] == 1)
    {
        // Build the admin links
        $admin = adminLinks($page, $url);
    }
    else
    {
        $admin = array('edit'=>NULL, 'delete'=>NULL);
    }

    // Format the image if one exists
    $img = formatImage($e['image'], $e['title']);

    if($page=='blog')
    {
        // Load the comment object
        include_once 'inc/comments.inc.php';
        $comments = new Comments();
        $comment_disp = $comments->showComments($e['id']);
        $comment_form = $comments->showCommentForm($e['id']);
    }
    else
    {
        $comment_form = NULL;
    }

?>

        <h2> <?php echo $e['title'] ?> </h2>
        <p> <?php echo $img, $e['entry'] ?> </p>
        <p>
            <?php echo $admin['edit'] ?>
            <?php if($page=='blog') echo $admin['delete'] ?>
        </p>
```

```php
        <?php if($page=='blog'): ?>
        <p class="backlink">
            <a href="./">Back to Latest Entries</a>
        </p>
        <h3> Comments for This Entry </h3>
        <?php echo $comment_disp, $comment_form; endif; ?>

<?php

} // End the if statement

// If the full display flag is 0, format linked entry titles
else
{
    // Loop through each entry
    foreach($e as $entry) {

?>

        <p>
            <a href="/simple_blog/<?php echo $entry['page'] ?>
/<?php echo $entry['url'] ?>">
                <?php echo $entry['title'] ?>

            </a>
        </p>

<?php

    } // End the foreach loop
} // End the else

?>

        <p class="backlink">
<?php

if($page=='blog'
    && isset($_SESSION['loggedin'])
    && $_SESSION['loggedin'] == 1):

?>
```

```
            <a href="/simple_blog/admin/<?php echo $page ?>">
                Post a New Entry
            </a>
<?php endif; ?>
        </p>

        <p>
            <a href="/simple_blog/feeds/rss.xml">
                Subscribe via RSS!
            </a>
        </p>

    </div>

</body>

</html>
```

When we navigate to `http://localhost/simple_blog/` in your browser, the admin links no longer appear (see Figure 11-3).

Figure 11-3. Your main page with the admin *links hidden from view*

Modifying comments.inc.php

Next, you want to hide the delete link from unauthorized users on any posted comments. You can do this by modifying the Comments class in comments.inc.php.

The only method you need to modify in the Comments class is showComments(). Add your session check by inserting the code in bold to showComments():

```php
// Generates HTML markup for displaying comments
public function showComments($blog_id)
{
    // Initialize the variable in case no comments exist
    $display = NULL;

    // Load the comments for the entry
    $this->retrieveComments($blog_id);

    // Loop through the stored comments
    foreach($this->comments as $c)
    {
        // Prevent empty fields if no comments exist
        if(!empty($c['date']) && !empty($c['name']))
        {
            // Outputs similar to: July 8, 2009 at 4:39PM
            $format = "F j, Y \a\\t g:iA";

            // Convert $c['date'] to a timestamp, then format
            $date = date($format, strtotime($c['date']));

            // Generate a byline for the comment
            $byline = "<span><strong>$c[name]</strong>
                        [Posted on $date]</span>";

            if(isset($_SESSION['loggedin'])
                && $_SESSION['loggedin'] == 1)
            {
                // Generate delete link for the comment display
                $admin = "<a href=\"/simple_blog/inc/update.inc.php"
                            . "?action=comment_delete&id=$c[id]\""
                            . " class=\"admin\">delete</a>";
            }
            else
            {
                $admin = NULL;
            }
        }
```

```
        else
        {
            // If no comments exist, set $byline & $admin to NULL
            $byline = NULL;
            $admin = NULL;
        }

        // Assemble the pieces into a formatted comment
        $display .= "
<p class=\"comment\">$byline$c[comment]$admin</p>";
    }

    // Return all the formatted comments as a string
    return $display;
}
```

Now you can navigate to an entry with a comment in your blog to see that the delete link is no longer visible (see Figure 11-4).

Figure 11-4. *The comment entry you display to unauthorized users*

Modifying admin.php

None of the actions performed by this page should be available to unauthorized users, so you want to require authorization before any of the functionality of admin.php can be accessed. Doing this is as simple as wrapping the entire page in a conditional statement.

Modify admin.php by adding the code in bold:

```php
<?php

session_start();

// If the user is logged in, we can continue
if(isset($_SESSION['loggedin']) && $_SESSION['loggedin']==1):

    /*
     * Include the necessary files
     */
    include_once 'inc/functions.inc.php';
    include_once 'inc/db.inc.php';

    // Open a database connection
    $db = new PDO(DB_INFO, DB_USER, DB_PASS);

    if(isset($_GET['page']))
    {
        $page = htmlentities(strip_tags($_GET['page']));
    }
    else
    {
        $page = 'blog';
    }

    if(isset($_POST['action']) && $_POST['action'] == 'delete')
    {
        if($_POST['submit'] == 'Yes')
        {
            $url = htmlentities(strip_tags($_POST['url']));
            if(deleteEntry($db, $url))
            {
                header("Location: /simple_blog/");
                exit;
            }
        }
```

```php
        else
        {
            exit("Error deleting the entry!");
        }
    }
    else
    {
        header("Location: /simple_blog/blog/$_POST[url]");
    }
}

if(isset($_GET['url']))
{
    $url = htmlentities(strip_tags($_GET['url']));

    // Check if the entry should be deleted
    if($page == 'delete')
    {
        $confirm = confirmDelete($db, $url);
    }

    // Set the legend of the form
    $legend = "Edit This Entry";

    $e = retrieveEntries($db, $page, $url);
    $id = $e['id'];
    $title = $e['title'];
    $img = $e['image'];
    $entry = $e['entry'];
}
else
{
    // Check if we're creating a new user
    if($page == 'createuser')
    {
        $create = createUserForm();
    }
```

```php
        // Set the legend
        $legend = "New Entry Submission";

        // Set the variables to null if not editing
        $id = NULL;
        $title = NULL;
        $img = NULL;
        $entry = NULL;
    }
?>
<!DOCTYPE html
    PUBLIC "-//W3C//DTD XHTML 1.0 Strict//EN"
    "http://www.w3.org/TR/xhtml1/DTD/xhtml1-strict.dtd">

<html xmlns="http://www.w3.org/1999/xhtml" xml:lang="en" lang="en">

<head>
    <meta http-equiv="Content-Type" content="text/html;charset=utf-8" />
    <link rel="stylesheet" href="/simple_blog/css/default.css" type="text/css" />
    <title> Simple Blog </title>
</head>

<body>
    <h1> Simple Blog Application </h1>

<?php

    if($page == 'delete'):
    {
        echo $confirm;
    }
    elseif($page == 'createuser'):
    {
        echo $create;
    }
    else:

?>
```

```
<form method="post"
    action="/simple_blog/inc/update.inc.php"
    enctype="multipart/form-data">
    <fieldset>
        <legend><?php echo $legend ?></legend>
        <label>Title
            <input type="text" name="title" maxlength="150"
                value="<?php echo $title ?>" />
        </label>
        <label>Image
            <input type="file" name="image" />
        </label>
        <label>Entry
            <textarea name="entry" cols="45"
                rows="10"><?php echo $entry ?></textarea>
        </label>
        <input type="hidden" name="id"
            value="<?php echo $id ?>" />
        <input type="hidden" name="page"
            value="<?php echo $page ?>" />
        <input type="submit" name="submit" value="Save Entry" />
        <input type="submit" name="submit" value="Cancel" />
    </fieldset>
</form>
<?php endif; ?>
</body>

</html>
<?php endif; // Ends the section available to logged in users ?>
```

At this point, you've barred anyone who isn't logged in from seeing administrative links and performing administrative tasks such as creating, editing, and deleting entries.

Creating a Login Form

Now that you require authorization for a user to view administrative links, you need to build in the functionality that allows your administrators to log in and gain access to those links.

To do this, you first need to create a login form where a user can enter her credentials to request access to the administrative links.

A logical location to place your login form is at http://localhost/simple_blog/admin. For the moment, admin.php shows a blank page if the user hasn't logged in because authorization is required before the page will do anything at all. You can fix that by placing the login form at the bottom of admin.php, inside an else block. Doing so shows a login screen to anyone who isn't logged in already.

Your login form requests a username and password and uses the POST method to send this information to update.inc.php, along with a hidden input named action that passes the value, login.

At the bottom of admin.php, just after the closing </html> tag, modify the file with the code in bold:

```
</html>

<?php

/*
 * If we get here, the user is not logged in. Display a form
 * and ask them to log in.
 */
else:

?>
<!DOCTYPE html
    PUBLIC "-//W3C//DTD XHTML 1.0 Strict//EN"
    "http://www.w3.org/TR/xhtml1/DTD/xhtml1-strict.dtd">

<html xmlns="http://www.w3.org/1999/xhtml" xml:lang="en" lang="en">

<head>
    <meta http-equiv="Content-Type"
        content="text/html;charset=utf-8" />
    <link rel="stylesheet"
        href="/simple_blog/css/default.css" type="text/css" />
    <title> Please Log In </title>
</head>

<body>

    <form method="post"
        action="/simple_blog/inc/update.inc.php"
        enctype="multipart/form-data">
        <fieldset>
            <legend>Please Log In To Continue</legend>
            <label>Username
                <input type="text" name="username" maxlength="75" />
            </label>
            <label>Password
                <input type="password" name="password"
                    maxlength="150" />
            </label>
```

```
            <input type="hidden" name="action" value="login" />
            <input type="submit" name="submit" value="Log In" />
        </fieldset>
    </form>

</body>

</html>

<?php endif; ?>
```

Now you can navigate to `http://localhost/simple_blog/admin` to see your login form in action (see Figure 11-5).

Figure 11-5. *Users not logged in see a login screen.*

Displaying Controls to Authorized Users

Your next steps are to modify `update.inc.php` to check whether the login credentials supplied via the login form are valid; if they are, you set `$_SESSION['loggedin']` to 1, which causes all administrative links and actions to become available to the user.

In `update.inc.php`, you add an `else if` block that checks whether it was the POST method that submitted the login form. You do this by checking whether the value of `$_POST['action']` is set to `login` and whether the values of the `username` and `password` fields were submitted with values.

If these criteria are met, you load the database credentials and open a connection. Next, you set up a SQL query that gets the number of matches found by comparing the submitted username and the SHA1() hash of the submitted password against the database.

■**Note** You must check the SHA1() hash of the password because that's what you saved in the database. There's no way to reverse a SHA1() hash, but the encryption algorithm always returns the same hash for a given string.

The user is authorized to view the blog if a match is returned, whereupon you can add $_SESSION['loggedin'] to the session and set its value to 1.

To accomplish this, you use session_start() at the top of update.inc.php, then add the else if block at the bottom, just above your block that checks whether you're creating a user.

Modify update.inc.php by adding the code in bold:

```php
<?php

// Start the session
session_start();

// Include the functions so we can create a URL
include_once 'functions.inc.php';

// Include the image handling class
include_once 'images.inc.php';

if($_SERVER['REQUEST_METHOD']=='POST'
    && $_POST['submit']=='Save Entry'
    && !empty($_POST['page'])
    && !empty($_POST['title'])
    && !empty($_POST['entry']))
{
    // Create a URL to save in the database
    $url = makeUrl($_POST['title']);

    if(strlen($_FILES['image']['tmp_name']) > 0)
    {
        try
        {
            // Instantiate the class and set a save dir
            $image = new ImageHandler("/simple_blog/images/");

            // Process the uploaded image and save the returned path
            $img_path = $image->processUploadedImage($_FILES['image']);
        }
```

```php
    catch(Exception $e)
    {
        // If an error occurred, output our custom error message
        die($e->getMessage());
    }
}
else
{
    // Avoids a notice if no image was uploaded
    $img_path = NULL;
}


// Include database credentials and connect to the database
include_once 'db.inc.php';
$db = new PDO(DB_INFO, DB_USER, DB_PASS);

// Edit an existing entry
if(!empty($_POST['id']))
{
    $sql = "UPDATE entries
            SET title=?, image=?, entry=?, url=?
            WHERE id=?
            LIMIT 1";
    $stmt = $db->prepare($sql);
    $stmt->execute(
        array(
            $_POST['title'],
            $img_path,
            $_POST['entry'],
            $url,
            $_POST['id']
        )
    );
    $stmt->closeCursor();
}
```

```php
    // Create a new entry
    else
    {
        // Save the entry into the database
        $sql = "INSERT INTO entries (page, title, image, entry, url)
                VALUES (?, ?, ?, ?, ?)";
        $stmt = $db->prepare($sql);
        $stmt->execute(
            array(
                $_POST['page'],
                $_POST['title'],
                $img_path,
                $_POST['entry'],
                $url
            )
        );
        $stmt->closeCursor();
    }

    // Sanitize the page information for use in the success URL
    $page = htmlentities(strip_tags($_POST['page']));

    // Send the user to the new entry
    header('Location: /simple_blog/'.$page.'/'.$url);
    exit;
}

// If a comment is being posted, handle it here
else if($_SERVER['REQUEST_METHOD'] == 'POST'
    && $_POST['submit'] == 'Post Comment')
{
    // Include and instantiate the Comments class
    include_once 'comments.inc.php';
    $comments = new Comments();

    // Save the comment
    if($comments->saveComment($_POST))
    {
        // If available, store the entry the user came from
        if(isset($_SERVER['HTTP_REFERER']))
        {
            $loc = $_SERVER['HTTP_REFERER'];
        }
```

```php
            else
            {
                $loc = '../';
            }

            // Send the user back to the entry
            header('Location: '.$loc);
            exit;
        }

        // If saving fails, output an error message
        else
        {
            exit('Something went wrong while saving the comment.');
        }
    }

// If the delete link is clicked on a comment, confirm it here
else if($_GET['action'] == 'comment_delete')
{
    // Include and instantiate the Comments class
    include_once 'comments.inc.php';
    $comments = new Comments();
    echo $comments->confirmDelete($_GET['id']);
    exit;
}

// If the confirmDelete() form was submitted, handle it here
else if($_SERVER['REQUEST_METHOD'] == 'POST'
    && $_POST['action'] == 'comment_delete')
{
    // If set, store the entry from which we came
    $loc = isset($_POST['url']) ? $_POST['url'] : '../';

    // If the user clicked "Yes", continue with deletion
    if($_POST['confirm'] == "Yes")
    {
        // Include and instantiate the Comments class
        include_once 'comments.inc.php';
        $comments = new Comments();
```

```
        // Delete the comment and return to the entry
        if($comments->deleteComment($_POST['id']))
        {
            header('Location: '.$loc);
            exit;
        }

        // If deleting fails, output an error message
        else
        {
            exit('Could not delete the comment.');
        }
    }

    // If the user didn't click "Yes", do nothing and return to the entry
    else
    {
        header('Location: '.$loc);
        exit;
    }
}

// If a user is trying to log in, check it here
else if($_SERVER['REQUEST_METHOD'] == 'POST'
    && $_POST['action'] == 'login'
    && !empty($_POST['username'])
    && !empty($_POST['password']))
{
    // Include database credentials and connect to the database
    include_once 'db.inc.php';
    $db = new PDO(DB_INFO, DB_USER, DB_PASS);
    $sql = "SELECT COUNT(*) AS num_users
            FROM admin
            WHERE username=?
            AND password=SHA1(?)";
    $stmt = $db->prepare($sql);
    $stmt->execute(array($_POST['username'], $_POST['password']));
    $response = $stmt->fetch();
    if($response['num_users'] > 0)
    {
        $_SESSION['loggedin'] = 1;
    }
```

```php
    else
    {
        $_SESSION['loggedin'] = NULL;
    }
    header('Location: /simple_blog/');
    exit;
}

// If an admin is being created, save it here
else if($_SERVER['REQUEST_METHOD'] == 'POST'
    && $_POST['action'] == 'createuser'
    && !empty($_POST['username'])
    && !empty($_POST['password']))
{
    // Include database credentials and connect to the database
    include_once 'db.inc.php';
    $db = new PDO(DB_INFO, DB_USER, DB_PASS);
    $sql = "INSERT INTO admin (username, password)
            VALUES(?, SHA1(?))";
    $stmt = $db->prepare($sql);
    $stmt->execute(array($_POST['username'], $_POST['password']));
    header('Location: /simple_blog/');
    exit;
}

else
{
    header('Location: ../');
    exit;
}

?>
```

You can test this code by navigating to http://localhost/simple_blog/admin and entering the username and password you inserted into the database previously (both values were set to admin). This redirects you to the main page and makes the Post a New Entry link visible again. If you open an entry, you can see that all the administrative links are visible again (see Figure 11-6).

Figure 11-6. After logging in, you can see the administrative links again.

Logging Users Out

After an authorized user completes his administrative tasks, he needs to be able to log out from the site. To enable this, all you need to do is unset $_SESSION['loggedin'], which hides the admin links and prevents any administrative actions from being performed until the user logs in again.

Adding a Log Out Link

You can simplify this process by adding a Log out link to your blog pages. This is as simple as adding an additional if block to index.php that displays a message notifying a user that she is logged in, as well as a link that allows her to log out.

You can keep the link visible by placing it right under the menu. In index.php, add the code in bold between the menu and the entries container:

```
<body>

    <h1> Simple Blog Application </h1>
    <ul id="menu">
        <li><a href="/simple_blog/blog/">Blog</a></li>
        <li><a href="/simple_blog/about/">About the Author</a></li>
    </ul>

<?php if(isset($_SESSION['loggedin']) && $_SESSION['loggedin']==1): ?>
    <p id="control_panel">
        You are logged in!
        <a href="/simple_blog/inc/update.inc.php?action=logout">Log
            out</a>.
    </p>
<?php endif; ?>

    <div id="entries">
```

Navigate to `http://localhost/simple_blog/` while logged in to see the new notification and Log out link (see Figure 11-7).

Figure 11-7. *When logged in, you now see a notification and a link to log out.*

Modifying update.inc.php to Log Out Users

The code you created in the last step means the Log out link will send your user to update.inc.php and use the GET method to pass a variable called action that is set to logout.

At the bottom of update.inc.php, add one more else if block that checks whether $_GET['action'] is set to logout; if so, use the session_destroy() function to destroy $_SESSION['loggedin'] and any other session variables, which reverts the user back to an unauthorized state and once again hides the administrative links and actions. From here, you simply send the user back out to the default page.

Insert the following code in bold into update.inc.php, just above the last else block:

```
// If the user has chosen to log out, process it here
else if($_GET['action'] == 'logout')
{
    session_destroy();
    header('Location: ../');
    exit;
}

else
{
    header('Location: ../');
    exit;
}

?>
```

You can test this code by clicking the Log out link on any page. Doing so takes you back to the main page and hides the administrative links (see Figure 11-8).

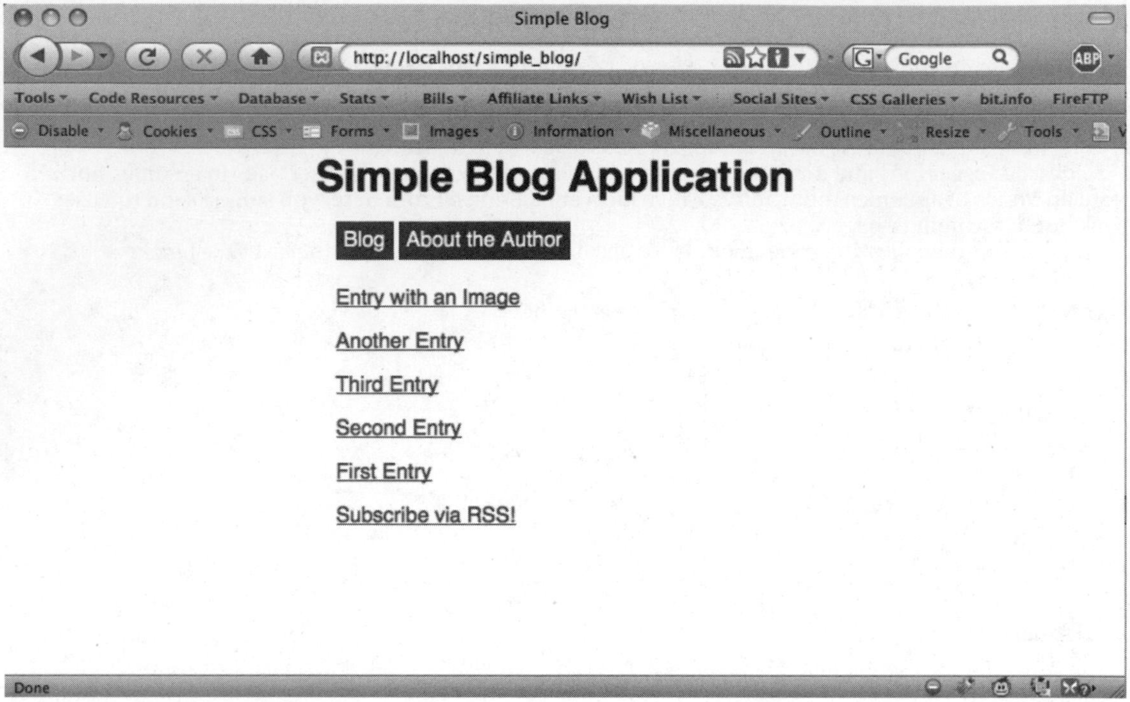

Figure 11-8. *Logging out hides the administrative links again.*

Summary

In this chapter, you created a very simple login system that allows you to add password protection to the administrative functions of your blog. This gives you better control over your blog by restricting access to the administrative links and actions.

At this point, your blog is nearly finished. In the next chapter, you will learn how to integrate spam-prevention, email validation, and some fun extras involving a few popular social media sites in an effort to connect further with your blog's readers.

CHAPTER 12

■ ■ ■

Finishing Touches

The last few steps are optional, but they add that final touches to the blog that will make it feel professional, inviting, and, most of all, useful.

In this chapter, you will learn how to add several fun features to the blog:

- An email validation script for posting comments

- Basic spam prevention measures for comment posting

- A "Post to Twitter" link, utilizing the `http://bit.ly` URL-shortening service

Email Validation

Validating a user's email address helps you avoid basic spam attempts. Some spam bots simply add garbage text into a form's inputs. By ensuring that the email input is filled out with a properly formatted email address, you can fend off the most primitive types of spam attacks.

However, you also want to keep in mind that people sometimes make typos, and if your comment form can't validate a user with a typo in her email address, you don't want to erase her comment completely and make her start over; this will frustrate your user and might prevent this person from joining the discussion on your blog.

To avoid this problem, you can save the comment in a session that you destroy only if the comment is posted successfully (or the session times out). This way, you won't penalize a real user who makes a simple mistake, giving her a chance to fix her mistake on the form before posting.

To validate email addresses before you save comments, you need to make the following modifications to the `Comments` class:

- Add a method to validate email addresses using a regular expression

- Modify the `saveComment()` method to call the validation function

- Save the contents of a comment form in session variables after posting

- Generate an error message if errors occur, so the user knows what went wrong

- Fill out the comment form with session values if they exist

- Destroy the session after a successful comment post

Adding a Method to Validate Email

Your first task is to write a new method that verifies whether the email address provided is a valid email format.

■**Note** This method doesn't verify that the email address is real; rather, it ensures that the format is valid. A user can still provide a fake email address, such as fake@email.com, and post a comment successfully.

You should make this method, called validateEmail(), private because you call it only from the Comments class. It's short and sweet: when called, it accepts the user's email address as an argument ($email) and matches the provided email address against a regular expression; the address is valid if the expression returns TRUE, but FALSE otherwise.

Open comments.inc.php and add validateEmail() just below the saveComment() method:

```
private function validateEmail($email)
{
    // Matches valid email addresses
    $p = '/^[\w-]+(\.[\w-]+)*@[a-z0-9-]+'
        .'(\.[a-z0-9-]+)*(\.[a-z]{2,4})$/i';

    // If a match is found, return TRUE, otherwise return FALSE
    return (preg_match($p, $email)) ? TRUE : FALSE;
}
```

The regular expression you use in this method looks incredibly complex, but you can break it down into three relatively simple sections: the part of the email address before the at (@) symbol, the part between the at (@) symbol and the period (.), and the top level domain (such as .com or .net).

The first section needs to match any hyphens (-) and word characters (symbolized by \w—this matches the letters, numbers, and underscore [_]) from the beginning of the string to the at (@) symbol. However, you should keep in mind that some email addresses use periods (.) as well, as in john.doe@email.com. This means you need to accommodate this email construction in your pattern, but not require it. Put this all together, and this section of the regular expression looks like this:

^[\w-]+(\.[\w-]+)*@

By placing the second part of the pattern in parentheses with the star (*) following, you can make this section required zero or more times, which effectively makes it optional.

■**Caution** Remember that the period (.) in regular expressions serves as a wildcard and matches nearly anything. To match only a period, be sure to escape the period with a backslash (\.).

The third section must match a domain name. Domain names cannot contain the underscore character (_), so this part of the pattern cannot use the word character shortcut (\w). Instead, you have to set up a character set manually that allows for letters, numbers, and the hyphen (-), and then require that one or more matches exist. As in the first section, your pattern must accommodate an optional set that matches the period (.) in the event a user's email address is from a subdomain, such as johndoe@sales.example.com. The third section of the pattern looks like this:

```
[a-z0-9-]+(\.[a-z0-9-]+)*
```

Finally, the pattern must match a top-level domain, such as .com or .net. This is as simple as creating a set of the letters a-z and requiring between two and four total characters that are at the end of the string; you express this requirement like this:

```
(\.[a-z]{2,4})$
```

Next, wrap this pattern in the required forward slash (/) delimiter, then append the i flag to make the pattern case-insensitive.

Validating Email Addresses

So far you've written a method to validate submitted email addresses. Next, you can modify saveComment() to call validateEmail(); this ensures that you save only comments with valid email addresses.

Inside saveComment(), add a conditional statement that performs an important check. If the returned value of validateEmail() is FALSE when the value of $p['email'] is passed, it terminates the function by returning FALSE.

Add these modifications by inserting the bold code into saveComment():

```
// Save comments to the database
public function saveComment($p)
{
    // Make sure the email address is valid first
    if($this->validateEmail($p['email'])===FALSE)
    {
        return FALSE;
    }

    // Sanitize the data and store in variables
    $blog_id = htmlentities(strip_tags($p['blog_id']),
        ENT_QUOTES);
    $name = htmlentities(strip_tags($p['name']), ENT_QUOTES);
    $email = htmlentities(strip_tags($p['email']), ENT_QUOTES);
    $comment = htmlentities(strip_tags($p['comment']),
        ENT_QUOTES);
```

```
// Generate an SQL command
$sql = "INSERT INTO comments (blog_id, name, email, comment)
        VALUES (?, ?, ?, ?)";
if($stmt = $this->db->prepare($sql))
{
    // Execute the command, free used memory, and return true
    $stmt->execute(array($blog_id, $name, $email, $comment));
    $stmt->closeCursor();
    return TRUE;
}
else
{
    // If something went wrong, return false
    return FALSE;
}
}
```

To test this, navigate to http://localhost/simple_blog/blog and select an entry. Now try to post a comment with a bad email address (such as "notarealemail") and click the Post Comment button. The script in update.inc.php will fail and output an error message because saveComment() returns FALSE when a valid email isn't supplied:

Something went wrong while saving the comment.

Saving Comments in Sessions

Next, you need to save the user's input in a session. As explained earlier, you do this so the user isn't forced to start from scratch if an error occurs when submitting the comment form.

In comments.inc.php, modify saveComment() by adding the following code in bold:

```
// Save comments to the database
public function saveComment($p)
{
    // Save the comment information in a session
    $_SESSION['c_name'] = htmlentities($p['name'], ENT_QUOTES);
    $_SESSION['c_email'] = htmlentities($p['email'], ENT_QUOTES);
    $_SESSION['c_comment'] = htmlentities($p['cmnt'],
        ENT_QUOTES);

    // Make sure the email address is valid first
    if($this->validateEmail($p['email'])===FALSE)
    {
        return FALSE;
    }
```

```
// Sanitize the data and store in variables
$blog_id = htmlentities(strip_tags($p['blog_id']),
    ENT_QUOTES);
$name = htmlentities(strip_tags($p['name']), ENT_QUOTES);
$email = htmlentities(strip_tags($p['email']), ENT_QUOTES);
$comment = htmlentities(strip_tags($p['comment']),
    ENT_QUOTES);

// Generate an SQL command
$sql = "INSERT INTO comments (blog_id, name, email, comment)
        VALUES (?, ?, ?, ?)";
if($stmt = $this->db->prepare($sql))
{
    // Execute the command, free used memory, and return true
    $stmt->execute(array($blog_id, $name, $email, $comment));
    $stmt->closeCursor();
    return TRUE;
}
else
{
    // If something went wrong, return false
    return FALSE;
}
}
```

Displaying the Stored Comment Information

You've saved the comment information in a session; now you can use the session variables to keep the comment form populated with the user's information. You can do this by modifying showCommentForm() to check whether the session variables are set, then store for output in the form.

You can add the code in bold to make showCommentForm() start showing stored comments:

```
// Display a form for users to enter new comments with
public function showCommentForm($blog_id)
{
    // Check if session variables exist
    if(isset($_SESSION['c_name']))
    {
        $n = $_SESSION['c_name'];
    }
    else
    {
        $n = NULL;
    }
```

```php
        if(isset($_SESSION['c_email']))
        {
            $e = $_SESSION['c_email'];
        }
        else
        {
            $e = NULL;
        }
        if(isset($_SESSION['c_comment']))
        {
            $c = $_SESSION['c_comment'];
        }
        else
        {
            $c = NULL;
        }

        return <<<FORM
<form action="/simple_blog/inc/update.inc.php"
    method="post" id="comment-form">
    <fieldset>
        <legend>Post a Comment</legend>
        <label>Name
            <input type="text" name="name" maxlength="75"
                value="$n" />
        </label>
        <label>Email
            <input type="text" name="email" maxlength="150"
                value="$e" />
        </label>
        <label>Comment
            <textarea rows="10" cols="45"
                name="comment">$c</textarea>
        </label>
        <input type="hidden" name="blog_id" value="$blog_id" />
        <input type="submit" name="submit" value="Post Comment" />
        <input type="submit" name="submit" value="Cancel" />
    </fieldset>
</form>
FORM;
    }
```

To test this, navigate to http://localhost/simple_blog/blog and select an entry. Enter a comment with a valid email address (you want to avoid the error screen for now), then click the Post Comment button to place a new comment on the blog entry.

After posting the comment, this script sends you back to the entry, where you can see the comment displayed both in the comment view as well as in the comment form. Your users might be confused if the form stays populated after a successful post, so you need to unset the session variables after a comment is stored properly.

You can do this by modifying saveComment() with the code in bold:

```
// Save comments to the database
    public function saveComment($p)
    {
        // Save the comment information in a session
        $_SESSION['c_name'] = htmlentities($p['name'], ENT_QUOTES);
        $_SESSION['c_email'] = htmlentities($p['email'], ENT_QUOTES);
        $_SESSION['c_comment'] = htmlentities($p['cmnt'],
            ENT_QUOTES);

        // Make sure the email address is valid first
        if($this->validateEmail($p['email'])===FALSE)
        {
            return FALSE;
        }

        // Sanitize the data and store in variables
        $blog_id = htmlentities(strip_tags($p['blog_id']),
            ENT_QUOTES);
        $name = htmlentities(strip_tags($p['name']), ENT_QUOTES);
        $email = htmlentities(strip_tags($p['email']), ENT_QUOTES);
        $comment = htmlentities(strip_tags($p['comment']),
            ENT_QUOTES);

        // Generate an SQL command
        $sql = "INSERT INTO comments (blog_id, name, email, comment)
                VALUES (?, ?, ?, ?)";
        if($stmt = $this->db->prepare($sql))
        {
            // Execute the command, free used memory, and return true
            $stmt->execute(array($blog_id, $name, $email, $comment));
            $stmt->closeCursor();

            // Destroy the comment information to empty the form
            unset($_SESSION['c_name'], $_SESSION['c_email'],
                $_SESSION['c_comment']);
            return TRUE;
        }
```

```
    else
    {
        // If something went wrong, return false
        return FALSE;
    }
}
```

You can test this script by posting a comment successfully. The comment should be displayed, but the form should be empty. Now enter a comment with a bad email address, which should throw up an error. From the error screen, navigate back to the entry you were testing with; you should see that no comment was posted, but the information you entered remains in the form.

Adding Error Messages

If you don't inform your users what went wrong, they might become confused and frustrated with your comment form. To counter this, you need to generate and display error messages when applicable; this will help the user fill out the form properly.

You're already using sessions, so here you can store error messages in an additional session variable, `$_SESSION['error']`. The saveComment() method lets you store any errors generated as an error code; you can then use the showCommentForm() to match an error with the appropriate error message you want to display on the form.

Identifying Errors in saveComment()

Begin by identifying the errors that might occur. The first error is an unexpected failure of the database query. Give this error the error code, 1. The second error occurs when the script encounters an invalid email, which you can identify with the error code 2. If necessary, you can add more error codes in the future.

You don't need to display an error if the user posts a comment successfully, so you don't store an error code when no errors occur. Also, you must unset the error session variable after a successful post to prevent the user from seeing the same error again, after the problem has been corrected.

Your script now dealings with error codes, rather than successful or unsuccessful scripts, so your script no longer needs to return TRUE or FALSE. Instead, you can make your script set a session variable with an error code and return nothing.

Implement these changes by adding the code in bold to saveComment():

```
// Save comments to the database
public function saveComment($p)
{
    // Save the comment information in a session
    $_SESSION['c_name'] = htmlentities($p['name'], ENT_QUOTES);
    $_SESSION['c_email'] = htmlentities($p['email'], ENT_QUOTES);
    $_SESSION['c_comment'] = htmlentities($p['cmnt'],
        ENT_QUOTES);
```

```php
// Make sure the email address is valid first
if($this->validateEmail($p['email'])===FALSE)
{
    $_SESSION['error'] = 2;
    return;
}

// Sanitize the data and store in variables
$blog_id = htmlentities(strip_tags($p['blog_id']),
    ENT_QUOTES);
$name = htmlentities(strip_tags($p['name']), ENT_QUOTES);
$email = htmlentities(strip_tags($p['email']), ENT_QUOTES);
$comment = htmlentities(strip_tags($p['comment']),
    ENT_QUOTES);

// Generate an SQL command
$sql = "INSERT INTO comments (blog_id, name, email, comment)
        VALUES (?, ?, ?, ?)";
if($stmt = $this->db->prepare($sql))
{
    // Execute the command, free used memory, and return true
    $stmt->execute(array($blog_id, $name, $email, $comment));
    $stmt->closeCursor();

    // Destroy the comment information to empty the form
    unset($_SESSION['c_name'], $_SESSION['c_email'],
        $_SESSION['c_comment'], $_SESSION['error']);
    return;
}
else
{
    // If something went wrong
    $_SESSION['error'] = 1;
    return;
}
}
```

Modifying update.inc.php

saveComment() no longer returns TRUE or FALSE, so you must modify update.inc.php to execute saveComment() rather than checking its output. Additionally, you need to account for the user pressing the comment form's Cancel button. When that happens, update.inc.php must unset the session variables to avoid problems.

Your first task is to fix issues with saving comments; make the following modifications, shown in bold and starting at line 94, to update.inc.php:

```php
// If a comment is being posted, handle it here
else if($_SERVER['REQUEST_METHOD'] == 'POST'
    && $_POST['submit'] == 'Post Comment')
{
    // Include and instantiate the Comments class
    include_once 'comments.inc.php';
    $comments = new Comments();

    // Save the comment
    $comments->saveComment($_POST);

    // If available, store the entry the user came from
    if(isset($_SERVER['HTTP_REFERER']))
    {
        $loc = $_SERVER['HTTP_REFERER'];
    }
    else
    {
        $loc = '../';
    }

    // Send the user back to the entry
    header('Location: '.$loc);
    exit;
}
```

Next, you can unset the session variables if a user presses the Cancel button by adding the code in bold to the last else block at the bottom of update.inc.php:

```php
else
{
    unset($_SESSION['c_name'], $_SESSION['c_email'],
        $_SESSION['c_comment'], $_SESSION['error']);
    header('Location: ../');
    exit;
}

?>
```

Matching Error Codes in showCommentForm()

Your script now stores error codes; next, you need to modify showCommentForm() to identify an error code and match it with a corresponding error message, which you then display on the comment form.

Begin by creating an array in which the error codes are the keys, and the messages are the values. Next, verify whether an error code was stored, and, if so, store the correct error message from the array in a variable ($error); otherwise, set the variable to NULL. Finally, insert the error message into the output for display.

Add these changes by inserting the code in bold into showCommentForm():

```
// Display a form for users to enter new comments with
public function showCommentForm($blog_id)
{
    $errors = array(
        1 => '<p class="error">Something went wrong while '
            . 'saving your comment. Please try again!</p>',
        2 => '<p class="error">Please provide a valid '
            . 'email address!</p>'
    );
    if(isset($_SESSION['error']))
    {
        $error = $errors[$_SESSION['error']];
    }
    else
    {
        $error = NULL;
    }

    // Check if session variables exist
    if(isset($_SESSION['c_name']))
    {
        $n = $_SESSION['c_name'];
    }
    else
    {
        $n = NULL;
    }
    if(isset($_SESSION['c_email']))
    {
        $e = $_SESSION['c_email'];
    }
```

```
        else
        {
            $e = NULL;
        }
        if(isset($_SESSION['c_comment']))
        {
            $c = $_SESSION['c_comment'];
        }
        else
        {
            $c = NULL;
        }

        return <<<FORM
<form action="/simple_blog/inc/update.inc.php"
    method="post" id="comment-form">
    <fieldset>
        <legend>Post a Comment</legend>$error
        <label>Name
            <input type="text" name="name" maxlength="75"
                value="$n" />
        </label>
        <label>Email
            <input type="text" name="email" maxlength="150"
                value="$e" />
        </label>
        <label>Comment
            <textarea rows="10" cols="45"
                name="comment">$c</textarea>
        </label>
        <input type="hidden" name="blog_id" value="$blog_id" />
        <input type="submit" name="submit" value="Post Comment" />
        <input type="submit" name="submit" value="Cancel" />
    </fieldset>
</form>
FORM;
    }
```

Now your users receive an error message if they make a mistake or something goes wrong with the submission. Try entering a bad email address to see your new error handling system in action (see Figure 12-1).

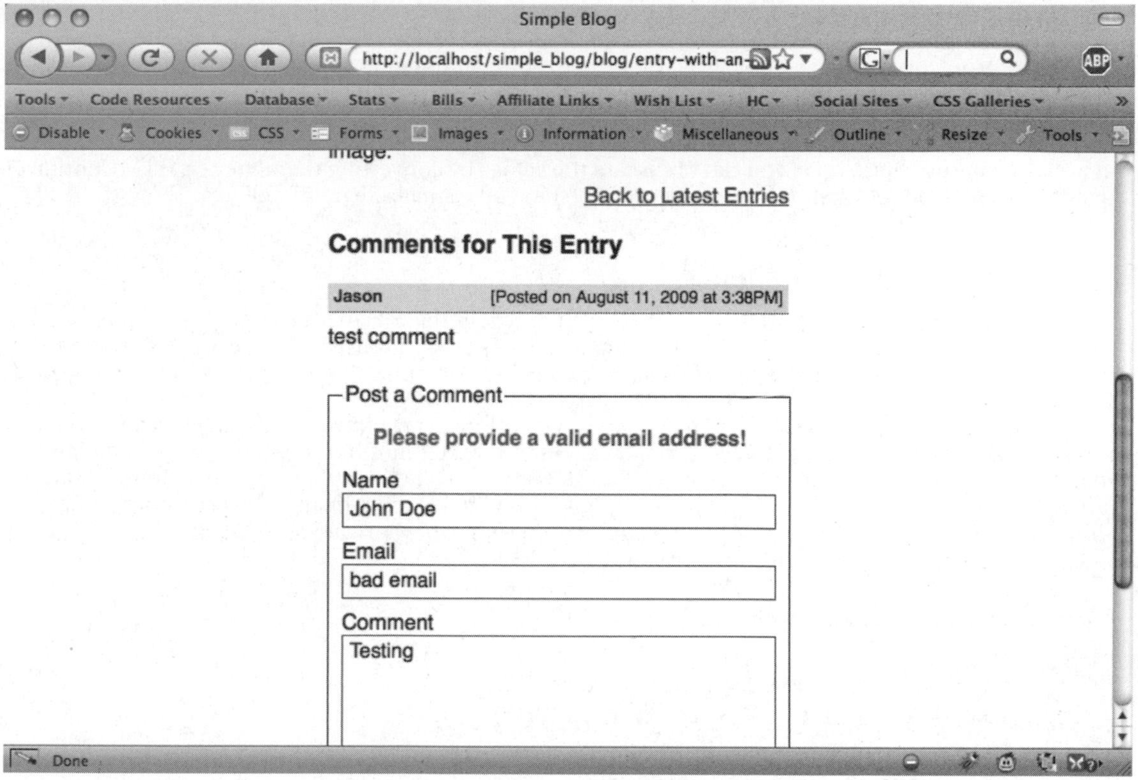

Figure 12-1. The error message displayed when a bad email address is entered

Basic Spam Prevention

Unfortunately, any web form is a potential target for spammers, both human and automated. If left unchecked, spammers can ruin a blog by flooding the comments with irrelevant links and other garbage. The spam buries legitimate comments and makes it difficult to find anything meaningful in the comment section, which can cause your users to give up on leaving or reading comments altogether.

To address this problem, you'll need to take some anti-spam measures on your comment form. There are myriad options available for spam prevention, ranging from user-dependent systems such as CAPTCHA[1] (the squiggly letters and numbers you've no doubt seen on some web forms), to server-side technologies such as Akismet[2] (which identifies spam pretty well without requiring the user to do anything).

In the spirit of learning, let's walk through how to build a custom form to curb spam, sometimes referred to as challenge-response. In this case, you present your user with a simple math question that must be answered to confirm that he isn't a spam bot.

---

[1] http://en.wikipedia.org/wiki/CAPTCHA
[2] http://akismet.com/

Creating a Basic Logic Question

It's not foolproof, but adding a basic logic question to your comment forms is a great way to trip up less sophisticated spam bots, without asking much of your users—it doesn't require too much effort to answer the question: "What is 2 + 3?"

Unfortunately, some spam bots are wily enough to parse the logic question and determine the answer. To confuse these bots, you can obfuscate the values by converting them to their HTML entities. Again, this isn't a perfect system, but it can prevent spam on a small site fairly well.

Generating Random Numbers

The first task is to generate a math question. To keep things simple, all answers to the math question should be less than 10. Keeping the question simple ensures that your users won't even have to think before answering the question, which is an important consideration: you don't want to make it any more difficult to post a comment than is *absolutely* necessary.

To keep things random and simple, you can create an array of two numbers between 1 and 4 using PHP's built-in mt_rand() function, which generates random numbers based on a low and high limit, then passes these results as arguments. You store the sum of the two numbers in a new session variable called $_SESSION['challenge'], and you use this variable to verify that the user supplied the proper response. You place the logic to challenge your user in a new private method called generateChallenge(), which you add to comments.inc.php:

```
private function generateChallenge()
{
    // Store two random numbers in an array
    $numbers = array(mt_rand(1,4), mt_rand(1,4));

    // Store the correct answer in a session
    $_SESSION['challenge'] = $numbers[0] + $numbers[1];
}
```

■**Note** PHP also has a function called rand() that works similarly to mt_rand(). It has been found that the results from rand() in some cases aren't actually very random, and that the results from mt_rand() tend to be more reliable when randomness is important.

Obfuscating the Values

So far you have two random numbers in an array; next, you need to *obfuscate* the values. Obfuscation in programming[3] is the practice of making code difficult to interpret. This is generally done as a security measure. You want to obfuscate the values on the current form to make it more difficult for a spam bot to parse your form and answer the challenge question.

Converting the random numbers to their ASCII[4] character code equivalents should help you baffle spam bots. ASCII stands for American Standard Code for Information Interchange, and it bridges

---

[3] http://en.wikipedia.org/wiki/Obfuscated_code
[4] http://en.wikipedia.org/wiki/ASCII

the gap between humans and computers. Computers can understand only numbers—every symbol is mapped to a numeric code. For example, the ASCII equivalent of a questions mark (?) is 63.

PHP provides a function to perform this conversion called ord(). To convert both numbers in the array $numbers, you use the array_map() function, which enables you to apply a function to each value in an array individually.

Obfuscate the numbers by adding the following code in bold to generateChallenge():

```php
private function generateChallenge()
{
    // Store two random numbers in an array
    $numbers = array(mt_rand(1,4), mt_rand(1,4));

    // Store the correct answer in a session
    $_SESSION['challenge'] = $numbers[0] + $numbers[1];

    // Convert the numbers to their ASCII codes
    $converted = array_map('ord', $numbers);
}
```

Adding the Math Question to the Form

Now that you have two obfuscated numbers, it's time to generate the HTML markup that displays the challenge question to the user.

The markup creates a text input field in which the user will type his answer to the challenge question. You label the text input with an obfuscated string that (you hope) will confuse a spam bot when it displays this question: "What is $n + m$?" n is the first random number, while m is the second.

Add the code in bold to generateChallenge() to return the markup for a challenge question:

```php
private function generateChallenge()
{
    // Store two random numbers in an array
    $numbers = array(mt_rand(1,4), mt_rand(1,4));

    // Store the correct answer in a session
    $_SESSION['challenge'] = $numbers[0] + $numbers[1];

    // Convert the numbers to their ASCII codes
    $converted = array_map('ord', $numbers);
```

```
    // Generate a math question as HTML markup
    return "

<label>&#87;&#104;&#97;&#116;&#32;&#105;&#115;&#32;
    &#$converted[0];&#32;&#43;&#32;&#$converted[1];&#63;
    <input type=\"text\" name=\"s_q\" />
</label>";
}
```

Adding the Challenge Question to the Form

At this point, you're ready to add the challenge question to the comment form. To do this, you need to modify showCommentForm() by creating a new variable, $challenge, to store the output of generateChallenge(), and then insert it into the form's HTML markup.

You add the challenge question by incorporating the code in bold to showCommentForm():

```
// Display a form for users to enter new comments with
public function showCommentForm($blog_id)
{
    $errors = array(
        1 => '<p class="error">Something went wrong while '
            . 'saving your comment. Please try again!</p>',
        2 => '<p class="error">Please provide a valid '
            . 'email address!</p>'
    );
    if(isset($_SESSION['error']))
    {
        $error = $errors[$_SESSION['error']];
    }
    else
    {
        $error = NULL;
    }

    // Check if session variables exist
    $n = isset($_SESSION['n']) ? $_SESSION['n'] : NULL;
    $e = isset($_SESSION['e']) ? $_SESSION['e'] : NULL;
    $c = isset($_SESSION['c']) ? $_SESSION['c'] : NULL;
```

```
        // Generate a challenge question
        $challenge = $this->generateChallenge();

        return <<<FORM
<form action="/simple_blog/inc/update.inc.php"
    method="post" id="comment-form">
    <fieldset>
        <legend>Post a Comment</legend>$error
        <label>Name
            <input type="text" name="name" maxlength="75"
                value="$n" />
        </label>
        <label>Email
            <input type="text" name="email" maxlength="150"
                value="$e" />
        </label>
        <label>Comment
            <textarea rows="10" cols="45"
                name="comment">$c</textarea>
        </label>$challenge
        <input type="hidden" name="blog_id" value="$blog_id" />
        <input type="submit" name="submit" value="Post Comment" />
        <input type="submit" name="submit" value="Cancel" />
    </fieldset>
</form>
FORM;
    }
```

You can test this code by loading an entry in your browser. Just below the comment text area, you can see a new input labeled with the challenge question (see Figure 12-2).

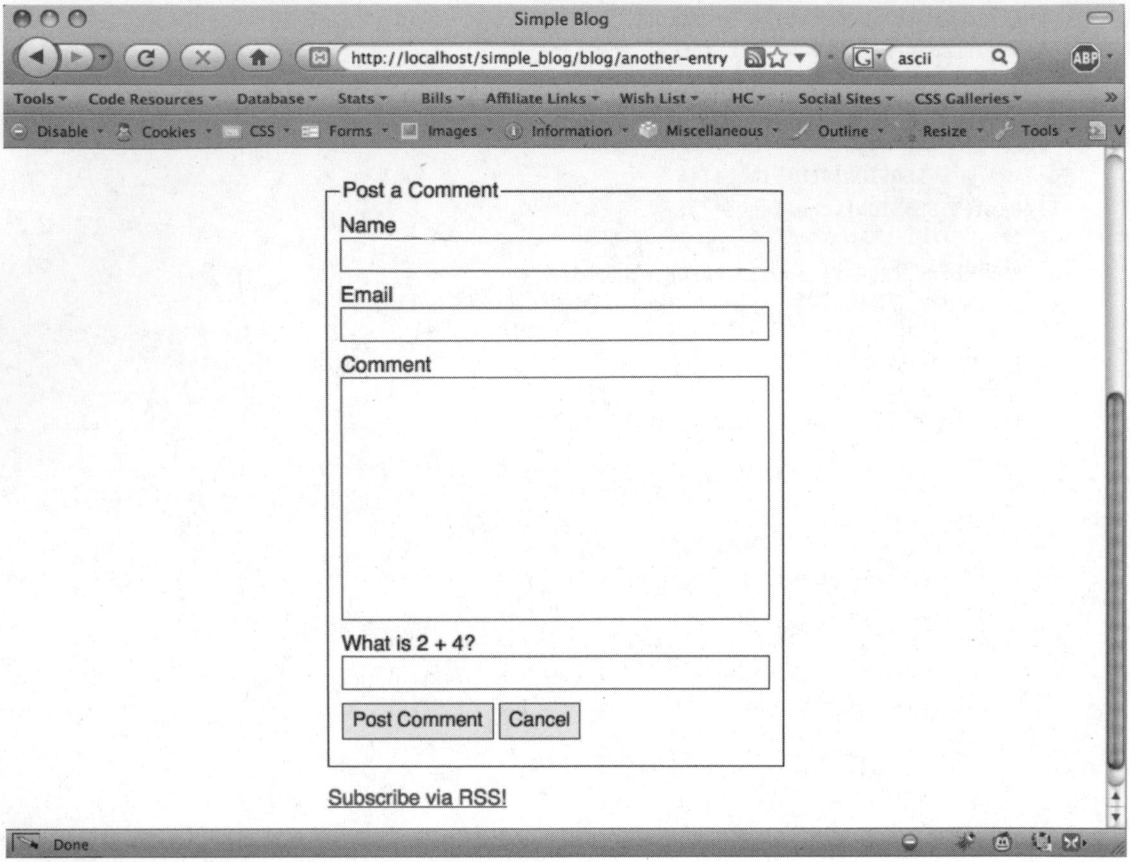

Figure 12-2. The challenge question displayed on the contact form

Verifying the Correct Answer

You've presented the user is being presented with a challenge question. The next step is to add a private method that compares the user's response to the challenge with the correct answer.

Call this method `verifyResponse()`. This method accepts the user's response to the challenge question generated in `generateChallenge()`, then it compares the value stored in `$_SESSION['challenge']` with the supplied response. If they match, the method returns TRUE; otherwise, it returns FALSE.

To avoid potential double-posting or other unexpected behavior, you should store the value of `$_SESSION['challenge']` in a new variable (`$val`), then destroy it using `unset()`.

CHAPTER 12 ■ FINISHING TOUCHES

Add the following method to comments.inc.php:

```
private function verifyResponse($resp)
{
    // Grab the session value and destroy it
    $val = $_SESSION['challenge'];
    unset($_SESSION['challenge']);

    // Returns TRUE if equal, FALSE otherwise
    return $resp==$val;
}
```

Adding the Verification into saveComment()

Next, you need to modify saveComment() so it calls verifyResponse() before saving the comment. This requires passing the proper information from the posted form, checking the method's return value, and storing an error code if the response doesn't match.

This error code doesn't fall within the existing two error codes, so you must define a new error code. For the sake of simplicity, make 3 your new error code for an incorrect response to the challenge question.

You can make these changes by adding the code in bold to saveComment():

```
// Save comments to the database
public function saveComment($p)
{
    // Save the comment information in a session
    $_SESSION['n'] = $p['name'];
    $_SESSION['e'] = $p['email'];
    $_SESSION['c'] = $p['comment'];

    // Make sure the email address is valid first
    if($this->validateEmail($p['email'])===FALSE)
    {
        $_SESSION['error'] = 2;
        return;
    }

    // Make sure the challenge question was properly answered
    if(!$this->verifyResponse($p['s_q'], $p['s_1'], $p['s_2']))
    {
        $_SESSION['error'] = 3;
        return;
    }

    // Sanitize the data and store in variables
```

```
$blog_id = htmlentities(strip_tags($p['blog_id']),
    ENT_QUOTES);
$name = htmlentities(strip_tags($p['name']), ENT_QUOTES);
$email = htmlentities(strip_tags($p['email']), ENT_QUOTES);
$comment = htmlentities(strip_tags($p['comment']),
    ENT_QUOTES);

// Generate an SQL command
$sql = "INSERT INTO comments (blog_id, name, email, comment)
        VALUES (?, ?, ?, ?)";
if($stmt = $this->db->prepare($sql))
{
    // Execute the command, free used memory, and return true
    $stmt->execute(array($blog_id, $name, $email, $comment));
    $stmt->closeCursor();

    // Destroy the comment information to empty the form
    unset($_SESSION['n'], $_SESSION['e'], $_SESSION['c'],
        $_SESSION['error']);
    return;
}
else
{
    // If something went wrong
    $_SESSION['error'] = 1;
    return;
}
}
```

Now the comment form will save a comment only if the user answers the challenge question correctly. The only thing left to do is to add an error message to correspond with error code 3, which you add in showCommentForm( ) by inserting the code in bold:

```
// Display a form for users to enter new comments with
public function showCommentForm($blog_id)
{
    $errors = array(
        1 => '<p class="error">Something went wrong while '
            . 'saving your comment. Please try again!</p>',
        2 => '<p class="error">Please provide a valid '
            . 'email address!</p>'
        ,
        3 => '<p class="error">Please answer the anti-spam '
            . 'question correctly!</p>'
    );
    if(isset($_SESSION['error']))
```

```
        {
            $error = $errors[$_SESSION['error']];
        }
        else
        {
            $error = NULL;
        }

        // Check if session variables exist
        $n = isset($_SESSION['n']) ? $_SESSION['n'] : NULL;
        $e = isset($_SESSION['e']) ? $_SESSION['e'] : NULL;
        $c = isset($_SESSION['c']) ? $_SESSION['c'] : NULL;

        // Generate a challenge question
        $challenge = $this->generateChallenge();

        return <<<FORM
<form action="/simple_blog/inc/update.inc.php"
    method="post" id="comment-form">
    <fieldset>
        <legend>Post a Comment</legend>$error
        <label>Name
            <input type="text" name="name" maxlength="75"
                value="$n" />
        </label>
        <label>Email
            <input type="text" name="email" maxlength="150"
                value="$e" />
        </label>
        <label>Comment
            <textarea rows="10" cols="45"
                name="comment">$c</textarea>
        </label>$challenge
        <input type="hidden" name="blog_id" value="$blog_id" />
        <input type="submit" name="submit" value="Post Comment" />
        <input type="submit" name="submit" value="Cancel" />
    </fieldset>
</form>
FORM;
    }
```

Try the form out by navigating to a blog entry in your browser and posting a comment. If you answer the challenge question incorrectly, the form displays an error message that explains what went wrong (see Figure 12-3).

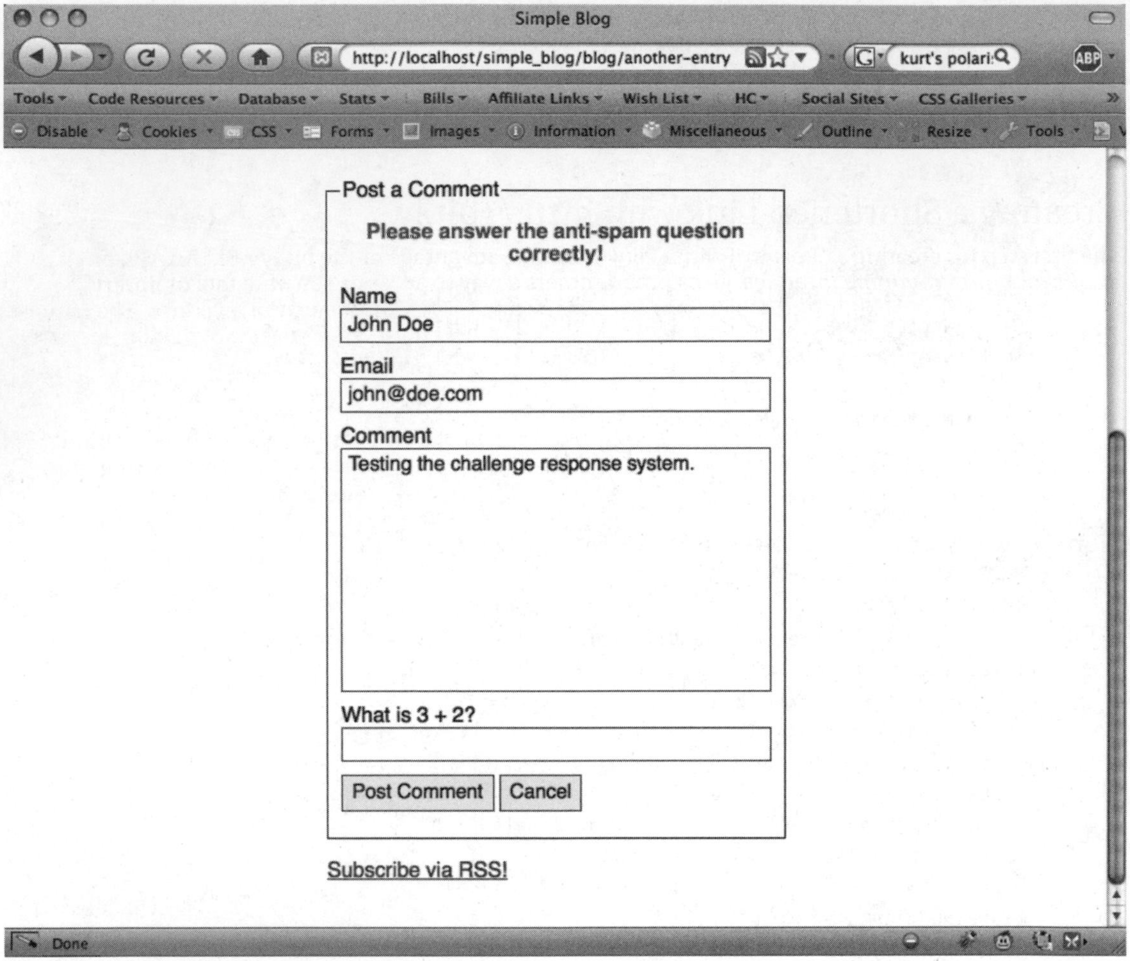

Figure 12-3. An error is displayed if the challenge question is answered incorrectly

"Post to Twitter" Link

Your next task is just for fun: it adds a "Post to Twitter" link to the bottom of each blog entry. When clicked, this link takes a user to her Twitter[5] home page and fills out her status field automatically with the title of the blog and a URL.

You use a shortened URL here because Twitter has a 140 character limit for status updates, and blog URLs have a tendency to be fairly long. To shorten your blog's URLs, you use the shortening service, `http://bit.ly`.

_____

[5] `http://twitter.com`

■**Note** Twitter is a social networking site that pioneered the concept of "micro-blogging," or status updates limited to 140 characters. As I write this, Twitter is one of the most popular and fastest-growing services on the web.

Creating a Shortened Link with http://bit.ly

The first step for creating a "Post to Twitter" link is to take advantage of the bit.ly API.[6] An API, or *application programming interface*, gives programmers a way to access a software tool or library.

In the case of bit.ly, the API defines a request string format that returns a response. The request string is the URL you want to shorten, as well as other information including the bit.ly version, log-in name, API key (an authorization code), and a response format.

You access the bit.ly API by creating a new function in functions.inc.php that you call shortenUrl(). This function accepts the URL you want to shorten as an argument.

When you create shortenUrl(), begin by building the request you want to send to the bit.ly API. Send your requests for URL shortening to http://api.bit.ly/shorten, along with a query string that contains all the information discussed so far—a log-in name, API key, and so on.

In functions.inc.php, create the function shortenUrl() and build the API request by inserting the cold in bold:

```php
function shortenUrl($url)
{
    // Format a call to the bit.ly API
    $api = 'http://api.bit.ly/shorten';
    $param = 'version=2.0.1&longUrl='.urlencode($url).'&login=phpfab'
        . '&apiKey=R_7473a7c43c68a73ae08b68ef8e16388e&format=xml';
}
```

■**Caution** The values passed for login and apiKey should be swapped out for your own bit.ly account credentials. You can obtain these for free by setting up an account at http://bit.ly.

Your next step is to send the request to bit.ly and load the response into memory. To do this, your script needs to connect to bit.ly remotely, which you can accomplish using the file_get_contents() function, which opens, reads, and returns the content of a file. By supplying the bit.ly API command to the function, you end up loading the response from the API into a variable.

---

[6] http://en.wikipedia.org/wiki/API

Next, add the following code in bold to shortenUrl() to open a connection to the bit.ly API and load the response:

```php
function shortenUrl($url)
{
    // Format a call to the bit.ly API
    $api = 'http://api.bit.ly/shorten';
    $param = 'version=2.0.1&longUrl='.urlencode($url).'&login=phpfab'
        . '&apiKey=R_7473a7c43c68a73ae08b68ef8e16388e&format=xml';

    // Open a connection and load the response
    $uri = $api . "?" . $param;

    $response = file_get_contents($uri);
}
```

The last step: Separate the shortened URL from the response. The requested format was XML, so the script needs a way to access the nodes within the XML response.

For example, you get this response you shorten the URL, http://google.com:

```xml
<bitly>
    <errorCode>0</errorCode>
    <errorMessage></errorMessage>
    <results>
        <nodeKeyVal>
            <userHash>11etr</userHash>
            <shortKeywordUrl></shortKeywordUrl>
            <hash>3j4ir4</hash>
            <nodeKey><![CDATA[http://google.com]]></nodeKey>
            <shortUrl>http://bit.ly/11etr</shortUrl>
        </nodeKeyVal>
    </results>
    <statusCode>OK</statusCode>
</bitly>
```

Each nested level of XML is essentially a container. This means that the whole response is in a container called bitly. You can find the results container inside the bitly container, which itself contains the nodeKeyVal container. nodeKeyVal contains shortUrl, which contains the shortened URL. This means that accessing the shortened URL from outside the XML requires that you access bitly, results, nodeKeyVal, and finally shortUrl.

Since PHP 5, developers have been able to use a library called SimpleXML, which makes it easy to traverse XML nodes. To extract the shortened URL from the XML response, you need to create an XML object using simplexml_load_string() and store it in the $bitly variable. Once you do this, you can drill down within the XML easily.

Add the code in bold to shortenUrl() to extract and return the shortened URL from the loaded response:

```
function shortenUrl($url)
{
    // Format a call to the bit.ly API
    $api = 'http://api.bit.ly/shorten';
    $param = 'version=2.0.1&longUrl='.urlencode($url).'&login=phpfab'
        . '&apiKey=R_7473a7c43c68a73ae08b68ef8e16388e&format=xml';

    // Open a connection and load the response
    $uri = $api . "?" . $param;
    $response = file_get_contents($uri);

    // Parse the output and return the shortened URL
    $bitly = simplexml_load_string($response);
    return $bitly->results->nodeKeyVal->shortUrl;
}
```

Now you can shorten any URL by passing it to this function, which returns the URL for use elsewhere in your scripts.

■**Note** bit.ly always returns the same short URL for a given web address, so it's perfectly acceptable to save the returned short URL in the database. Additionally, bit.ly provides a JavaScript API that lowers the impact on bit.ly's service and eliminates a server request from your script.

Generating an Automatic Status Update for Twitter

With shortened URLs just a function call away, you're ready to generate the "Post to Twitter" link at the bottom of each blog. You generate this link from another function, which you name postToTwitter(). This function accepts the title of the entry as its only argument.

This function uses values from the $_SERVER superglobal to determine the current entry's URL, then shortens it. It then appends the shortened URL to the entry title, URL encodes the whole string using urlencode(), and adds a link to Twitter as the value of the status variable.

The Twitter link points to http://twitter.com/?status=, which takes any logged in Twitter user to his homepage and fills his status box with the contents of the status variable in the query string.

In functions.inc.php, write the postToTwitter() function by adding the code in bold:

```
function postToTwitter($title)
{

    $full = 'http://'.$_SERVER['HTTP_HOST'].$_SERVER['REQUEST_URI'];
    $short = shortenUrl($full);
    $status = $title . ' ' . $short;
    return 'http://twitter.com/?status='.urlencode($status);
}
```

Displaying the Link on Entries

The last thing you need to do is insert the generated link into the entry display. Do this by modifying index.php. Only fully displayed blog entries should have "Post to Twitter" links, so add a call to postToTwitter() only inside the conditional block that checks whether $fulldisp is set to 1.

Inside the block, add a call to postToTwitter() if the current page is the blog and store the return value in $twitter. If the user is on the about page, set the $twitter variable to NULL.

Then, simply insert the $twitter variable into the HTML output to add the link:

```
// If the full display flag is set, show the entry
if($fulldisp==1)
{

    // Get the URL if one wasn't passed
    $url = (isset($url)) ? $url : $e['url'];

    if(isset($_SESSION['loggedin']) && $_SESSION['loggedin'] == 1)
    {
        // Build the admin links
        $admin = adminLinks($page, $url);
    }
    else
    {
        $admin = array('edit'=>NULL, 'delete'=>NULL);
    }
```

```php
    // Format the image if one exists
    $img = formatImage($e['image'], $e['title']);

    if($page=='blog')
    {
        // Load the comment object
        include_once 'inc/comments.inc.php';
        $comments = new Comments();
        $comment_disp = $comments->showComments($e['id']);
        $comment_form = $comments->showCommentForm($e['id']);

        // Generate a Post to Twitter link
        $twitter = postToTwitter($e['title']);
    }
    else
    {
        $comment_form = NULL;
        $twitter = NULL;
    }

?>

        <h2> <?php echo $e['title'] ?> </h2>
        <p> <?php echo $img, $e['entry'] ?> </p>
        <p>
            <?php echo $admin['edit'] ?>
            <?php if($page=='blog') echo $admin['delete'] ?>
        </p>
        <?php if($page=='blog'): ?>
        <p class="backlink">
            <a href="<?php echo $twitter ?>">Post to Twitter</a><br />
            <a href="./">Back to Latest Entries</a>
        </p>
        <h3> Comments for This Entry </h3>
        <?php echo $comment_disp, $comment_form; endif; ?>

<?php

} // End the if statement
```

To see this in action, load an entry in your browser (see Figure 12-4).

Figure 12-4. The "Post to Twitter" link on fully displayed blog entries

Summary

Congratulations! You've just built your first dynamic blog, complete with administrative controls, image handling, a commenting system, and social media integration.

By now, you should feel comfortable with the basics of PHP, as well as some of the more advanced features, such as regular expressions and image processing. You've officially added a new tool to your web development skill set.

All that's left to do now: start using your new blog!

Index

■Special Characters

! operator, 53
-> (arrow) notation
    object-oriented PHP, 214
s
_ (underscore) character
    denoting private properties, 213
    domain names, 343
<<< (heredoc) syntax, 36

■A

a (anchor) element/tag
    making RSS feed available to non-browsers, 279–280
About the Author page, 162, 164, 179, 185
absolute property, ImageHandler class, 224
abstraction
    database-access abstraction layer, 116
action variable
    deleting entries in database, 201
ADD INDEX clause, 103, 157
addition operator, 48
admin page see admin.php file
admin table, 311, 316
admin.php file
    adding file input to admin form, 207
    building HTML form to add administrators, 312
    creating, 128
    deleting entries in database, 197, 198, 201
    displaying entries saved in database, 139
    hiding controls from unauthorized users, 325
    login form restricting administrative access, 328
    modifying access rule, 190–191

modifying to save page asssociations, 165–168
    passing URL values to, 190–191
    populating form with entry to edit, 191–194
    retrieving unique ID for new entry, 138
    setting up access rule, 173
    uploading images, 207
administrative access, restricting, 311–340
    adding administrators, 312–317
    creating admin table, 311
    creating login form, 328–330
    displaying controls to authorized users, 330–337
    hiding controls from unauthorized users, 318–328
    logging users out, 337–340
administrative links
    creating, 187–188
    displaying, 188–190
    displaying controls to authorized users, 330
    hiding from users, 311, 318
administrators

    adding administrators, 312–317
    creating login form, 328–330
    displaying controls to authorized users, 330–337
    hiding controls from unauthorized users, 318–328
    logging users out, 337–340
    navigating site without losing privileges, 318
    saving new administrators in database, 315–317
adminLinks() function, 187–188
Akismet, 353
algorithms, encryption, 316, 331

369

ALTER TABLE statement, MySQL, 103
    ADD INDEX clause, 103, 157
anchor element/tag
    making RSS feed available to non-browsers,
        279–280
AND (&&) operator, 52
Apache, 3, 5
    installing, 6
        verifying installation, 13
arguments, function prototypes, 43
arithmetic assignment operators, 47, 48
arithmetic operators, 47, 48
array_map() function, 148, 355
array_pop() function, 267
array_push() function, 146
arrays, 38–41
    $_COOKIE, 84, 93–95
    $_FILES, 85–89, 208–211
    $_GET, 77–82, 84
    $_POST, 82–84
    $_REQUEST, 84–85
    $_SERVER, 74–77
    $_SESSION, 89–93
    $GLOBALS, 73
    associative arrays, 59
    debugging arrays, 75
    multidimensional arrays, 40, 59
    superglobal arrays, 69–95
arrow (->) notation
    object-oriented PHP, 214
ASP-style delimiters, 31
assignment operators
    arithmetic assignment operators, 47, 48
    assignment by reference, 49
    concatenating, 54
associative arrays, 59
AUTO_INCREMENT, MySQL, 102
auto-complete, 16

■B

backreferences, rewrite rules
    accessing, 173
    passing URL values to admin.php with
        .htaccess, 191
    setting up rule for page-and-entry URLs,
        174
bind_param() method, MySQLi, 115
bind_result() method, MySQLi, 116
binding parameters, 115

bit.ly API
    creating shortened link, 363–365
BLOB type, MySQL, 102
block comments, 46
    DocBlocks, 220
blog, 6
blog project see simple_blog project
blog_id column, comments table, 284
Boolean values, 37
break statement, 60
break tag, HTML, 34
browsers
    making RSS feed available to, 278–279
    outputting data to, 41–46
    storing information on user's machine, 93,
        95
built-in function references, 16
business layer
    mapping functions to output saved entries,
        141
    writing business functions, 148–149
business logic, 140

■C

CAPTCHA, 353
Cascading Style Sheets see CSS
case (switch) statement, 61
channel tag, RSS feeds, 265
CHAR type, MySQL, 101
character classes, 174, 191
characters
    matching non-word characters, 181
    matching word characters, 173
checkSaveDir() method, ImageHandler class,
    228–236
class keyword, OOP, 212
classes
    character classes, 174
    Comments class, 285
    ImageHandler class, 218–240
classes, OOP, 211, 212
    class constructors, 214
    using classes/objects in scripts, 215–218
    visibility declarations, 213
client-side scripting, 4–5
close() method, MySQLi, 113, 116
closeCursor() method, PDO, 117, 136
code folding, 16
coding logic

separation in programming, 139–140
commands
    echo() statement, 42
    print() statement, 41
    print_r() function, 49
    printf() statement, 43
    sprintf() statement, 45
comment column, comments table, 284
comments, 46–47
    adding error messages to comments form,
        348–353
    block comments, 46
    building comment entry form, 286–287
        modifying index.php to display, 287–289
    deleting comments, 304–310
        creating confirmation form, 305–306
        modifying update.inc.php to handle,
            307–310
        removing comments from database, 306
    displaying comments for entries, 296–298,
        300–302
        modifying index.php for, 302–304
    displaying stored comment information,
        345
    DocBlocks, 220
    email address validation for posting, 341–
        353
    inline comments, 46
    retrieving comments for entries, 293–296
    saving in sessions, 344
    shell-style comments, 47
    spam prevention, 353–362
    storing new comments, 289–291
        modifying update.inc.php for, 291–293
Comments class

    building, 285
    confirmDelete() method, 304, 305, 307
    deleteComment() method, 304, 306, 308
    generateChallenge() method, 354, 355
    retrieveComments() method, 293
    saveComment() method, 289, 343, 347, 348,
        359
    showCommentForm() method, 286, 345,
        350, 356, 360
    showComments() method, 296, 300, 301,
        323
    validateEmail() method, 342
    verifyResponse() method, 358
comments table, 283–285
    storing new comments in, 289

comments.inc.php file
    adding method code to file
        confirmDelete(), 305
        deleteComment(), 306
        generateChallenge(), 354, 355
        retrieveComments(), 294
        saveComment(), 289, 344, 347, 348, 359
        showCommentForm(), 286, 345, 350,
            356, 360
        showComments(), 297, 300, 301
        validateEmail(), 342
        verifyResponse(), 359
    creating, 285
    hiding delete link from unauthorized users,
        323
comparison operators, 47, 50
concatenating assignment operator, 54
concatenation, 35
concatenation operator, 54
confirmation form
    deleting comments from, 305–306
confirmDelete() function, 197, 198, 200
confirmDelete() method, Comments class, 304,
        305, 307
connecting PHP scripts to MySQL, 109–118
    index.php file, 149
    script to process entry form input, 134–135
connections, database logic, 139
constructors, OOP, 214
content type, 237
content type header, 88, 265
content, syndicating, 264–281
continue statement, 62
control structures, 54–66
    break statement, 60
    continue statement, 62
    do-while loop, 57
    else/else if statements, 55
    for loop, 58
    foreach loop, 59
    goto statement, 65
    if statement, 55
    include/include_once constructs, 63
    require/require_once constructs, 63
    return statement, 63
    switch statement, 61
    while loop, 56
controls

    displaying to authorized users, 330–337

hiding from unauthorized users, 318–328
conversion specifications, 43
$_COOKIE superglobal array, 93–95
    array containing the contents of, 84
CREATE DATABASE statement, MySQL, 100
CREATE TABLE statement, MySQL, 100–102
    IF NOT EXISTS clause, 101
created column, entries table, 126, 128, 272
createUserForm() function, 312, 315
credentials
    storing database credentials, 134
CSS (Cascading Style Sheets), 129, 132
    displaying entries saved in database, 139
curly braces {}
    checking braces used in pairs, 196
custom URLs
    creating friendly URLs using .htaccess, 170–175
    creating friendly URLs automatically, 175–183

■D

data types
    MySQL, 102
    MySQLi, 115
database connections
    creating blog entries, 266
database credentials
    checking if login credentials valid, 331
    storing, 134
database layer
    writing database functions, 141–148
database logic, 139
database-access abstraction layer, 116
databases
    see also MySQL
    adding administrators, 312–317
    adding columns to tables, 157, 176
    adding commenting system to blog, 283
    avoiding storage of redundant data, 118–121
    CREATE DATABASE statement, 100
    creating admin table, 311
    creating comments table, 283–285
    creating in phpMyAdmin, 126
    deleting entries, 197–204
    displaying entries, 138–139
    DROP DATABASE statement, 99
    mapping functions to output saved entries, 140

modifying update.inc.php to save URLs in, 182
    MySQL, 109–111
    MySQLi, 111–116
    PDO (PHP Data Objects), 116–118
    planning database tables, 118–122
    removing comments, 306
    storing comments, 289–291
    storing/retrieving images, 240–247
    supporting multiple database types, 116
    updating entries in, 194–197
    using page to filter database records, 159–164
datatype specifiers, 45
datatypes, 32
    arrays, 38–41
    Boolean values, 37
    floating point numbers, 37
    integers, 37
    strings, 33–37
date column, comments table, 284
date() function, 274, 298–299
DATE_RSS constant, 274
dates
    creating custom date formatting string, 298–299
DATETIME type, MySQL, 102
day formatting characters, 298
db.inc.php file, 134, 149, 266
debugging, arrays, 75
decrementing operators, 47, 52
DEFAULT keyword, 157
delete link, 188, 189
    deleting entries in database, 197, 198, 200
    hiding from unauthorized users, 323
DELETE statement, MySQL, 109
deleteComment() method, 304, 306, 308
deleteEntry() function, 201, 203
deleting comments, 304–310
deleting database entries, 197–204
delimiters, 30, 31
delimiters, regex, 182
design patterns, 140
development environment, setting up, 3–28
die() function, 110
directives
    RewriteBase, 172
    RewriteEngine, 171
    RewriteRule, 172, 173, 174, 190, 264
    short_open_tag, 31

displaying output, 140, 149–154
division operator, 48
DocBlocks, 220
doImageResize() method, 254, 255, 256, 258
domain names
    use of _ (underscore) character, 343
double-quote syntax, 34
doubles, 37
do-while loop, 57
DROP DATABASE statement, MySQL, 99
dst_ arguments, imagecopyresampled(), 255, 256
dynamic web pages, 4
dynamic websites, 3

■E

echo() statement, 42
Eclipse, 18
    choosing project workspace, 20
    creating project, 23–26
    DocBlocks, 220
    downloading, 19
    installing, 18–21
    showing resources starting with period, 171
    unpacking PDT archive, 19
edit link
    creating administrative links, 188
    displaying administrative links, 189
else/else if statements, 55
email
    validateEmail() method, 342–343
email column, comments table, 284
embedding PHP scripts, 29–31
encoding
    URL encoding, 78
encryption algorithm, 316, 331
enctype, 207
entries table
    automatically populated fields, 128
    created column, 126, 128, 272
    creating in phpMyAdmin, 127
    creating input form for, 128–132
    deleting entries in database, 197–204
    displaying records saved in database, 138–139
    entry column, 126, 128
    id column, 125, 128
    image column, adding, 241

modifying functions to accept page parameters, 158–164
    page column, adding, 157
    planning for blogging application, 125–127
    saving entries to, 132
    script to process entry form input, 132–138
        connecting to database, 134–135
        retrieving unique ID, 136
        saving values in entries table, 135
        verification of input, 133
    structure in phpMyAdmin, 127
    title column, 125, 128
    updating entries in database, 194–197
    url column, adding, 176
entries, simple_blog project
    deleting related comments, 304–310
    displaying comments for, 296–298, 300–304
    retrieving comments for, 293–296
    storing new comments, 289–291
entry column, entries table, 126, 128
    saving values in entries table, 135
    verification of entry form input, 133, 134
EOD identifier, 36
equal comparison operator, 50
error control operators, 47, 51
error handling, OOP
    throw keyword, 222
error suppression operators, 52
error value, $_FILES, 85
error_reporting() function, 70, 71
errors
    adding error messages to comments form, 348–353
    checking for error during file upload, 221–222
    handling errors with try...catch, 226–228
    turning off errors, 70
escaping characters in strings, 33
exceptions
    try...catch statement, 226–228
execute() method
    MySQLi, 116
    PDO, 117
        saving values in entries table, 136
exit() command
    alias for, 110
Extensible Markup Language (XML), 264
extensions
    determining file extensions, 237

■ F

F (forbidden) flag, URL rewriting, 173
feed readers *see* RSS aggregators
feeds *see* RSS feeds
feeds folder, 264
fetch() method, MySQLi, 116
    retrieving unique ID for new entry, 136
file extensions, determining, 237
file permissions, 231
file uploads *see* uploading files
file_get_contents() function, 363
filepath property, ImageHandler class, 224
files
    see also admin.php file; comments.inc.php
        file; db.inc.php file; functions.inc.php
        file; images.inc.php file; index.php file;
        rss.php file; update.inc.php file
    accessing uploaded file, 208–211
    checking file uploaded and without errors,
        88
    checking file uploaded is JPG image, 88
    creating PHP file, 26–27
    saving uploaded file to file system, 223–225
    setting up rules for URL rewriting, 172
$_FILES superglobal array, 85–89, 208–211
    checking whether file was uploaded, 208,
        209–211
    methods using DocBlocks, 220
filters
    using page as filter, 158, 159–164
flags, URL rewriting, 173, 174
FLOAT type, MySQL, 102
floating point numbers, 37
folder permissions, 231
folders
    checking if folder already exists, 228–231
    creating directory in, 232
    creating to store images, 228–236
for loop, 58
forbidden (F) flag, URL rewriting, 173
foreach loop, 59
    creating blog entries, 268, 270
form tag
    changing enctype to accept file uploads, 207
formatImage() function, 246–247
formatting dates, 298–299
forms
    creating input form for entries table, 128–
        132

populating form with entry to edit, 191–194
    script to process entry form input, 132–138
friendly URLs
    creating custom URLs using .htaccess, 170–
        175
    creating custom URLs automatically, 175–
        183
    previewing blog entries with, 175
FTP option, XAMPP, 13
function prototypes, 43
function references, 16
functions, 66
    accessing information about, 29
    mapping to output saved entries, 140
    modifying to accept page parameters, 158–
        164
    recursive functions, 148
    return statement, 63, 66
    returning values from, 67
    scope of variables declared within, 71
    user-defineds, 66–67
    writing business functions, 148–149
    writing database functions, 141–148
functions, custom
    see also methods
    adminLinks(), 187–188
    confirmDelete(), 197, 198, 200
    createUserForm(), 312
    deleteEntry(), 201, 203
    formatImage(), 246–247
    makeUrl(), 181
    postToTwitter(), 365, 366
    retrieveEntries(), 141–148
    sanitizeData(), 141, 148–149
    shortenUrl(), 363, 364, 365
functions, list of PHP
    array_map(), 148, 355
    array_pop(), 267
    array_push(), 146
    date(), 274
    die(), 110
    file_get_contents(), 363
    getimagesize(), 250
    header(), 155
    htmlentities(), 111
    imagecopyresampled(), 255
    imagecreatefromjpeg(), 88
    imagecreatefromxyz() functions, 252
    imagecreatetruecolor(), 255
    imagedestroy(), 88

imagejpeg(), 88
imagexyz() functions, 253
is_dir(), 230
list(), 72
md5(), 316
min(), 251
mkdir(), 231
move_uploaded(), 224
mt_rand(), 354
mysql_close(), 111
mysql_connect(), 110
mysql_error(), 110
mysql_fetch_array(), 111
mysql_free_result(), 111
mysql_query(), 111
mysql_real_escape_string(), 111
mysql_select_db(), 110
ord(), 355
preg_replace(), 180
rand(), 354
session_destroy(), 92
session_start(), 90
setcookie(), 93
sha1(), 316
simplexml_load_string(), 364
strip_tags(), 111, 148
strtolower(), 181
strtotime(), 274
time(), 93
unset(), 92, 358
urldecode(), 78
urlencode(), 78
functions.inc.php file
    accepting page info. in URL, 158
    adminLinks() function, 187, 188
    confirmDelete() function, 200
    createUserForm() function, 312
    creating blog entries, 266
    creating different viewing styles for pages, 185
    deleteEntry() function, 203
    formatImage() function, 246
    including in index.php, 149
    modifying to handle URLs, 176–178
    postToTwitter() function, 366
    reinforcing logical separations, 141
    retrieveEntries() function, 143, 144, 145, 147, 244, 272
    sanitizeData() function, 149
    shortenUrl() function, 363, 364, 365

using page to filter database records, 159, 160, 161
writing database functions, 141

■G

generateChallenge() method, Comments class, 354, 355
GET method, 77
$_GET superglobal array, 77–82
    accepting page info. in URL, 159
    array containing the contents of, 84
    checking if set using ternary operator, 166, 192, 194
    deleting comments in database, 307
    deleting entries in database, 197
    logging users out, 339
    modifying index.php to check for url not id, 178
    passing entry IDs in URL, 150
getImageExtension() method, 237
getImageFunctions() method, 253, 254
getimagesize() function, 250, 253
getNewDims() method, 250, 251, 252, 254
GIF images
    determining file extension of uploads, 237
global scope, 70, 71
$GLOBALS superglobal array, 73
goto statement, 65
greater than comparison operators, 50
GUID (Globally Unique Identifier), 271

■H

header() function
    describing RSS feeds, 265
    redirects, 155
heredoc syntax, 36, 200
hidden inputs, 165, 166
    deleting entries in database, 200
    inserting, 193
    storing page in, 167
highlighting
    syntax highlighting, 16
hour formatting characters, 299
.htaccess file
    creating, 171–175
    creating friendly URLs using, 170–175
    declaring base-level folder for URL rewriting, 172
    description, 170

passing URL values to admin.php with, 190–191

setting up rules

for admin.php access, 173

for page-and-entry URLs, 174

for page-only URLs, 174

for URL rewriting, 172

turning on URL rewriting, 171

htdocs folder

choosing Eclipse PDT project workspace, 20

creating new projects automatically in, 21

HTML

break tag, 34

script tags, 31

HTML forms

adding administrators, 312–315

enctype, 207

inserting hidden inputs, 165, 166

UPLOAD_ERR_OK constant, 221

htmlentities() function, 111

creating blog entries, 268

storing new comments, 289

HTTP_HOST value, $_SERVER, 74

HTTP_REFERER value, $_SERVER, 75, 77, 292, 305

HTTP_USER_AGENT value, $_SERVER, 75

■ I

id column, comments table, 284

id column, entries table, 125, 128

identical comparison operator, 50, 51

IDEs, 15

PDT IDE, 18

if else statement, 166

IF NOT EXISTS clause

CREATE TABLE statement, 101

if statement, 55

compressing into one line, 150

image column, entries table, 241

image uploads *see* uploading images

imagecopyresampled() function, 255, 256

imagecreatefromjpeg() function, 88

imagecreatefromxyz() functions, 252

imagecreatetruecolor() function, 255

imagedestroy() function, 88

ImageHandler class, 218–240

checking for error during file upload, 221–222

checkSaveDir() method, 228–231, 232

doImageResize() method, 254

getImageExtension() method, 237

getImageFunctions() method, 253

max_dims property, 249

processUploadedImage() method, 219

renameFile() method, 237

save_dir property, 219

saving uploaded file to file system, 223–225

imagejpeg() function, 88

images

creating folder to store, 228–236

determining file extensions, 237

ensuring image name is unique, 237

formatImage() function, 246–247

modifying update.inc.php to save images, 225–226

renaming, 236–240

resizing, 248–259

adding property for maximum dimensions, 249

choosing image function to use, 252–254

determining new image dimensions, 249–252

resampling image at proper size, 254–258

saving uploaded images, 219

storing and retrieving from database, 240–247

modifying index.php to display images, 246–247

modifying retrieveEntries() to retrieve images, 244–246

modifying update.inc.php to save path to images, 241–244

uploading, 207

writing class to handle, 218

images.inc.php file

calling formatImage() function, 247

checking for error during file upload, 221

creating, 218

declaring getImageFunctions(), 253

defining ImageHandler properties, 219

modifying update.inc.php to save images, 226

saving uploaded file to file system, 223, 224

imagexyz() functions

choosing image functions to use, 253

inc folder

creating, 132

db.inc.php file, 134

functions.inc.php file, 141
 storing database credentials, 134
 update.inc.php file, 132, 135
include construct, 63
 including database credentials, 135
include_once construct, 63
 creating blog entries, 266
 trying to reference nonexistent file with, 51
 writing presentation code, 149
incrementing operators, 47, 52
index.php file
 accepting page info. in URL, 158–159
 calling postToTwitter(), 366
 calling retrieveEntries(), 150
 calling sanitizeData(), 151
 displaying administrative links, 188
 displaying entries saved in database, 138
 ensuring page variable is passed, 166
 hiding administrative links from users, 318
 logging users out, 337
 making RSS feed available to browsers, 278–
  279
 making RSS feed available to non-browsers,
  279–280
 modifying links between pages, 162
 modifying to display comment form, 287–
  289
 modifying to display entry comments, 302–
  304
 modifying to display images, 246–247
 modifying to handle URLs, 178–180
 opening connection to database, 149
 redirects, 155
 retrieving unique ID for new entry, 136, 138
 writing presentation code, 149, 152, 153
indexing columns, MySQL, 103
 ADD INDEX command, 157
inheritance, OOP, 213
inline comments, 46
input tag
 maxlength attribute, 128
INSERT statement, MySQL, 103–105
 VALUES keyword, 103
installations

 Eclipse PDT, 18–21
 PHP, Apache, and MySQL, 6
 XAMPP, 6–15
instantiation of objects, OOP, 214
INT type, MySQL, 102
integers, 37

integrated development environments *see* IDEs
interfaces

 procedural interface, 109
IP address, 13
 accessing IP address of site visitors, 74
is_dir() function, 230

■J

JavaScript
 client-side scripting, 4
JOIN clause, MySQL, 108
JPEG images
 determining file extension of uploads, 237
JPG files, 88

■K

key to value pairing, 38
keywords, OOP *see* OOP keywords

■L

L (last rule) flag, URL rewriting, 173, 174
LAST_INSERT_ID() function, 136
Lerdorf, Rasmus, 3
less than comparison operators, 50
LIMIT clause, DELETE statement, MySQL, 109
link tag
 making RSS feed available to browsers, 278–
  279
links
 creating administrative links, 187–188
 creating shortened link with http://bit.ly,
  363–365
 displaying administrative links, 188–190
 modifying links between pages, 162
 Post to Twitter link, 362–368
list() function, 72, 73
 descriptions of methods using DocBlocks,
  220
 determining image dimensions, 250
 retrieving information supplied about
  uploaded file, 221
local scope, 71
localhost
 verifying Apache/PHP running, 13
logging users out, 337–340
logic
 business logic, 140

database logic, 139
presentation logic, 140
reinforcing logical separations, 141
separation of coding logic, 139–140
logical operators, 47, 52
login form, 328–330
looping
break statement, 60
continue statement, 62
do-while loop, 57
for loop, 58
foreach loop, 59
while loop, 56

■M

magic methods, 214
magic_quotes_gpc setting, 15
makeUrl() function, 181, 182
manual, PHP, 29
max_dims property, ImageHandler class, 249
maxlength attribute, input tag, 128
md5() function, 316
menus
adding menu to web pages, 184
methods
see also functions, custom
descriptions of methods using DocBlocks, 220
doImageResize(), 254
getImageExtension(), 237
getImageFunctions(), 253
getNewDims(), 250, 251, 252
magic methods, 214
processUploadedImage(), 219
renameFile(), 237
methods, Comments class
confirmDelete(), 304, 305, 307
deleteComment(), 304, 306, 308
generateChallenge(), 354, 355
retrieveComments(), 293
saveComment(), 289, 343, 347, 348, 359
showCommentForm(), 286, 345, 350, 356, 360
showComments(), 296, 300, 301
validateEmail(), 342–343
verifyResponse(), 358
methods, OOP
accessing, object-oriented PHP, 214
defining class methods, 214

min() function, 251
mkdir() function, 231
mod_rewrite documentation, 172
Model-View-Controller (MVC) pattern, 140
modulus operator, 48
month formatting characters, 298
move_uploaded file() function, 224
mt_rand() function, 354
multidimensional arrays, 40
nesting foreach statements, 59
multiplication operator, 48
Multitier Architecture pattern, 140
MySQL
see also databases
adding columns to tables, 157, 176
AUTO_INCREMENT keyword, 102
binding parameters, 115
connecting PHP scripts to, 109–118
data storage, 97
data types, 102
description, 5
eliminating performance issues, 118
indexing columns, 103
installing, 6
verifying installation, 14–15
introduction, 98
manipulating data in MySQL tables, 98–109
planning database tables, 118–122
PRIMARY KEY keywords, 102
MySQL extension, 109–111
die() function, 110
htmlentities() function, 111
mysql_xyz() functions, 110, 111
recommended further reading, 122
security weaknesses, 109
SQL injection, 111
strip_tags() function, 111
MySQL statements
ALTER TABLE, 103
CREATE DATABASE, 100
CREATE TABLE, 100–102
DELETE, 109
DROP DATABASE, 99
INSERT, 103–105
JOIN clause, 108
SELECT, 105–107
avoiding shortcut selector (SELECT *), 122
UPDATE, 107
USING clause, 108

MySQL timestamp
    creating pubDate from, 274
mysql_close() function, 111
mysql_connect() function, 110
mysql_error() function, 110
mysql_fetch_array() function, 111
mysql_free_result() function, 111
mysql_query() function, 111
mysql_real_escape_string() function, 111
mysql_select_db() function, 110
MySQLi, 111–116
    bind_param() method, 115
    bind_result() method, 116
    close() method, 113, 116
    data types, 115
    execute() method, 116
    fetch() method, 116
    PDO compared, 116
    prepare() method, 115
    query() method, 113
    recommended further reading, 122
    using methods, 113
    using prepared statements with, 113–116

■N

name column, comments table, 284
name value, $_FILES, 85
NC (nocase) flag, URL rewriting, 173, 174
negative lookahead, regex, 181
new keyword, OOP, 215
new line character (\n), 34
New PHP File dialog, 26
New Project window, 23
nocase (NC) flag, URL rewriting, 173, 174
NOT NULL constraint, 157
nowdoc syntax, 36
NULL, declaring variables as, 160

■O

obfuscation, 354
OOP (object-oriented programming), 211–218
    accessing property or method, 214
    calling a method in, 113
    class constructors, 214
    classes and objects, 211, 212
    compared to procedural code, 112
    defining class methods, 214
    enabling reference to self without knowing
        name, 214
    error handling, 222
    object instantiation, 214
    use of arrow (->) notation, 214
    using classes/objects in scripts, 215–218
    visibility declarations for class members,
        213
    writing class to handle images, 218
OOP keywords
    class keyword, 212
    new keyword, 215
    private keyword, 212, 213
    protected keyword, 213
    public keyword, 213
    this keyword, 214
    throw keyword, 222
    var keyword, 213
open-source software, 3
operators, 47–54
    ! operator, 53
    addition operator, 48
    AND (&&) operator, 52
    arithmetic assignment operators, 47, 48
    arithmetic operators, 47, 48
    comparison operators, 47, 50
    concatenating assignment operator, 54
    concatenation operator, 54
    decrementing operators, 47, 52
    division operator, 48
    equal comparison operator, 50
    error control operators, 47, 51
    error suppression operators, 52
    greater than comparison operators, 50
    identical comparison operator, 50, 51
    incrementing operators, 47, 52
    less than comparison operators, 50
    logical operators, 47, 52
    modulus operator, 48
    multiplication operator, 48
    OR (||) operator, 52
    string operators, 47, 54
    subtraction operator, 48
    XOR operator, 53
OR (||) operator, 52
ord() function, 355
output commands, 41–46
    echo(), 42
    print(), 41
    print_r(), 49
    printf(), 43
    sprintf(), 45

■P

page column, entries table, 157
page-and-entry access, 174
page-only access, 174
pages *see* web pages
parameters
    binding parameters, 115
    descriptions of methods using DocBlocks, 220
parsing errors
    checking {} used in pairs, 196
password column, admin table, 311

passwords

    adding administrators, 316
    SHA1() hash of, 331
paths
    relative paths, 137
patterns, programming, 140
patterns, regular expressions
    see also regex
    enclosing patterns in delimiters, 182
    makeUrl() function, 181
    matching non-word characters, 181
    preg_replace() function, 181
    URL rewriting, 172
PDO (PHP Data Objects), 116–118
    closeCursor() method, 117
    connecting to database, 149
    database-access abstraction layer, 116
    execute() method, 117
    MySQLi compared, 116
    potential issues when using, 116
    prepare() method, 117
    recommended further reading, 122
PDT IDE, 18
    installing Eclipse PDT, 18–21
performance, MySQL
    avoiding shortcut selector (SELECT *), 122
    eliminating performance issues, 118
permissions, file/folder, 231
photos, uploading, 88
PHP, 3–4
    comments, 46–47
    control structures, 54–66
    creating PHP file, 26–27
    creating PHP script, 27–28
    datatypes, 32
    DocBlocks, 220

file/folder permissions, 231
installing, 6
    verifying installation, 13
magic methods, 214
operators, 47–54
PDO (PHP Data Objects), 116–118
reserved words, 66
setting up development environment, 3–28
superglobal arrays, 69–95
user-defineds, 66–67
viewing source code in PHP project, 166
PHP delimiters, 30
PHP files *see* files
PHP functions *see* functions
PHP functions, list of *see* functions, list of PHP
PHP manual, 29
PHP Project window, 24
PHP scripts *see* scripts
PHP_SELF value, $_SERVER, 75
phpMyAdmin
    creating entries table in, 127
    creating new database in, 126
PNG images
    determining file extension of uploads, 237
POST method, 82
    deleting entries in database, 201
    verification of entry form input, 133, 134
    verifying form was submitted using, 88
$_POST superglobal array, 82–84
    array containing the contents of, 84
    checking if login credentials valid, 330
    deleting comments in database, 308
    deleting entries in database, 201
    inserting hidden inputs in HTML forms, 165, 168
    using prepared statements with MySQLi, 113, 116
    verification of entry form input, 134
Post to Twitter link, 362–368
    creating shortened link with http://bit.ly, 363–365
postpending variables, 51
postToTwitter() function, 365, 366
preg_replace() function, 180
prepare() method, MySQLi, 115
prepare() method, PDO, 117, 135
prepared statements, 111, 116
    using page to filter database records, 160
    using with MySQLi, 113–116
prepending variables, 51, 52

preprocessing, 4
presentation layer
    mapping functions to output saved entries, 141
    writing presentation code, 149–154
presentation logic, 140
PRIMARY KEY keywords, MySQL, 102
print() statement, 41
print_r() function, 49
    debugging arrays, 75
printf() statement, 43
private keyword, OOP, 212, 213
procedural interface, 109

    compared to OOP, 112, 212
processing data
    business logic, 140
processUploadedImage() method,
        ImageHandler class, 219, 221

    calling checkSaveDir(), 232
    calling doImageResize(), 258
    calling getImageExtension(), 238
    calling renameFile(), 238
    determining file extensions, 237
programming
    OOP, 211–218
    planning scripts, 139–154
    separation of logic in, 139–140
programming patterns
    Model-View-Controller (MVC) pattern, 140
    Multitier Architecture pattern, 140
projects
    choosing Eclipse PDT project workspace, 20
    creating Eclipse project, 23–26
    creating PHP project, 23
    PHP Project window, 24
    viewing source code in PHP project, 166
promoting web sites, 170
properties, OOP
    accessing, 214
    class properties, 212
    private keyword, 212
    visibility declarations for, 213
protected keyword, OOP, 213
pubDate
    creating from MySQL timestamp, 274
public keyword, OOP, 213
publishing date, RSS feeds, 272

Q

query() method, MySQLi, 113
quotes
    double-quote syntax, 34
    single-quote syntax, 33

R

rand() function, 354
random numbers, 354
real numbers, 37
Really Simple Syndication *see* RSS
recursive functions, 148
redirects, 155
redundant data
    avoiding storage of, 118–121
reference
    assignment by reference, 49
regex (regular expressions), 171
    creating character classes, 191
    enclosing patterns in delimiters, 182
    further information on, 172
    making expressions lazy, 174
    matching either nothing or something, 190
    matching non-word characters, 181
    matching word characters, 173
    negative lookahead, 181
    optionally matching period (.) in, 342
    patterns, 172
    setting up rules for URL rewriting, 172
    signifying end of string, 190
    use of symbols in regex
        $, 172, 173, 174, 190
        *, 342
        +, 173, 181
        ?, 174
        ?!, 181
        \, 172
        \s, 181
        \w, 173, 181
        (), 172
        [], 174, 191
        ^, 173
        |, 172, 190
    using in validateEmail() method, 342
    wildcards in, 342
relational database management systems, 97
relative paths, 137
releases, production vs. development, 4
REMOTE_ADDR value, $_SERVER, 75

renameFile() method, ImageHandler class, 237
replacements, URL rewriting, 173
    makeUrl() function, 181
    preg_replace() function, 181
$_REQUEST superglobal array, 84–85
REQUEST_METHOD value, 83
require/require_once constructs, 63
reserved words, 66
resizing images, 248–259
    determining dimensions, 249–252
    determining functions to use, 252–254
    resampling image at proper size, 254–258
retrieveComments() method, 293, 296
retrieveEntries() function, 141–148, 150
    adding $page variable as argument in
        index.php, 159
    creating blog entries, 266, 267
    creating different viewing styles for pages,
        185
    modifying index.php to check for url not id,
        178
    modifying to accept URL not id, 176
    modifying to retrieve images, 244–246
    modifying to return created column, 272
    populating form with entry to edit, 192
    using page to filter database records, 159
return statement, 63, 67
return values
    descriptions of methods using DocBlocks,
        220
RewriteBase directive, 172
RewriteEngine directive, 171
RewriteRule directive
    creating RSS feeds, 264
    modifying rule for admin.php access, 190
    setting up rule for admin.php access, 173,
        174
    setting up rule for page-only URLs, 174
    setting up rules for URL rewriting, 172
rewriting URLs *see* URL rewriting
RFC-822 format, 272, 274
RSS (Really Simple Syndication), 263
    creating RSS feeds, 264–277
    format for, 264
    publishing RSS feeds, 278–280
RSS aggregators, 263
    making RSS feed available to non-browsers,
        279–280
RSS feeds
    creating, 264–277

creating feed items, 266–277
    describing feeds, 265–266
    making available to browsers, 278–279
    making available to non-browsers, 279–280
    publishing, 278–280
    publishing date, 272
    using URL as GUID, 271
rss tag, version attribute, 265
rss.php file
    creating blog entries, 266, 267, 268
    creating RSS feeds, 264
    describing RSS feeds, 265
    inserting GUID, 271
    reformatting and adding date, 275
rules
    accessing backreferences, rewrite rules, 173
    flags, 173
    modifying rule for admin.php access, 190–
        191
    patterns, 172
    replacements, 173
    setting up rule for admin.php access, 173
    setting up rule for page-and-entry URLs,
        174
    setting up rule for page-only URLs, 174
    setting up rules for URL rewriting, 172

■S

S (skip) flag, URL rewriting, 173
sanitizeData() function, 141, 148–149, 151
Save Entry button, 133, 134
save_dir property, ImageHandler class, 219

    creating folder to store images, 230
    saving uploaded file to file system, 223
saveComment() method, 289
    email address validation for posting
        comments, 343, 347, 348
    modifying update.inc.php to call, 291
    spam prevention using simple math
        question, 359
scaling, 125
    planning scripts, 139
scope
    global scope, 70
    local scope, 71
    variable scope, 70–73
script tags, HTML, 31
scripted languages, 4
scripting

client-side scripting, 4–5
server-side scripting, 4–5
scripts
    choosing SDK/IDE, 15
    connecting PHP scripts to MySQL, 109–118
    creating PHP script, 27–28
    email address validation for posting
        comments, 341–353
    embedding PHP scripts, 29–31
    planning scripts, 139–154
        mapping functions to output saved
            entries, 140
        redirects, 155
        separation of logic in programming,
            139–140
        writing business functions, 148–149
        writing database functions, 141–148
        writing presentation code, 149–154
    script to process entry form input, 132–138
    using classes/objects in scripts, 215–218
SDKs (software development kits)
    benefits of, 15
    choosing SDK, 15, 18
    Eclipse SDK, 18
search engine optimization (SEO), 170
search engines
    indexing URLs, 170
SELECT statement, MySQL, 105–107
    avoiding shortcut selector (SELECT *), 122
    JOIN clause, 108
    USING clause, 108
    WHERE clause, 106
Select Workspace Directory window, 21
SEO (search engine optimization), 170
$_SERVER superglobal array, 74–77
    checking REQUEST_METHOD value, 83
    creating folder to store images, 230
    saving uploaded file to file system, 223
    verification of entry form input, 134
server-side scripting, 4–5

$_SESSION superglobal array, 89–93
    adding error messages to comments form,
        348
    displaying controls to authorized users, 330,
        331
    displaying stored comment information,
        345
    hiding administrative links from users, 318
    logging users out, 337
    saving comments in sessions, 344

spam prevention using simple math
    question, 354, 358
session_destroy() function, 92
    logging users out, 339
session_start() function, 90
    displaying controls to authorized users, 331
    hiding administrative links from users, 318
sessions, 89–93, 318
SET keyword, UPDATE statement, MySQL, 107
setcookie() function, 93
sha1() function, 316

SHA1() hash, passwords, 331
shell-style comments, 47
short tags, 31
    XML declarations conflict with, 265
short_open_tag directive, 31
shortenUrl() function, 363, 364, 365
showCommentForm() method, 286
    email address validation for posting
        comments, 345, 350
    spam prevention using simple math
        question, 356, 360
showComments() method, 296, 300, 301
    hiding delete link from unauthorized users,
        323
    storing output of, 302
simple_blog database
    admin table, 311
    comments table, 283–285
    creating in phpMyAdmin, 126
    deleting entries, 197–204
    displaying entries, 138–139
    entries table, 125–132
        adding image column, 241
        adding page column, 157
        adding url column, 176
        creating input form for, 128–132
simple_blog project
    About the Author page, 162, 164
    admin.php file, 128
        adding file input to, 207
        modifying to save page asssociations,
            165–168
        modifying access rule, 190–191
    administration
        creating administrative links, 187–188
        displaying administrative links, 188–190
        restricting administrative access, 311–
            340
    blog entries

creating, 266–277

previewing with friendly URL, 175

commenting system, 283–310

email address validation for posting comments, 341–353

creating directory to store images, 232

creating friendly URLs automatically, 175–183

functions.inc.php file, 141, 143, 144, 145, 147

modifying to handle URLs, 176–178

.htaccess file

creating, 171–175

creating friendly URLs using, 170–175

passing URL values to admin.php with, 190–191

inc folder, 132

index.php file, 138

modifying to handle URLs, 178–180

populating form with entry to edit, 191–194

Post to Twitter link, 362–368

previews page loaded with URL variables, 161

programming pattern, 140

redirects, 155

RSS feeds, 264, 265–266

making available to browsers, 278–279

making available to non-browsers, 279–280

script to process entry form input, 132–138

connecting to database, 134–135

retrieving unique ID, 136

saving values in entries table, 135

verification of input, 133

spam prevention, 353–362

syndicating content, 264–281

update.inc.php file, 132, 135

modifying to save URLs in database, 182

updating entries in database, 194–197

web pages

adding menu to, 184

creating different viewing styles for, 185–186

modifying functions to accept page parameters, 158–164

saving page asssociations, 168–169

simplexml_load_string() function, 364

single-quote syntax, 33

size value, $_FILES, 85

skip (S) flag, URL rewriting, 173

software development kits *see* SDKs

source code

viewing in PHP project, 166

spam prevention

Akismet, 353

CAPTCHA, 353

email address validation for posting comments, 341–353

using simple math question, 354–362

sprintf() statement, 45

SQL injection, 111

src_ arguments, imagecopyresampled(), 255, 256

string operators, 47, 54

strings, 33–37

double-quote syntax, 34

escaping characters in, 33

heredoc syntax, 36

nowdoc syntax, 36

single-quote syntax, 33

string concatenation, 35

strip_tags() function, 111, 148, 289

strtolower() function, 181

strtotime() function, 274, 300

subtraction operator, 48

superglobal arrays, 69–95

$_COOKIE, 93–95

$_FILES, 85–89

$_GET, 77–82

$_POST, 82–84

$_REQUEST, 84–85

$_SERVER, 74–77

$_SESSION, 89–93

$GLOBALS, 73

switch statement, 61

syndicating content, 264–281

syntax highlighting, 16

■T

tables, MySQL

adding columns, 157, 176

admin table, 311

ALTER TABLE statement, 103

automatically populated fields, 128

comments table, 283–285

CREATE TABLE statement, 100–102

data storage, 97

DELETE statement, 109

entries table, 125–127

indexing columns, 103
INSERT INTO phrase, 103–105
JOIN clause, 108
manipulating data in, 98–109
modifying data in, 107
planning database tables, 118–122
retrieving data, 105
    from multiple tables, 108
SELECT statement, 105–107
UPDATE statement, 107
tags
strip_tags() function, 148
ternary operator, 150, 166
TEXT type, MySQL, 102
textarea tag, 128, 193
this ($this) variable, 214
throw keyword, OOP, 222
time formatting characters, 299
time() function, 93
title column, entries table, 125, 128
saving values in entries table, 135
verification of entry form input, 133, 134
tmp_name value, $_FILES, 85
ToyRobot class, 212
declaring private property in, 213
writeName() method, 215, 216
ToyRobot.php file, 212
try...catch statement, 226–228
Twitter, 363
generating automatic status update for, 365–368
Post to Twitter link, 362–368
postToTwitter() function, 365, 366
type value, $_FILES, 85

U

underscore (_) character
denoting private properties, 213
unique ID
retrieving for new entry, 136
unset() function, 92, 93, 358
UPDATE statement, MySQL, 107
importance of WHERE clause, 108
update.inc.php file, 132
accessing uploaded files, 208–211
adding error messages to comments form, 349
checking if login credentials valid, 330, 331
handling comment deletion, 307–310

handling new comments, 291–293
including database credentials, 135
logging users out, 339
redirects, 155
retrieving unique ID for new entry, 137
saving images, 225–226
saving new administrators in database, 315, 316
saving page asssociations, 168–169
saving path to images, 241–244
saving URLs in database, 182
saving values in entries table, 135
testing checkSaveDir() method, 233–236
updating entries in database, 195
UPLOAD_ERR_OK constant, 221
uploading files, 85
accessing uploaded file, 208–211
adding file input to admin.php, 207
changing enctype to accept file uploads, 207
checking file uploaded and without errors, 88
checking file uploaded is JPG image, 88
checking for error during upload, 221–222
checking whether file was uploaded, 208
move_uploaded() function, 224
retrieving file information, 221
saving uploaded file to file system, 223–225
saving uploaded images, 219
uploading images
creating folder to store images, 228–236
determining file extensions, 237
ensuring image name is unique, 236
handling errors with try...catch, 226–228
saving uploaded images, 219
uploading photos, 88
url column, entries table, 176
URL encoding, 78
URL rewriting
accessing backreferences, 173
declaring base-level folder, 172
flags, 173
further information on, 172
patterns, 172
replacements, 173
setting up rule for admin.php access, 173
setting up rule for page-only URLs, 174
setting up rules for rewriting, 172
turning on, 171
using .htaccess file, 170
urldecode() function, 78

urlencode() function, 78
URLs
    accepting page info. in URL, 158–159
    accessing URL variables, 78–82
    blog previews page loaded with URL
        variables, 161
    creating friendly URLs using .htaccess, 170–
        175
    creating friendly URLs automatically, 175–
        183
    ensuring variable passed when link clicked,
        166
    entering URL without trailing slash, 174
    modifying functions.inc.php to handle,
        176–178
    modifying index.php to handle, 178–180
    modifying update.inc.php to save, 182
    passing entry IDs in, 150
    passing URL values to admin.php with
        .htaccess, 190–191
    previewing blog entries with friendly URL,
        175
    search engine indexing of, 170
    search engine optimization, 170
    setting up rule for page-and-entry URLs,
        174
    shortenUrl() function, 363, 364
    using as GUID for blog entries, 271
user-defineds, 66–67
username column, admin table, 311

users, restricting administrative access

    adding administrators in database, 312–317
    creating login form, 328–330
    displaying controls to authorized users,
        330–337
    hiding administrative links from users, 318
    hiding controls from unauthorized users,
        318–328
    hiding delete link from unauthorized users,
        323
    logging users out, 337–340
USING clause, SELECT statement, MySQL, 108

■V

validateEmail() method, Comments class, 342–
    343
validation

email address, for posting comments, 341–
    353
VALUES keyword
    INSERT INTO phrase, MySQL, 103
var keyword, OOP, 213
VARCHAR type, MySQL, 101, 102
variables, 32
    accessing URL variables, 78–82
    arrays, 38–41
    Boolean values, 37
    concatenating, 36
    declaring as NULL, 160
    ensuring passed when link clicked, 166
    floating point numbers, 37
    integers, 37
    placing an operator sign before/after, 51
    postpending, 51
    prepending, 51, 52
    scope, 70–73
    storing values in, 32
    strings, 33–37
    superglobal arrays, 69
verifyResponse() method, Comments class, 358
version attribute, rss tag, 265
View option, browser menu, 166
views
    creating different viewing styles for pages,
        185–186
void keyword, 42

■W

web pages
    accepting page info. in URL, 158–159
    accessing publicly displayed pages, 174
    adding menu, 184
    checking page before displaying delete, 189
    creating different viewing styles for, 185–186
    differentiating between multi-and single-
        entry pages, 185
    modifying admin.php to save page
        asssociations, 165–168
    modifying functions to accept page
        parameters, 158–164
    modifying links between, 162
    moving information from page to page, 69
    passing data between pages using GET, 77
    passing data between pages using POST, 82
    saving page asssociations, 168–169
    supporting multiple pages, 157

using page to filter database records, 159–164

web site marketing, 170

web sites

accessing IP address of site visitors, 74

adding menu to pages, 184

creating friendly URLs using .htaccess, 170–175

creating friendly URLs automatically, 175–183

dynamic websites, 3

identifying site referring visitor, 74, 77

modifying functions to accept page parameters, 158–164

name of host site, 74

storing information on user's machine, 93, 95

WHERE clause, MySQL

DELETE statement, 109

SELECT statement, 106

UPDATE statement, 108

using page to filter database records, 159

while loop, 56

whitespace, 36

Windows

setting magic_quotes_gpc Off, 15

word characters

matching non-word characters, 181

matching word characters, 173

Workspace Launcher window, 20

workspaces

choosing Eclipse PDT project workspace, 20

writeName() method, ToyRobot class, 215, 216

■XYZ

XAMPP, 6

downloading, 7

FTP option, 13

installing, 6–15

testing installation, 11–13

verifying Apache/PHP running, 13

verifying MySQL running, 14

XAMPP Control Panel, 11

xampp folder, 7, 11

XML (Extensible Markup Language), 264

XML declaration, 265

XOR operator, 53

year formatting characters, 299

You Need the Companion eBook

Your purchase of this book entitles you to buy the companion PDF-version eBook for only $10. Take the weightless companion with you anywhere.

We believe this Apress title will prove so indispensable that you'll want to carry it with you everywhere, which is why we are offering the companion eBook (in PDF format) for $10 to customers who purchase this book now. Convenient and fully searchable, the PDF version of any content-rich, page-heavy Apress book makes a valuable addition to your programming library. You can easily find and copy code—or perform examples by quickly toggling between instructions and the application. Even simultaneously tackling a donut, diet soda, and complex code becomes simplified with hands-free eBooks!

Once you purchase your book, getting the $10 companion eBook is simple:

❶ Visit **www.apress.com/promo/tendollars/**.

❷ Complete a basic registration form to receive a randomly generated question about this title.

❸ Answer the question correctly in 60 seconds, and you will receive a promotional code to redeem for the $10.00 eBook.

Apress®
THE EXPERT'S VOICE™

233 Spring Street, New York, NY 10013

Offer valid through 4/10.